Tahoe

Tahoe

An Environmental History

Douglas H. Strong

University of Nebraska Press
Lincoln and London

Chapter 3 has previously been published, in
somewhat different form, as "Preservation Efforts at
Lake Tahoe, 1880 to 1980," Journal of Forest
History 25 (April 1981): 78–97.

The paper in this book meets the guidelines for
permanence and durability of the Committee on
Production Guidelines for Book Longevity of the
Council on Library Resources.

Library of Congress Cataloguing in Publication Data

Strong, Douglas Hillman.
    Tahoe, an environmental history.

    Bibliography: p.
    Includes index.
    1. Regional planning—Tahoe, Lake, Region
(Calif. and Nev.) 2. Environmental protection—
Tahoe, Lake Region (Calif. and Nev.) 3. Tahoe,
Lake, Region (Calif. and Nev.)—History. I. Title.
HT392.5.T3S77   1984   333.7'09794' 38   83-6523
ISBN 0-8032-4141-0

Publication of this book was aided by a grant from
The Andrew W. Mellon Foundation.

Dedicated to my mother and father,
Gertrude D. Strong and Edward W. Strong,
who introduced me to the mountains

Contents

Illustrations

Maps

Preface

Lake Tahoe is exceptional. For more than a century, visitors have acclaimed its beauty, and its fame has spread worldwide. This remarkable lake on the northern California–Nevada line attracts millions of visitors annually, more than any other natural scenic area of similar size in the United States.

Like Lake Baikal in the Soviet Union and Lake Como in northern Italy, Lake Tahoe is surrounded by mountains. The setting is picturesque, and the crystal blue water of Tahoe is breathtaking. Its depth (1,645 feet) is exceeded by only nine lakes in the world, among them Great Slave Lake in Canada and Crater Lake in Oregon. In spite of its high elevation (6,229 feet above sea level at maximum), Tahoe never freezes over; its water is perpetually in motion, precluding the formation of ice except on the fringes. Because of its depth and size (twenty-two miles long and twelve miles wide), Tahoe holds an immense volume of water; unleashed, it would flood the state of California to a depth of more than fourteen inches. The lake's outlet, the Truckee River, flows into landlocked Pyramid Lake and into irrigation canals in Nevada.

The natural setting of Lake Tahoe is remarkable, but its story is far from idyllic. Tahoe's scenic beauty has been its undoing. Widespread commercial development to accommodate the crowds of people that flock to its shores has resulted in an alarming rate of environmental deterioration. Water quality, to cite a highly publicized issue, has declined rapidly, even though the city of South Lake Tahoe has one of the most sophisticated sewage treatment plants in the world. In fact, algae attached to rocks and algae blooms in the lake have become unfortunate facts of life.

A fundamental question arose early in Tahoe's history that continues unanswered to this day: to whom does Tahoe belong, and how should it be used? Those local residents and outside investors who have wished to develop its resources have favored private ownership of property and "free enterprise." They have argued that the Tahoe Basin rightfully belongs to those with title to the land and that the legal owners should be free to use the land as they see fit, whether this means cutting its timber or building a high-rise casino-hotel.

Not everyone, however, has welcomed the transformation of the Tahoe Basin through deforestation and urbanization. Even in the early days of settlement, a few individuals argued that the priceless heritage of Tahoe belongs to the people of California and Nevada and to the nation at large. They insisted that the Tahoe Basin, or major portions of it, should be set aside in parks or forest reserves. Still others advocated controlled growth that would allow economic development without incurring high environmental costs or loss of scenic amenities.

The struggle among these contending forces has given rise to a related critical question: who should decide Tahoe's future? Resolution of this problem has been difficult, for the people of the Tahoe Basin lack a sense of community or common purpose; political authority is divided among five counties bordering the lake, two state governments, and the national government. As a result, although more than 72 percent of the land area is publicly owned, there is still no consensus on who should decide the future of the Tahoe Basin or what that future should be.

Certainly Tahoe's environmental problems stretch the imagination. Severe soil erosion, irreversible water degradation, and deteriorating air quality threaten its fragile environment. In addition, social problems proliferate: traffic congestion, rising crime rates, shortage of middle- and low-income housing, and high seasonal unemployment. As Charles Goldman, an expert on the water quality of the lake, has stated, "In a sense Tahoe represents in

In spite of serious environmental problems, Lake Tahoe retains vistas of exceptional beauty, as revealed in this view from Rubicon Point. James Hildinger.

microcosm the environmental problems of the 20th century, both on a national and international basis."[1] Goldman minced no words in describing the current condition of the lake: "Lake Tahoe is being polluted. To deny this fact is comparable to saying that a man receiving a daily dose of arsenic in his breakfast coffee is not being slowly poisoned. If the poisoning continues, the steady accumulation in the man's system will eventually kill him. If the pollution of Lake Tahoe is not stopped now, the pollutants will continue to accumulate in the lake, and in time the lake will turn from clear blue to turbid green."[2]

Almost a hundred years earlier, another university scientist, Joseph LeConte, recalled a visit to Tahoe in 1870 in quite different words and from an altogether different world:

> Oh, the exquisite beauty of this lake!—its clear waters, emerald-green, and the deepest ultramarine blue; its pure shores, rocky or cleanest gravel, so clean that the chafing of the waves does not stain in the least the bright clearness of the waters; the high granite mountains, with serried peaks, which stand close around its very shore to guard its crystal purity. . . . of all the places I have yet seen, this is the one which I could longest enjoy and love the most.[3]

No one can be impartial about Lake Tahoe. Having visited the region from the late 1930s on, to hike, ski, boat, and swim, I have marveled at its scenic wonders. At the same time, I have sadly witnessed the rapid deterioration of its environmental quality. As an environmental historian, I recognize the earlier circumstances that once encouraged private ownership and development of most of the lakeshore property. Yet I believe that Tahoe, because of its exceptional scenic and recreational value, belongs to all Americans. It should be carefully husbanded to preserve these values; the ecological health of the lake should take precedence over the wishes of private property owners. My purpose here is not to cast blame for past mistakes, but to explain how and why the Tahoe Basin evolved from an isolated mountain region in the nineteenth century to the rapidly growing year-round recreational and urban area it is today—and to explain how and why this spawned a particularly intractable set of problems.

The story of Tahoe that follows begins with the natural history of the basin and its annual visitations by the Washo Indians. The first two chapters describe the settlement and development of the basin from the early days to 1960. Chapters Three and Four discuss responses to threats to the environment, as well as efforts to establish national and state parks and national forests in the basin. The last two chapters explain some of the efforts and difficulties of planners, politicians, and others who have wrestled in recent years with the environmental problems that have resulted from population growth and urbanization.

A short book on such a complex topic necessarily must be selective and interpretive: it cannot include discussion of all persons, places, or events of significance in Tahoe's environmental history. A bibliographical essay for each chapter lists the sources that were most useful to me and suggests further reading for anyone who wishes to pursue the topic in greater depth. The notes at the end of the book are limited primarily to citations for direct quotations. Many of these references, especially to newspapers, are not duplicated in the bibliography.

It is my hope that a better understanding of Tahoe and its complexities will enhance our understanding of other areas and their environmental problems. More immediately, I hope this brief history can in some way help those people, both within and outside the Tahoe Basin, who are working to achieve control over growth and development so that Lake Tahoe can remain a scenic and recreational treasure of national significance. It is not too late to preserve one of America's most precious resources.

Space does not permit the mention of everyone who assisted me in the course of this study, particularly the many librarians and archivists who gave unstintingly of their time. I wish to give special thanks, however, to Barbara Lekisch, former librarian of the Lake Tahoe Area Council library, who aided my research from beginning to end.

Several other people provided valuable assistance, including Donald J. Pisani on the history of water use, Joseph H. Engbeck, Jr., on California state parks, and Andrew R. Schmidt on U.S. Forest Service land acquisition. Glenn S. Smith opened Forest Service records to me and responded to numerous questions. I am particularly indebted to Thomas R. Cox, Sari Sommarstrom, and Kenneth C. and Lynne Smith, who read the entire manuscript and offered constructive criticism.

A grant from the William Randolph Hearst Foundation helped finance research at the National Archives in Washington, D.C., and in northern California and western Nevada. A sabbatical leave from San Diego State University provided the necessary time to complete research and a preliminary draft of the book. The Forest History Society granted permission to use material from my article "Preservation Efforts at Lake Tahoe: 1880 to 1980," *Journal of Forest History* 25 (April 1981): 78–97.

I am grateful to my daughter, Beret, who graciously volunteered to type an early draft of the manuscript, and to Carey Charlesworth and Joan Crowder for their editorial assistance. Finally, I am indebted to my wife, Karlan, for her perceptive criticisms of the book and her enthusiastic assistance in its completion.

1 The Tahoe Basin:
Natural History and Early Days

The Lay of the Land

The striking beauty of Lake Tahoe has resulted from millions of years of geologic changes. The Sierra Nevada, on which Tahoe is nestled, consists of an uptilted granite batholith about four hundred miles long. The eastern edge of the batholith forms a tremendous fault scarp, which can be viewed from the Carson and Washoe valleys east of Tahoe, and the remainder of it slopes gradually westward toward California's Central Valley. At the southern end and on the eastern sides of the Tahoe Basin, granite from this uplifted material constitutes most of the bedrock. At the northern and northwestern sides, as well as at scattered sites elsewhere, evidence of volcanic activity remains: small cinder cones mark the sites of the most recent eruptions. The Tahoe Basin resulted from faults that allowed it to drop, less than three million years ago, forming what is called a graben or trough. The graben rests between a dual crest of the Sierra Nevada—the main crest to the west and the Carson Range to the east. Since that time, additional uplifting and volcanic activity have altered the landscape.

Within the past two million years, extensive glaciation and deposition have further transformed the topography. Sheets of ice more than a thousand feet thick covered mountain valleys and all but the highest peaks on the western side of the basin. The ice scoured out

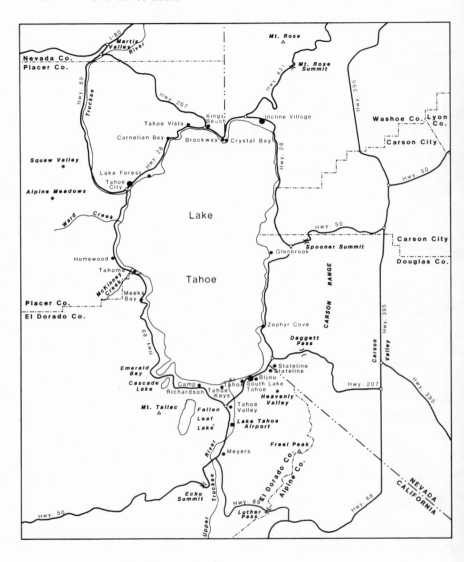

The Lake Tahoe Basin

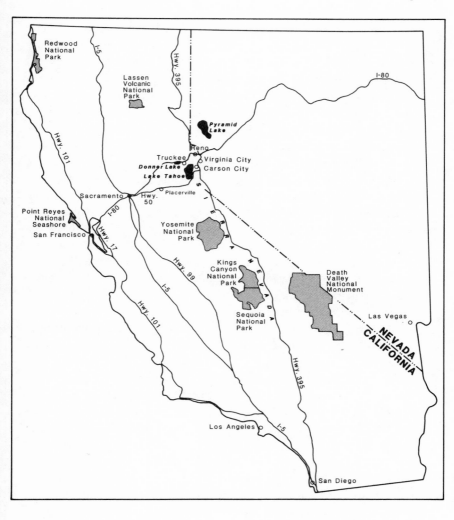

Lake Tahoe in relation to California and western Nevada

cirques and steep slopes, as well as the basins below where Fallen Leaf Lake, Cascade Lake, Emerald Bay, and smaller lakes and ponds formed. The fragments of rock and silt carried by the ice and water eventually came to rest in moraines, and one of these can be seen just east of the present Lake Tahoe airport. Due to the "rain shadow" cast by the main crest of the Sierra, the Carson Range to the east held only small glaciers, if any, on the shaded sides of the peaks and so remains relatively gentle and rolling in contrast to the highly sculptured peaks to the west of the lake.

At the north end of the basin, large streams of ice descended from Squaw Valley and neighboring valleys to block the canyon on the Truckee River (the outlet of Lake Tahoe), forming an ice dam that at one time raised the water level of the lake several hundred feet above its current depth. When this and ice dams formed by other glacial advances gave way, great granite boulders hurtled downstream with the floodwaters and came to rest beyond the present-day site of Reno. At other times the level of the lake fluctuated several hundred feet because volcanic flows of basalt blocked the outlet, only to erode gradually away. Today andesitic mudflows and lava form a natural dam at the outlet of the lake, at Tahoe City.

With the end of the Pleistocene or glacial epoch more than ten thousand years ago, silt and sand from the melting glaciers eroded rapidly, depositing layer after layer of sediment on the relatively flat lake bottom. Sediment collecting at the edge of the lake formed deltas, the largest of which is now the site of the city of South Lake Tahoe. The potential for erosion in the basin has remained high because the soil tends to be shallow and coarse, lacking humus and other materials that hold moisture and bind the soil together. The processes of erosion and deposition continue inevitably as the Sierra wears down, particularly where decomposed granite is exposed to running water.

The Lake Tahoe Basin, formed by these geologic forces and defined as the land and water area that contributes to the outflow from the lake, is small—slightly more than 500 square miles of land and water in relation to the surface area of Lake Tahoe, which is

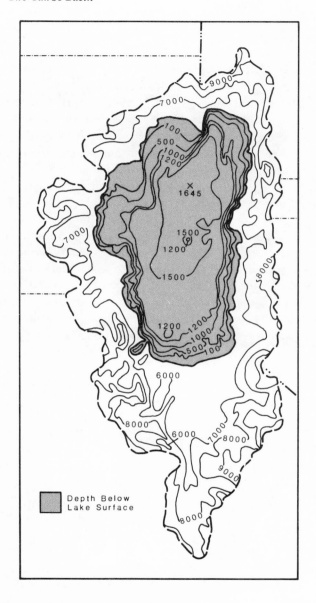

Topography of the Lake Tahoe Basin

The fault scarp to the west of Carson Valley rises sharply to Lake Tahoe, which rests between the Carson Range and the crest of the Sierra Nevada. Special Collections, University of Nevada–Reno Library.

roughly 191 square miles. Most of the terrain in the basin is quite steep; about half the land has a slope greater than 20 percent. Land development in recent years has therefore been concentrated on the more level land along the lakeshore, especially at the southern end of the basin. The perimeter of the basin is rugged, particularly in the Desolation Wilderness area to the west, and is relatively unaffected by human contact.

Most of Tahoe's water arrives via storms originating in the northern Pacific Ocean and bearing moist marine air that drops heavy loads of snow during the winter months, especially at higher elevations. Winter temperatures are moderate, especially near the lake, seldom dropping below zero degrees Fahrenheit for any length of time. During the spring thaw, the melting snow feeds more than sixty inlets to the lake, primarily on the wetter western side of the basin. Summers, on the other hand, are quite dry except for occasional thunderstorms, and the mean daily temperature hovers comfortably above seventy near the lake. But the same climate that limits temperature extremes also limits the growth of vegetation. Because of the high elevation (above six thousand feet), frost restricts the growi..g season to from 70 to 120 days. The combination of scarce precipitation in summer, the short growing season, and rather poor soil yields slow-growing vegetation that does not grow again easily if disturbed or destroyed.

Although vegetation in the basin is mixed because of differences in temperature and precipitation, coniferous forests clearly dominate. Jeffrey pine and white fir prevail along the western lake shore. Sugar pine, widespread prior to the advent of logging, remains only in scattered clumps. Incense cedar grows well on the warmer, well-drained slopes, and Sierra juniper, quaking aspen, mountain hemlock, Ponderosa pine, red fir, and lodgepole pine are commonly seen. Subalpine wildflowers and sagebrush coexist in the basin. In addition to forest lands, Tahoe has chapparal, meadows, and marshes.

Many animals and birds originally flourished in this varied habitat. Bears, deer, mountain lions, and smaller mammals, as well as Canada geese, eagles, ducks, and many other land and water birds, were once numerous. More than three hundred species of wildlife still inhabit the basin, although several are now listed as rare or endangered. The peregrine falcon and the wolverine, among others, no longer reside in the basin because of the deterioration of their habitat. Native and exotic fish still flourish, though their numbers have been depleted from earlier days: rainbow trout, Kokanee salmon, lake trout, whitefish, brook trout, and others. The native cutthroat trout, once the principal species in Lake Tahoe, has been eliminated through overfishing, dams, human interference with spawning activities and grounds, and the competition of exotic fish species.

Barring some unusual natural event like a volcanic eruption or a new glacial epoch, the ecosystem of the basin would change very gradually under natural conditions, remaining relatively stable over millennia. The clarity and purity of Tahoe's water could be maintained for a long time if the ecological cycles remained stable. But the basin has undergone rapid transformation in recent years, and the lake is no longer stable. To examine this transformation and its consequences is to focus attention on one species: Homo sapiens.

The Washo Indians

To the Washo Indians, Lake Tahoe was a sacred place, a provider of food, and their most important gathering point each year. The lake and neighboring valleys on the eastern edge of the Sierra were the heart of Washo lands. According to their belief, the Washos had lived in this territory since creation; anthropologists estimate that they camped seasonally in the Tahoe Basin for several thousand years.

The lives of the Washos were closely integrated with their environment. In the absence of domesticated animals, agriculture, and such skills as pottery making and metallurgy, the Washos depended on hunting, gathering, and fishing. They survived for generations without depleting their sources of sustenance. Like most hunters and gatherers, they normally kept their population, probably no more than three thousand at its peak, well under the maximum for which they could provide given their technology and resource base. Nevertheless, survival depended on frequent moves to replenish food stocks and keen knowledge of the changing conditions of weather, plants, and animals.

Having passed the long winter season camped in valleys just east of the Sierra, and needing to reprovision, the Washos would make their annual trek to Lake Tahoe. From the land to the north, as far away as Honey Lake, came the Washo group called "Wel mel ti," who normally established their summer camps on Tahoe's north shore. The "Pau wa lu" climbed the steep slope of the Sierra from Carson Valley and camped on the east shore, and the "Hung a lel ti" left what is now the Woodfords and Markleeville area to settle temporarily on Tahoe's south shore. Thus the scattered groups of Washos came together at "Da ow a ga" (the edge of the lake)— which whites later mispronounced, calling it Tahoe.

Young men and women would gather at Tahoe first, as the snows melted. This left more food in the winter camps for the older people and the children, who would follow as the weather improved. By June all the Washos would be encamped near the shores of Tahoe, many families returning to establish campsites that are marked today by bedrock mortars. With a plentiful food supply at the lake, the Washos could enjoy visiting with their neighbors and participation in competitive sports, dancing, and courtship.

More than at any other time of the year, during their summer camps the Washos joined as one people in a specific location and were involved in the same task: fishing. All members of a family would work intensively during the short time in June when the fish ran upstream to spawn in the creeks that entered the lake. Cutthroat trout and suckers were so plentiful that they could be caught easily with spears, nets, hooks, and conical baskets. That portion of the catch not cooked on hot coals and eaten immediately was split open and dried in the open air for later use.

With the end of the spawning run and as the snow melted in the higher elevations, some families left their Tahoe campsites to fish, hunt, and gather in the surrounding mountains. Others returned to lower country along the headwaters of the Carson and Truckee rivers and elsewhere. The women concentrated on gathering seeds, berries, roots, tea, vegetables, and other plants. Individual families moved continually from place to place, harvesting such items as wild onions, cattails, strawberries, sugar pine sap, gooseberries, and sunflower seeds.

As summer wore on and the fishing continued to decline, increasing numbers of families returned east of the Sierra to hunt for deer, rabbits, and other game, to gather plants yet untouched that season, and to await the piñon nut harvest. With the approach of fall, Washo families congregated again, this time in the piñon forests on the low mountains east of Tahoe in what is now western Nevada.

Washo Indian women made exceptional baskets. Special Collections, University of Nevada–Reno Library.

Here each family collected thousands of pounds of piñon nuts, the main food supply for the winter ahead, and then hauled the nuts to winter camps. There the Washos spent long hours making their exceptionally fine baskets, as well as arrowheads and other implements. And there they awaited the spring thaw, when they would once again begin their annual trek to the shores of Lake Tahoe.

Thus the Washos followed the seasons, continuing a way of life in the same locality for uncounted generations. They shared available food; anyone who was selfish would face disapproval and possibly the withdrawal of group assistance, an action that could mean ruin in a land where life depended on cooperation. Only occasionally did intruders or severe food shortage threaten them. If necessary, the Washos would defend their territory, especially the prized fishing sites at Tahoe and the piñon forests to the east. But normally they remained at peace.

The traditional Washo ways could not be sustained once white settlers had arrived. White people fenced the land, cut piñon trees, killed game, and claimed Indian fishing grounds, and their livestock destroyed many of the plants upon which the Indians depended. The Washos lacked the population, political organization, and technology necessary for effective resistance. They did the best they could to maintain their way of life, adapting to the position of an ethnic minority living on the fringes of white society.

Still, the Washos retained a cultural identity, and many continued their yearly trek to the shores of Lake Tahoe. As late as 1915, anthropologist Samuel Barrett reported that he walked miles of Tahoe's shores searching for Indian camps. "When I arrived," Barrett noted, "I would find some patriarch patiently chipping arrowheads or making a bow preparatory to going on a hunt for deer in the adjacent forest."[1] By the 1920s, the annual migrations had ended; the older people had died and the younger men stayed in nearby valleys in western Nevada to work on ranches, on highway maintenance crews, at summer resorts, and in other wage labor.

In spite of the troubled times that befell the Washos, they survived. In recent years many have settled in three "colonies," governed today by a tribal council, within their former lands. Several are interested in maintaining a sense of their heritage and are working with the Forest Service on a proposal for an Indian cultural center at Taylor Creek, an inlet of Lake Tahoe, once the site of an Indian summer encampment.

Opening the Tahoe Basin

The discovery of gold at Sutter's Mill in 1848 brought with it a flood of overland travelers to California who wanted to cross the high, dangerous Sierra Nevada as quickly and easily as possible on their way to the goldfields. In time, Tahoe gained a share of the

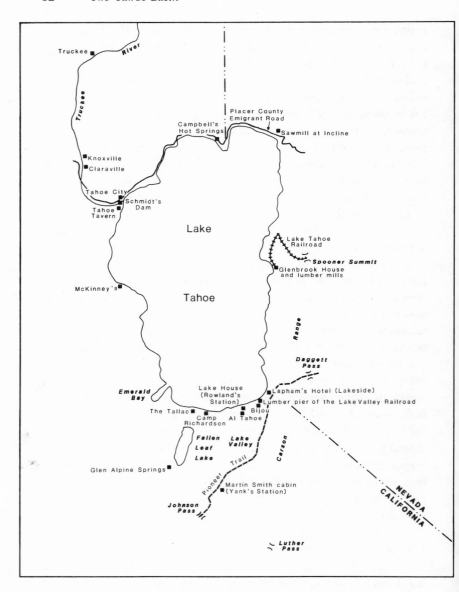

Historical Sites

traffic from the east, but not until the development in the 1860s of a reverse migration from California to the Comstock Lode, Virginia City's mining bonanza, did Tahoe begin to be widely known and visited.

No one knows when the first white person set foot in the land of the Washos. In 1827 the fur trapper Jedediah Smith made the first crossing of the mountains, west to east, in the vicinity of Ebbetts Pass, not far south of the Tahoe Basin. Early in 1844, when Lt. John C. Frémont camped near a river that flowed from the mountains to the west of the Great Basin, Washo Indians drew a map for him revealing that the stream originated in a mountain lake (Tahoe) some three or four days' travel away. Frémont led his party south to the Carson River and then, disregarding the Indians' warning of deep snow, west into the mountains.

While seeking an observation point from a peak (probably Red Lake Peak) on the approach to a pass on February 14, Frémont noted, "We had a beautiful view of a mountain lake at our feet, about fifteen miles in length, and so entirely surrounded by mountains that we could not discover an outlet."[2] This is the first recorded sighting of Lake Tahoe by a white man.

Late that year, several families (the Stevens-Murphy-Townsend party) forged a new route across the Sierra. Rather than follow the tracks of earlier parties, they listened to the advice of an elderly Indian who directed them to a river (which they named after him), the Truckee. The main group with the wagons followed a tributary directly west to Donner Lake and then made the first successful wagon crossing of the Sierra. A small group on horseback, four men and two women, followed the main river to its outlet from Lake Tahoe; they were perhaps the first white people to venture onto the shore of the lake. Apparently they skirted the west shore to McKinney Creek and then left the basin on their way to Sutter's Fort in the Sacramento Valley.

The discovery of gold in 1848 led to an intensified search for a good route through the northern Sierra, but the Tahoe Basin itself attracted little interest. Not only did the eastern front of the Sierra as approached from Carson Valley provide a formidable barrier, but anyone who surmounted that obstacle on the way to Tahoe had to climb a second pass to the west in order to cross the Sierra. Nevertheless, a few people followed Scott's route (the Placer County Emigrant Road), first used in 1849, which skirted the northern end of the lake.

Road construction in the vicinity of Tahoe was dominated at first by private promoters and local boosters in pursuit of business. But the advantages of establishing a transportation link with settlements in the eastern United States soon spurred the efforts of California's state government. While early national discussions of a transcontinental railroad focused on routes that avoided the forbidding Sierra Nevada, Californians explored their eastern border and a possible central route across the mountains.

Almost nothing was known of this territory. When surveyor William Eddy traveled to Carson Valley in summer 1852 to determine the state's eastern border, he had to conclude "reluctantly" that the valley lay twelve to fifteen miles outside California. That year, John Calhoun Johnson, a rancher, received credit for pioneering a short central route across Johnson (now Echo) Pass that connected Placerville and Carson Valley. This trail, "Johnson's cut-off," opened the south end of the Tahoe Basin.

The California legislature provided in 1855 for construction of a wagon road from the Sacramento Valley to the eastern border of the state. Private donors and local counties helped fund the road. In June 1857, the first stagecoach crossed Johnson Pass to Lake Valley (at the southern end of Lake Tahoe) and then climbed Luther Pass, to the south of the lake, to the west fork of the Carson River on the way to what is now Woodfords. A new day had begun for Lake Tahoe, for the route was in full use by wagons the following year.

Several alternative routes soon followed as road builders sought easier and more direct passage across the mountains. By 1860 a toll wagon road crossed the southern part of the Tahoe Basin on the route of the present Pioneer Trail, crossing the Carson Range at Daggett Pass to the Kingsbury Grade and Genoa in the Carson Valley. This variant quickly attracted business, including the short-lived Pony Express that ran between St. Joseph, Missouri, and Sacramento.

The subsequent construction of a wagon road over Donner Pass to the north foreshadowed a major shift of freight and passenger travel to the Central Pacific Railroad. The railroad completed track over the same pass to Lake's Crossing (now Reno) in 1868. The Tahoe Basin then ceased to be the major way station in crossing the Sierra. But small settlements along some of its roads remained, providing a nucleus for subsequent growth.

The Tourist Trade

Martin Smith, a Pennsylvanian, built Tahoe's first log cabin in upper Lake Valley in 1851 in order to provide food and lodging to the few travelers who ventured past. Three years later Asa Hawley, anticipating the construction of a wagon road to Tahoe, settled nearby and opened a trading post. He could claim the distinction of being the only permanent inhabitant at the lake once Smith had left for the winter season.

As Lake Valley became a stopover point on the road between Carson City and Placerville in ensuing years, a few others settled there. They made little visible impact on the land. In describing the south shore of the lake in summer 1857, a visitor noted: "A dense pine forest extends from the water's edge to the summits of the surrounding mountains, except in some points where a peak of more than ordinary elevation rears its bald head above the waving forest."[3] Two years later another visitor who camped at the southeastern end of the lake described it as "the most beautiful shore we ever beheld" and noted the complete absence of any boats or "any improvements" about the lake.[4]

The rush to the Comstock that began in 1859, drawing thousands of people from California to what later became the territory of Nevada, had great impact on Tahoe. Then as now, events of the outside world heavily influenced developments within the basin.

The freighting business, the budding tourist industry, and the lumber industry there all resulted directly from the remarkable growth of Virginia City, a community that reached a sizable population as if overnight. Essentially everything needed by this instant city had to be transported over the Sierra from California, reversing the earlier east-to-west traffic. A steady flow of heavily loaded wagons hauled everything from mining machinery, firewood, and food to brass beds, chandeliers, and silk. Prices soared, and fortune hunters poured over Johnson Pass on the way past Lake Tahoe to the bonanza in Nevada.

When William Brewer of the California Geological Survey visited Tahoe in 1863, he estimated that five thousand teamsters had steady employment in the "Washoe" trade and other commerce to the east of the Sierra. Teams of six to ten horses pulled loads of three to eight tons in "huge cumbrous wagons" that clogged the toll road. By summer 1864, about a hundred inns and lodging stations lined the route from Placerville, including Yank's Station (at Meyers), Lake House (at Al Tahoe, which is named after Al Sprague, a hotel owner), Lapham's Hotel (at Stateline), and Glenbrook House (at Glenbrook).

When completion of the Central Pacific Railroad essentially ended the freight wagon business, many innkeepers moved to the shoreline of the lake. Here they could provide accommodations in boardinghouses for seasonal workers and for vacationing families who were beginning to discover the pleasures of summer in the mountains. It was only a half-day's ride from the hot, dry hills of Nevada's Virginia City to the lake; and Californians, especially from San Francisco, were also beginning to consider Tahoe a summer vacation site.

Easterners, who had discovered such attractions as Niagara Falls, Lake George, the Catskills, and Virginia's Natural Bridge earlier in the century, increasingly turned their attention to the American west. Natural wonders—the hot springs and geysers of Yellowstone, the Big Trees of Calaveras Grove, and especially the cliffs and waterfalls of Yosemite Valley—competed with the cultural attractions of Europe for the tourist trade. And, with increas-

Tourists aboard the steamer Tahoe *flocked to the rail to view Rubicon Point.* Nevada State Museum.

ing frequency, tourists to Yosemite included Tahoe on their itineraries.

Steamship travel came of age at Tahoe in 1873, when two new ships joined the smaller existing steam vessels. The largest steamer, the *Governor Stanford,* carried the mail and followed a regular schedule, leaving Tahoe City for such settlements and attractions as Campbell's Hot Springs, Glenbrook, Lapham's Landing, Rowland's Station, and McKinney's. The ports of call changed somewhat over the years as new resorts appeared, but the boat service continued to attract people to the basin.

Although the site today of bumper-to-bumper traffic, the Lake Hotel–Bijou store–post office knew quieter days at the turn of the century.
California Historical Society, San Francisco.

Road transportation near the shore of the lake also improved. By the mid-1870s roads connected Glenbrook to Tallac Point (near the present-day site of Camp Richardson) and McKinney's to Campbell's Hot Springs (now Brockway). Trails cut across the rugged slopes of Emerald Bay and around the northeast corner of the lake, completing a circuit of Tahoe.

Stage lines connected Tahoe to the outside world and completed the transportation network. Benton's stage left Carson City in time to connect with the steamer at Glenbrook for a tour of the lake and with Bailey and Moody's stage from Tahoe City to Truckee. Going the other way, tourists could leave the Truckee rail depot at seven in the morning, tour the lake by steamer, and be ready to leave Glenbrook the following morning on the stage for Carson and Virginia City, connecting again with the Central Pacific Railroad.

As the Tahoe Basin attracted more and more interest and tourists, diverse resorts appeared along the shores of the lake. Growing numbers of eastern visitors joined the members of San Francisco's elite and the wealthy mining and business interests of the Comstock at the lake's "best" hotels: Glenbrook House (advertised as the Saratoga of the West), the Tallac, and the Grand Central Hotel in Tahoe City. People of more modest means vacationed in rustic hotels and cottages or camped. By the end of the 1880s a reported one hundred people each day took the stage from Truckee to Tahoe City. By this time, both the road system and the pattern of settlement had been well established.

Mining, Farming, and Fishing

While the focus was shifting from the short-lived rush of teamsters along the Comstock Road to quieter, family-oriented businesses along the shores of the lake, other enterprises developed that encouraged settlement in the Tahoe Basin. In June 1863 two prospectors discovered an apparently rich ore deposit on the east bank of the Truckee River near its junction with Squaw Creek. When William Brewer passed there not long after, he found hundreds of men crowded into "Knoxville," a ragged tent community of several saloons, a couple of "hotels," clothing stores, a butcher shop, a bakery, and sundry other enterprises. Despite the great excitement and the claims of a second Comstock, Brewer felt that the prospects looked dim and concluded that he "surely would not invest money" in anything he had seen. He had a similar reaction to Claraville, a mile upstream, and to Centerville and Elizabethtown, sites of supposed silver strikes in the mountains between the north shore of Lake Tahoe and Martis Valley farther north.

Although the shanty towns were quickly abandoned when ore samples proved worthless, several of the disappointed miners drifted only as far as the north end of the Tahoe Basin, an area visited previously by occasional fur trappers and prospectors. Soon a small community (Tahoe City) appeared; lots in town reportedly sold for $50 each, a hundred-foot wharf projected into the lake, and in 1864 the Tahoe City Hotel offered accommodations. With the completion of the Central Pacific Railroad through Truckee in 1868, the growth of Tahoe City as a resort seemed assured. By 1871 the "city" could boast a hotel, a store, a saloon, a livery stable, and several scattered private homes.

Although mining never became an active enterprise in the basin, markets created by teamsters gave rise to agriculture. At first, small meadowlands and vegetable gardens served the individual toll stations and inns along the Placerville–Carson Road in Lake Valley. As business increased, the land under cultivation and the acreage of grasslands used to pasture cattle and dairy cows also expanded.

Soon farms and ranches appeared around the perimeter of the lake wherever wild hay could be harvested and livestock grazed. All over the basin, meadowlands were quickly preempted and put to use, usually in units of 160 to 320 acres. Few people paid attention to the exact boundaries of their tracts; many neglected even to acquire legal title. With hay selling by the pound and fresh food at a premium, land changed hands rapidly, and speculation prevailed.

By the early 1870s the *Truckee Republican* reported that fifteen dairies operated at Lake Valley, each with an average of sixty milk cows and forty head of young stock. Farmers shipped butter to Carson City or Virginia City. Each dairy reportedly maintained about 500 acres of meadowland from which it harvested wild or timothy hay. With the increasing interest in Tahoe land, the value of the meadowlands rose to as much as $20 per acre, an early sign of land price escalation. By the mid-1870s the dairies of Lake Valley supported two coopers' shops at the head of the lake that manufactured firkins of white pine in which to ship the butter to market. In spite of gradual deterioration in quality of the pasturage, livestock grazing remained important well into the twentieth century, and small Tahoe dairies continued to supply local and eastern Sierra markets for several decades.

Fishing provided another small but important industry in the basin, but it flourished initially and then declined rapidly. As soon as the Comstock opened in 1859, Italian, Portuguese, and other

Dairies and livestock depended on scattered meadowland, such as this hayfield at Glenbrook. Special Collections, University of Nevada–Reno Library.

commercial fishermen were plying the waters of Lake Tahoe near the south shore. Men in small boats hauled in thousands of native trout, which, when not consumed locally, were marketed in Carson Valley and Virginia City. Indians reportedly netted large numbers of fish throughout the year in the Upper Truckee River and other inlets, and these were sold to local innkeepers.

In ensuing years, Lake Tahoe supported twenty or twenty-five full-time fishermen during the summer season. Many considered the fish supply unlimited and thus applauded the shipment of trout to hotel dining rooms as far afield as San Francisco and Chicago. Sports fishermen also exacted a toll, for there was no legal limit to the number that could be taken by hook and line. One fisherman caught 148 pounds of fish in three hours. An occasional native cut-throat trout weighed more than 20 pounds.

The California Fish Commission had placed a hundred thousand whitefish in Tahoe and nearby waters and large numbers of young trout and salmon in the Truckee River by 1880. In subsequent years, the commission established two hatcheries at the lake and experimented with the introduction of such new species as eastern brook trout and mackinaw (lake trout). Yet when Chancey Juday investigated fishing conditions at Lake Tahoe in 1904, he found only two species being taken in quantity, lake trout and silver trout. Even so, about eighty boats remained actively engaged in fishing, and commercial fishermen continued to ship fish from the basin.

Not until 1917 did the California legislature ban commercial fishing at Tahoe. By then the damage had been done; and the native cutthroat verged on extinction by the 1930s. Excessive catches, dams, disturbance of spawning grounds, and the voracious appetite of mackinaw, which devour fingerlings, contributed to the decline. Subsequent large-scale plants of fish in Tahoe proved disappointing: survival rates were low. Perhaps, in a quiet way, the decline of the fish populations signaled the potential impact of growing numbers of people on all the native species of the basin.

The Lumber Industry

Fishing and agriculture within the Tahoe Basin remained relatively small enterprises throughout the late nineteenth century, but the lumber industry came to dominate human activity. Although second growth timber eventually covered most of the scars left by loggers, little virgin timber survived. Both the vegetation and the eroding slopes on which the timber once stood underwent rapid change.

The earliest mills, established by 1860 at the south end of the lake, supplied building materials for local settlements and early trading posts. With the discovery of the Comstock Lode, however, the development of mines and of the neighboring towns provided an insatiable lumber market. As early as 1861, Augustus Pray and partners built a water-powered sawmill on the east shore at the site now known as Glenbrook. Here they cut as much as ten thousand

Lumber mills at Glenbrook in the 1870s and 1880s provided timber for Virginia City and the Comstock Lode. Nevada State Museum.

board feet a day, which they transported by wagon over the summit to the east and down Clear Creek to Carson Valley. The same year, Samuel Clemens (Mark Twain) staked a timber claim nearby—then watched in fascination as it went up in smoke after his unattended campfire jumped out of control. Clemens later called Tahoe "the fairest picture the whole earth affords," yet the consequence of his brief sojourn on its shores was the scorching of nearby mountain slopes.

Mining of the Comstock Lode increased the demand for wood. An immense quantity of timber was required for square-set timbering, a mining technique used to shore up the ceiling of underground excavations; quantities of wood were also used for building materials, as fuel for steam pumps in the mines, and for other purposes. At the end of the long winter of 1867, Chinese merchants sold the roots of previously cut trees near Virginia City for $60 per cord.

When the scattered piñon and juniper trees near Virginia City and the forest on the east side of the Carson Range fell quickly to loggers and the price of lumber skyrocketed, mining interests looked hungrily at the vast and essentially untouched forests within the Tahoe Basin. The editor of the *Washoe Times* remarked, on a visit to the lake: "At present the timber and lumber capabilities of the borders of Lake Tahoe seem illimitable."[5] The only problem was how to quickly and economically transport the timber across many miles of rough, steep terrain to where it was needed.

The invention of the V-shaped flume eased the transport problem. The expanding mills at Glenbrook shipped lumber and cordwood by wagon to Spooner Summit, where it was loaded into a flume for a quick watery ride down Clear Creek Canyon to the lumber yards just south of Carson City. From there, heavily loaded wagons hauled the wood up the steep road to the Virginia City area.

The railroad, together with the V-shaped flume, provided the key to the possible exploitation of Tahoe's forests. By January 1870, trains operated by the Virginia and Truckee Railroad hauled ore from the Comstock to the stamp mills on the Carson River and returned with wood from the Sierra. By 1873 and the Big Bonanza strike, more than thirty trains per day were using the twenty-one miles of single track between Carson City and Virginia City.

To a considerable extent the history of the lumber industry at Tahoe is the story of Duane L. Bliss and the Carson and Tahoe Lumber and Fluming Company. After a turn at prospecting and storekeeping in California, Bliss operated a stamp mill and then helped establish a bank near Virginia City. When his bank was absorbed by the Bank of California, Bliss joined Henry M. Yerington to construct the railroad from Carson City to Virginia City. That completed, they shifted their interest to the lumber business at Tahoe. In this they were joined by Darius Ogden Mills, president of the Bank of California.

Their newly formed Carson and Tahoe Lumber and Fluming Company (CTLFC), with Bliss as president and general manager, purchased large tracts of timberland on the slopes of the eastern side of the basin and bought the mills at Glenbrook House and other

The wood-burning engine "Tahoe" hauled lumber to Spooner Summit.
Nevada State Museum.

properties. In time CTLFC held more than fifty thousand acres in
the basin, including many miles of shoreline, some of which had
cost as little as $1.25 per acre. The company purchased additional
acreage from the Central Pacific Railroad in the northern and
northwestern parts of the basin: alternate sections of land that
originally had been granted by the federal government to promote
construction of the first transcontinental railroad. Before long
CTLFC had acquired other sections from preemptors. The company furnished money to people who would purchase a half-section
of land from the government and then turn it over to them. It also

purchased acreage from people who took up property under the Timber Culture Act and other federal and state land laws.

With control of a vast acreage of timberland and a transportation system extending from Spooner Summit to Virginia City, the next task of CTLFC was to streamline logging operations within the Tahoe Basin. In 1874 survey crews inspected the steep grades between Glenbrook and Spooner Summit, and the following summer large crews completed construction of nearly nine miles of narrow-gauge track over eleven trestles and through a 487-foot tunnel along the climb to the pass. Teamsters with the aid of powerful block and tackle hauled three locomotives and many log cars up the steep mountainside from Carson Valley to Tahoe—a noteworthy accomplishment.

Loggers cut trees in various parts of the basin and brought them to the lakeshore by flume, greased skids, or teams of oxen. There the trees were gathered in large booms and pulled across the lake by steamer to the Glenbrook mills, where they were sawed into timber. The newly completed Lake Tahoe Railroad then hauled the lumber to a large receiving yard at Spooner Summit, nearly a thousand feet higher than the lake. After being dumped into the flume, which was fed by feeder flumes from Marlette Lake to the north and from the mountain streams to the south, the wood made the twelve-mile journey with a three-thousand-foot drop in elevation to the Carson Valley. Finally, the Virginia and Truckee Railroad carried the lumber and cordwood twenty miles to the Comstock market.

As CTLFC exhausted the readily available timber near Glenbrook, it extended operations to the south shore and the west side of the lake. A member of the Wheeler Survey in 1876, part of the federal government's geographical surveys west of the one-hundredth meridian, described a large lumber camp at Sugar Pine Point where trees were cut into twenty- to thirty-foot sections and hauled to the shore on strong wagons with solid wooden wheels, pulled by six or eight yoke of oxen. As a collection point for the timber to be rafted by steamer to Glenbrook, Meeks Bay also became a focal point of the CTLFC operation.

Denuded hillsides show the result of destructive logging practices in 1876 at Spooner Summit, site of the junction of the CTLFC's railroad and flume. Nevada State Museum.

At Tahoe Valley on the south shore, CTLFC engaged Matthew Gardner and others to supply an immense quantity of lumber. In 1875 Gardner agreed to supply "60 million feet of logs" over the next six years. To fulfill his contract, he built a standard-gauge railroad from a pier at the lakeshore (at present-day Camp Richardson) back into the woods along the west side of the valley. An

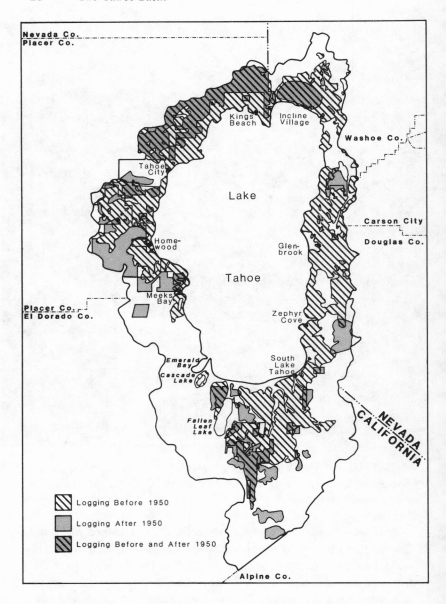

Logging in the Lake Tahoe Basin

average of seventy-two carloads could be unloaded daily. The rails were constantly shifted to reach uncut forest land until, in the mid-1880s, Gardner's lumbering enterprise finally came to an end.

A short distance to the east, George W. Chubbuck built a narrow-gauge railroad from Bijou to tap the timber in the southeastern corner of the basin. His Lake Valley Railroad, built in 1886, was soon taken over by CTLFC, which rebuilt it and extended the track toward Meyers. At Bijou, the loaded logging cars could be run out on an eighteen-hundred-foot pier into the lake, where the logs were dumped into the water.

Although Bliss's mills dominated the Tahoe lumber industry, several small operators cut timber throughout the basin. One competitor stood out from all the others. Walter Scott Hobart organized the Sierra Nevada Wood and Lumber Company and established a mill at Incline at the northeastern end of the lake. From there he shipped timber to the Comstock by an ingenious system. First a narrow-gauge railroad carried logs to the mill from timbered slopes to the northwest and from Sand Harbor, which served as a gathering point for logs from company land at the south end of the basin. The mill had a double-tracked incline railway. Powered by a stationary forty horse-power steam engine that operated a bull wheel, the railway hoisted the logs up a steep hill, gaining fourteen hundred feet in elevation. From the top of the railway the timber was moved via flume and railroad to the Comstock.

The incline railway, completed late in 1880, soon hauled large quantities of lumber. Hobart controlled more than ten thousand acres of timberland and kept 250 loggers busy at the peak of operations, but by the mid-1890s the timber supply had been so depleted that the company dismantled its track. The logging operation moved north of the lake to Overton, later called Hobart Mills. Left behind were remnants of the former forest, abandoned mills, decaying flumes, and vertical scars on Incline Mountain that are still visible from the western side of the lake.

Sometime later the California State Forester criticized the logging practices of the Sierra Nevada Wood and Lumber Company—practices not uncommon in the Tahoe Basin. Loggers cut all trees of marketable size, leaving the area nearly denuded. In the process, mostly because of carelessness in felling and skidding trees, they destroyed a large part of the young growth. Slash, consisting of broken timber, branches, and tree tops, remained in a jumbled mass where it fell—a hindrance to the reproduction of new trees and a fire hazard.

At roughly the same time Hobart moved his logging business from the Tahoe Basin, CTLFC closed. Not only had the best of the timberland been cut over, but the primary customer, the Comstock mines, had declined steadily after the golden years of the 1870s. According to conservative estimates, more than thirty million board feet came from the Glenbrook and Incline mills annually during the peak years, and tens of thousands of cords of firewood were cut each year. During the twenty years of prosperity of the Comstock Lode, lumber (including sawed mine timbers) valued at more than $80 million came from the forests of the Tahoe and Truckee basins, helping to produce the approximately $400 million in mineral wealth that came out of the mines.

In the late 1890s, the population of Virginia City declined. Abandoned homes were sometimes used for firewood. At the south shore of Tahoe, which had yielded an estimated twenty-one million board feet in a single season, logging camps, mills, flumes, and railroads lay abandoned among the stumps of the cutover land. Nearby acreage, littered with discarded equipment and logging waste, sold for no more than $1.50 an acre. The number of people making a living in the basin dropped sharply, many roads quickly became impassable, and former roadside inns and post offices disappeared. After an investment of an estimated million dollars by Bliss and friends and a short period of great activity, much of the Tahoe Basin had again become an area of sparse population and scattered rustic resorts and summer homes. It would be another fifty years before the basin would again experience such momentous changes or destruction.

When E. A. Sterling, a former assistant in the U.S. Bureau of Forestry, inspected the basin in 1904, he reported that the forest cover had been materially changed because of both lumbering and fires. Only on the inaccessible upper slopes did the original forest, mainly firs, remain untouched by lumbermen. In regard to the best timber close to the lake, he remarked: "The forest is much reduced in density; brush and reproduction are competing for possession in the openings; the sugar pine has disappeared almost entirely, and is scantily represented in the reproduction; the finest of the Jeffrey and yellow pine and white fir has been removed, fir production in general [is] replacing the pine; while considerable areas have reverted entirely to brush."[6]

The brush, commonly called chapparal, competed with young seedlings. Fortunately, loggers had left enough defective trees to provide sufficient seed for reproduction. As a result, in the absence of fire, a dense new forest, ten to twenty feet high by 1904, had risen. White firs held competitive advantage, producing an abundance of seeds, growing well in the shade, and surviving in relatively poor seedbeds. These trees grew from amid the chapparal and the old slash left by logging operators, providing a forest cover that promised to restore the scenic beauty, if not the quality of timber, that had once graced the slopes of the Tahoe Basin.

But because of the denseness of the new growth and the abundance of the slash, the new forest was vulnerable to fires as never before. In September 1889, for example, the *Sacramento Record-Union* reported: "Witnesses fresh from the Lake Tahoe region inform us that almost that entire section is a scene of desolation on account of the destruction of fires. . . . At the head of Emerald Bay last week a fire was raging of many miles extent, destroying the finest park of tree growth in all that region."[7] The article noted the potential consequences of the loss of vegetation: floods, soil erosion, reduction in wildlife, destruction of valuable timber, and desolation of the finest scenery.

A fire that started near Meyers in September 1898 swept up the mountains to the east. When Charles H. Shinn, a U.S. forest agent, visited the basin in 1902, he reported sighting many small and smoldering fires, especially on the California side of the basin, often "four to ten in one day's travel."[8] The debris left from logging operations fed the fires, creating sufficient heat to destroy humus and harden clay in the soil. A fire southeast of Bijou burned for more than three weeks in 1903.

Sheepherders, who intentionally set many of the fires to encourage the growth of new vegetation, also damaged the forests by bringing their sheep to the mountains early in the season. The animals destroyed more than they ate, sliding on the wet slopes and trampling the young grasses. By autumn no feed remained, and visitors to the basin had to carry hay and barley for their horses.

The damage to young trees as a result of overgrazing was evident. The most overstocked range had almost no new seedlings, whereas ranges spared from overgrazing revealed a mass of young trees, often two or three thousand to the acre, which choked out the competing underbrush. The brush, which was less dense on the more arid eastern side of the basin, did provide a useful ground cover to reduce erosion, although it also hindered second growth of timber.

When forest agent Sterling completed his 1904 investigation, he foresaw little hope for protecting the forest, for he believed that local sentiment opposed state laws to regulate and protect it. He advocated increased federal activity in the basin, at least in one corner already set aside as a forest reserve. By this time, the question of government ownership and regulation of land in the Tahoe Basin had become a critical issue.

Another important legacy of the logging era was a pattern of land ownership that affected development around the lake in the twentieth century. On the east shore in particular, Bliss and Hobart had dominated, purchasing their land outright. There, property remained in large blocks; because little could be done with the land after the timber had been removed, there was no reason to divide it for sale. As a consequence, large landholdings were available later for both a state park and a national forest, and for such major development projects as Incline Village. At the south shore, in contrast, the rights to cut timber had often been leased rather than purchased, the land ownership tended to be more segmented. Cutover land retained value for grazing, and some tracts on level terrain close to the lake were attractive for building summer cottages. In general, individual landholdings on the California side tended to be smaller than on the east shore, which left the door open for the patchwork of small developments and subdivisions that followed.

The passing of the logging era marked the end of a period in which a relatively few men—farmers, sheepherders, miners, fishermen, and loggers—attempted to profit from Tahoe's natural resources. Prospectors never found the mineral wealth they sought. Fishermen gradually depleted the resources on which they depended. Loggers quickly decimated the forest and in the process eliminated the employment base it had briefly provided. By the turn of the century, Tahoe no longer offered attractive opportunities for the exploitation of natural resources. Future development, including the urbanization of parts of the basin, rested instead, upon the slowly growing tourist trade.

2 Urbanization of the Tahoe Basin, 1900–1960

Summer Resorts and Transportation, 1900–1930

Tourism soon dominated the economic life of Tahoe. Duane Bliss and his family, recognizing the collapse of the lumber industry in the basin, shifted their financial interests to the burgeoning summer recreation business. The *Tahoe,* a graceful, 169-foot steamship owned by the Blisses, was launched at Glenbrook in 1896. Adorned with the finest brass and mahogany, this elegant ship could carry two hundred passengers at about twenty knots and was aptly called the "queen of the lake." She had Moroccan leather upholstry and fine Belgian carpets; no expense had been spared to provide the finest appointments. For nearly forty years, the *Tahoe* made her rounds of the lake, delivering the mail and carrying passengers.

His dominance of transportation on the lake assured, Bliss linked the Tahoe Basin by rail to the outside world. He dismantled the Lake Tahoe Railroad at Glenbrook and the two logging railroads at the south shore. The locomotives, cars, rails, and other equipment provided the nucleus for the Lake Tahoe Railway and Transportation Company, recently incorporated by the Bliss family. Bliss acquired a right-of-way from Truckee to Tahoe City across land owned by the Truckee Lumber Company, and by May 1900 construction crews had laid fifteen miles of track. The new narrow-gauge railroad operated from May 15 to November 15 each year, primarily to serve the tourist trade.

The final link in the circle of tourist enterprises of the Bliss family was the Tahoe Tavern, a luxury hotel completed in 1901. This large four-story building, situated just south of Tahoe City, combined elegance with rusticity. As the Tavern advertised: "Imagine a long rambling building of shingles the color of pine bark, twenty-foot porches, whose supports are the roughsawed native wood, all set in the primeval forest, with the magnificent sweep of Lake Tahoe in front, and you have the picture of this hotel."[1] A San Francisco businessman could leave his family at the Tavern for the summer and commute there on weekends. The Friday night train arrived in time for breakfast at the lake, and the return train on Sunday night took him home in time for work on Monday morning.

Tahoe offered a rare combination of attractions: accessibility, first-class accommodations, and remarkable scenic beauty. A Southern Pacific promotional book noted: "Tahoe is yet of the wilderness, and this is its chief charm. It is at the doors of cities, easy of access and hospitable, provided with the comforts of a luxury-loving age, while preserving the virtues of the simple life and freedom from the scrambling conceits of over refinement."[2]

The Tahoe Tavern continued a tradition of prestigious hotels at Lake Tahoe. The refurbished Tallac hotel, near present-day Camp Richardson, advertised its own "ballroom, ladies' billiard and pool room, four latest improved bowling alleys, sun parlors, stage and dressing rooms for theatricals, $10,000 worth of French plate mirrors and 500 electric lights."[3]

In spite of the railroad and luxury hotels, major portions of the shoreline remained relatively isolated. Many of the roads that had been maintained during the logging boom had fallen into disrepair. No road connected the north and south shores, and access to the basin by any means except rail from Truckee to Tahoe City remained uncomfortable and undependable. Tahoe promoters eagerly looked for ways to open the basin further to the outside world.

Though proposals for constructing electric railways abounded,

The elegant Tahoe Tavern attracted wealthy tourists to the north shore of Lake Tahoe. California Historical Society, San Francisco.

the future of transportation at Tahoe depended on the development of roads and the introduction of automobiles. The once renowned interstate wagon road from Placerville to Carson Valley that had served the south shore during its former period of prosperity lay in ruins. In 1895, the California legislature created the Lake Tahoe State Wagon Road across Echo Summit, and gradually the route was improved. To the north, the other major wagon road to Tahoe, over Donner Summit, also had been neglected. Not until 1909 did the state legislature provide funds to select and survey a route (later called Highway 40) and then construct a state highway across Donner Pass to Truckee. (Today, Interstate 80 crosses the Sierra a short distance to the north of the original state highway.) In 1913, the completion of a road around Emerald Bay opened a popular 260-mile circle route from Sacramento to Tahoe.

The Pierce Arrow Auto Stage Line by 1919 carried passengers from the rail depot in Sacramento over the newly completed American River Highway (Highway 50), advertised as "one of the finest mountain roads in all California," to the Tallac hotel on the south shore. At Tahoe, the stage line serviced Fallen Leaf Lodge, The Grove, Bijou, Camp Bell, Connally's, Young Brothers, Lakeside, and Al Tahoe.

The appearance little by little of several new resorts signaled changes under way within the basin. The older resorts, expensive to maintain, did not offer the accommodations desired by many in the new wave of tourists who were arriving by bus and automobile. The Tahoe Tavern continued to cater to its wealthy clientele, but the Tallac hotel closed its doors in the early 1920s and was razed by its owners. In its place such family-oriented areas as Camp Richardson and Meeks Bay Resort sprang up to assume a share of the tourist business.

Summer Homes and Housing Tracts

As the number of summer resorts gradually increased, so did the number of families looking to the Tahoe Basin for summer

Auto travel on the shores of Lake Tahoe proved an adventure in 1916. California State Library.

home sites. Before the turn of the century, prominent San Franciscans were acquiring private estates near the shores of Tahoe, particularly on the northwest side. Land sales multiplied on the north shore as well. In the early 1890s, for example, the Lake Tahoe Chautauqua Improvement Company offered capital stock of $100,000 in a summer resort at Carnelian Bay. As an added incentive, promoters offered free building sites to investors who purchased a substantial number of shares in the company. Noting that steep mountain grades still discouraged the growth of Tahoe as a summer resort area, the company proposed an electric railway from Reno to Carnelian Springs that would, at least in theory, become the central point on the perimeter of the lake.

Author A. J. Wells had noted the construction of several attractive summer homes around the edge of the lake by 1906 and the rise of a more or less permanent population. Wells predicted that, as at Lake George, Lake Geneva, Lake Como, and other resorts, "so at Tahoe there will be a summer city, and boulevards about the lake will be builded and amusement houses will invade the wilderness, and all the gregarious instincts of man will find free play as well as the beauty-loving side of his nature."[4]

Thoughts of the lucrative development of major tracts and subdivisions soon enticed investors to Tahoe. In 1906 John T. Read and Brothers, a Reno real estate and mining brokerage, took out a full page advertisement in the *Daily Nevada State Journal* for their Emerald City Tract, claiming that this tract of eighty-two lots on the north shore of Emerald Bay was the only subdivision of Tahoe property on the market. Seventy-five-foot lakefront lots were offered for $200–500 each.

The *San Francisco Call* reported in May 1912 that two leading San Francisco real estate firms had acquired the old Bliss timberland and planned to divide forty-four thousand acres into large summer villa sites suitable for millionaires and others. In addition, a plan for town sites for people of moderate means led to a prediction that Tahoe would become "a mecca for hundreds of thousands of people every season." An editorial in the *Call* praised the idea, noting that "until now there has been no systematic exploitation of the real estate of the lake shore."[5] Admitting that America had no counterpart to the cultural attraction of Europe, the *Call* nevertheless insisted that America's natural scenery rivals that of Switzerland, Austria, and Norway. The editorial closed by suggesting that California had a duty to open the Lake Tahoe region to people from less favored regions.

A smaller development on the south shore marked a different and more successful kind of project. After Al Sprague built the Al Tahoe hotel in 1908, southern California investors acquired the property and subdivided several nearby lots. The Al Tahoe Development Company owned its own electricity generating plant and prided itself on catering only to the select population in the small community it promoted. In the 1920s, the Al Tahoe area and near-by Bijou, not far from the site of present-day Stateline, continued to prosper with investment by such people as Frank Globin from Sacramento. Globin bought several hundred acres of wooded land and the small inn at Al Tahoe, sight unseen. During summer 1924 he renovated his new property and served the moderate number of tourists who happened by. Globin also owned the local water company, then serving twenty-four customers, and he encouraged improvement of the road over Echo Summit.

Although real estate promotion remained slow, land prices in popular locations near the lake rose steadily. Claire MacDonald, granddaughter of an early lumberman, complained in 1924 that a hundred-foot lakefront lot at Homewood cost $5,000. Instead, she purchased a large hillside lot for $400 and had the frame of a small three-room cottage constructed by carpenters; materials and labor cost another $700. Obviously, the opportunity to acquire property at Tahoe remained open to persons of moderate means.

The 1930s

In spite of the depression, south Tahoe had emerged as an increasingly popular area by the early 1930s.[6] Meyers, Al Tahoe, Bijou, and Zephyr Cove were thriving; even Stateline began to show signs of life. Summer home construction increased, and the need for a school became apparent. Not since the logging era ended in the 1890s had there been any educational facilities at south Tahoe. Now local residents built a small school near the junction of highways 89 and 50; it served as many as thirty-five students in summer and six or eight in winter. School began in July and continued until mid-December, then closed for three months in the heart of winter and reopened from mid-March until June.

If the local newspaper, the *Tahoe Tattler,* can be believed, the

Tahoe Basin experienced a minor building boom in the five years prior to American entry into World War II in 1941. The headlines reveal a pattern of boosterism and confidence in the future: "Building Boom Sweeps Over Tahoe," "Winter Resort Assured For Tahoe," and "New Crop of Tahoe Homes Completed as Fall Building Starts." The Lake Valley Chamber of Commerce, organized in 1938, provided the south shore with a counterpart to the Chamber of Commerce already operating on the north shore.

According to the Lake Tahoe Sierra Association, a booster organization, there were more than forty resorts around the edge of the lake in 1940, and nearly all were in California. Campgrounds at the Camp Richardson Resort and elsewhere were popular, and motels like Wagner's Auto Camp, Tahoe Alps Court, and Rustic Cottage Court multiplied in number. The Greyhound Bus Company advertised an eight-hour trip from San Francisco, charging $7.75 for the round trip.

The "building boom" of the late 1930s should be kept in perspective, however. The *Tattler* estimated then that fifty new homes had been built throughout the basin in 1939, ranging from a ten-room "palace" to a one-room cabin. Approximately 150 businesses operated on the lake shores. Total real estate values were estimated at upward of $20 million, with Placer County in the lead. The summer population probably peaked at more than twenty thousand; the winter population may have been two thousand. Tahoe remained a large mountain lake ringed by small, scattered communities. A local dance, the construction of a single home, or summer guests in individual homes still warranted comment in the local newspaper, and Lake Tahoe retained its rustic atmosphere.[7]

The major stumbling block to plans for further development appeared to be inadequacies of the road system, both to and within the basin. Tahoe business interests called for proper road signs and a white line down the center of the narrow roadways. Of more importance, a three-year construction program to realign and improve Highway 50 over Echo Pass reached fruition in 1940. The California Highway Commission finally authorized year-round maintenance for Highway 50 over Echo Summit and Highway 89 from Truckee to Tahoe City, but American entry into the war delayed implementation for the duration of hostilities.

The quiet days at Tahoe were numbered. The Bliss family's railway, which had been taken over by the Southern Pacific Railroad Company in 1925 and converted to a standard-gauge track, could no longer operate competitively despite special winter excursion trains, liberal stopover privileges, and other attractions. The last train from Truckee to Tahoe City ran in 1942; the track was torn up for scrap iron to aid the war effort. Lake steamers, so much a part of Tahoe tradition, also proved uneconomical, unable to compete with the convenience of automobiles, trucks, and buses. Even the *Tahoe* became expendable after she lost her mail contract. The Bliss family, out of sentiment, repurchased the once proud ship in 1940 and consigned her to a watery grave in Tahoe's depths rather than sell her for scrap.

Not everyone was pleased with the signs of growth and change at Tahoe. In a series of articles and editorials during summer 1938, the *Tattler* complained that uncontrolled growth on the north shore threatened the quality of recreational opportunities at the lake. The newspaper praised those landowners who advocated zoning restrictions for property around Kings Beach and Carnelian Bay to prevent it from turning into a "desert of brass horns, gaudy umbrellas, [and] rooting tooting pop guzzlers."

North shore residents and promotion interests waged a heated battle over zoning. A committee of property owners chaired by Mrs. Will T. Mooney favored restricted zones for business and multiple family units and a ban on amusement concessions, stables, and billboards over six feet square. It also advocated fire inspection, septic tanks, garbage disposal, and inspection of building plans before a building permit would be issued.

But the opposition, led by Walter Hempkill, carried the day. Hempkill argued for the Kings Beach–Brockway Property Owners Protective Association that Kings Beach should have no restrictions whatsoever on growth, instead allowing in "new blood" in the form of the "laboring man." Amusement parks, he claimed, would aid community development, and building restrictions would prevent the "small fellow" from building even a modest summer cottage. At that time no legal restrictions existed on the kinds of structures that could be built, and twenty-five-foot lots appeared in parts of Kings Beach. From the perspective of business leaders, growth meant profit.

Another problem became increasingly apparent in this prewar period: poor communication among the various segments of the basin and lack of a sense of community. In the early days, each major resort had published its own promotional leaflet, yet all shared a vested interest in promoting the steamer and the beauty of the lake. Now, however, the editor of the *Tattler* complained that people in Bijou had no idea of important developments at Brockway and possibly had not even heard of Kings Beach, a thriving business area. Of course the reverse was true also. Although the Lake Tahoe Sierra Association tried to help resolve the problem, its members concentrated on their own interests and devoted little time to the lake as a whole. The *Tattler's* editor had no answer but noted that eventually "something must be done to tie the entire lake community together."[8]

With the advent of war, gasoline rationing had an immediate effect: Tahoe was deserted except for a few caretakers, occasional tourists, and military personnel. As one resort owner later stated, "We hibernated for five years." Only Highway 40, considered essential for defense purposes, remained open, and Highway 50 closed each winter. Even bus service to south Tahoe was terminated. For those who managed to visit Lake Tahoe at this time, the experience must have been similar to what it had been at the beginning of the century.

Winter Recreation

Skiing, a popular recreational activity within the basin, contributed substantially to the remarkable growth there after 1945. Skiing actually began in the Sierra almost as soon as Scandinavian sailors had disembarked from ships in San Francisco harbor on their way to dig for gold. John A. Thompson, a Sacramento rancher and a native Norwegian, gained fame as Snowshoe Thompson, carrying the mails across the Sierra to Carson Valley for twenty winters prior to his death in 1876. Using heavy ten-foot skis and a single six-foot pole, Thompson carried a pack weighing as much as a hundred pounds across the mountains in the worst winter weather. Known for his feats of endurance, he would carry no blankets, sleeping in shelters along the way or, as the tale has it, dancing all night on a rock to keep from freezing in a blizzard. Others introduced downhill skiing and—preferring to compete with one another instead of Thompson—ran in the short races that became popular by the late 1860s.

In spite of their early beginnings at Tahoe, winter sports took hold only slowly, primarily because the first heavy snows each winter essentially closed the basin to the outside world. Tahoe resorts had no regular winter recreational activities. Of course, anyone so inclined could strap on a pair of skis or snowshoes and go into the woods. Ski trails radiated outward from the few resorts willing to provide comfort to winter travelers, but skiing was as much a matter of transportation as of recreation. Truckee staged a winter carnival, including ski racing and jumping, in the years before World War I, and both toboggans and skis could be rented at Truckee and Lake Tahoe.

The Tahoe Tavern sponsored a Christmas fete of ski and bobsled races, hockey contests, exhibition skating, tobogganing, sleigh rides, and other winter sports in 1928. North Tahoe staged its first annual national ski-jumping tournament in 1930, with an international field of fifteen contestants and large numbers of spectators. Olympic Hill had a ski-jumping hill, and before the end of the decade ski runs appeared at White Hills near Spooner Summit and at Bijou. The White Hills run offered a T-bar lift, but that commercial advantage was undercut by a lack of snow, and the business eventually succumbed. The small operation at Bijou survived until the ski boom of the 1950s.

Outside the Tahoe Basin, increasing numbers of winter recreationists drove into the mountains to enjoy snow-related activities. The California Ski Association, organized in 1930, staged its first competitive tournament in 1933 under the auspices of the Auburn Ski Club and the Lake Tahoe Ski Club. The association had eighteen member clubs by the end of the decade. On Highway 40, lodges built at Norden by the University of California and the Sierra Club, near a hotel at Soda Springs that had been constructed not long before, provided the nucleus for a ski area on Donner Summit. Such nearby ski resorts as Donner Ski Ranch and Sugar Bowl served winter sports enthusiasts. On Highway 50, members of the Placerville Ski Club, also founded in 1930, drove as far to ski as the road was open. By 1938 the state kept the road open to Twin Bridges; there a longtime resident jacked up a Model-T Ford and operated a rope tow with one of its wheel hubs. At Camp Sacramento, west of Echo Summit, a small ski resort called Eidelweiss opened by 1941; it closed during the war, then reopened featuring the first chair lift near south Tahoe, but it failed later because of insufficient snow.

Roads to both the north and south shores remained open all year following the war. Several small lifts operated, including those at Granlibakken, Meyers, and Echo Summit. Ski resorts had opened nearby at spots like Mount Rose and the Sierra Ski Ranch. By the mid-1950s, some nineteen ski resorts existed in a great loop around the Tahoe Basin and within it. Tahoe was becoming one of the major winter sports areas in the United States.

One small resort on the south shore of the lake, Bijou Park Skiway, was particularly successful. Chris Kuraisa, who purchased the Skiway, formed a corporation with George Canon, Rudy Gersick, and Curly Musso by 1955. Together they leased land at the bottom of a wooded mountain that rises to the east of Heavenly Valley Creek. The new resort opened in 1956 with two rope tows, a chair lift, and a small hut at the top. That first season ten thousand skiers used the resort, and the firm netted $23,000, largely from the $4 charged for an all-day pass on the chair lift. From this promising beginning, Heavenly Valley expanded rapidly. Within twenty years the resort served ten thousand skiers a day.

Another remarkable story of growth took place just outside the basin, in Squaw Valley. This valley remained a hay ranch and dairy farm for decades, ignored by almost everyone. Then in 1948, Wayne Poulson and Alex Cushing organized the Squaw Valley Development Corporation. Poulson, an avid skier, supplied the land, and Cushing, a New York socialite and lawyer, provided the financial backing. Soon a substantial lodge and chair lift opened to the public. And in 1955, to the surprise of nearly everyone, the International Olympic Committee selected Squaw Valley as the site for the 1960 Winter Olympic Games. An El Dorado county supervisor called it "about the biggest thing that could happen to Lake Tahoe and vicinity." Others noted the millions of dollars of free publicity for the area that would result. The state legislature of California appropriated a million dollars to begin a construction program to transform Squaw Valley into one of the major ski centers in the United States.

Heavenly Valley backers, just beginning construction of their first chair lift, took heart, for they knew that the whole winter recreation industry in the basin would benefit. Following the 1960 Winter Olympics, the ski industry grew explosively, and the impact on Tahoe Basin was tremendous. Winter traffic jams, for example, became accepted as part of a new way of life. Although the winter population did not equal the crowds of summer, it helped establish a base for year-round business enterprises and a growing permanent population. Together with gambling, winter recreation became the major attraction for the winter tourist trade.

Gambling

Gambling came to the American west with the earliest pioneers. Lumbermen and miners gained a reputation for enthusiasm over games of chance: travelers along the Comstock Road played poker at Yank's Station and other wayside inns. Gambling, like all other enterprises in the Tahoe Basin, declined with the end of the lumbering era, but it never disappeared completely.

Nevada legalized gambling in 1869 and then banned it in 1910, but from all accounts the changes in legal status made little difference to the practice. Clubs in Reno operated as speakeasies, allowing gambling behind closed doors. Then in 1931 the Nevada legislature legalized gambling once again, at the same time as it lowered the residency requirement for divorce to six weeks. These measures encouraged visitation to Nevada during the hard times of the great depression. On the first night of legal gambling, Californians were plentiful in the crowds.

Although gambling at this time was small-scale, and although Las Vegas remained a town of only five thousand people in the southern Nevada desert, gambling soon became the backbone of Nevada's economy. In 1936 Harold Smith opened a casino on Virginia Street in Reno with penny roulette and a couple of slot machines. He advertised nationally in the 1940s, and the familiar "Harold's Club or Bust" billboards helped place Reno on the map. While many small clubs went bankrupt, Harold's Club was enjoying five thousand visitors daily in 1945. By 1950 the number had risen to twenty thousand.

William Harrah, who had operated a bingo parlor in southern California, moved to Reno in 1937 and opened Harrah's Tango Club. Harrah began a small casino business in 1942 and expanded rapidly. Adopting Harold Smith's strategies and introducing some of his own, Harrah soon attracted the largest crowds in Reno. In 1955 he expanded his operation to the Lake Tahoe Basin, where gambling already existed.

Gambling had been an accepted practice at the lake since the early days, and it continued over the years despite its sometimes shady reputation. Local sheriffs would arrive too late (so it seemed) to find reported gambling activity on the California shore. In the mid-1920s, Clyde Beecher built the Nevada Club on the Nevada side of the state line at the south shore, a forerunner of the Tahoe-area casinos. At the state line on the north shore, the Cal-Neva Club emerged in the 1930s as the lake's busiest night spot, attracting celebrities like Clara Bow and Will Rogers. The *Tahoe Tattler* reported in 1941 that "Lake Tahoe's No. 2 industry is nightlife

The Nevada Club at Stateline lay hidden in the forest in the 1930s.
Nevada Historical Society.

(No. 1 resorts). To the lake's 20-odd full-fledged nightspots (bars, casinos, dance halls, etc.) flock each week-end an estimated 3000 persons, who spend anywhere from 25 cents for a glass of beer to $50,000 in an expensive game."[9]

This was nothing in comparison to what would follow. After World War II, a number of small casinos appeared at Stateline on the south shore. Ownership changed often as businesses failed or were absorbed by neighbors. For example, the Tahoe Village became Casino de Paree, then the Glass Slipper, then Cooter Jones. Eddie Sahati introduced big-name entertainers at his Stateline Country Club. Nearby, the owners of the Gateway Club—Curly Musso and George Canon—brought weekend skiers to their casino by bus. The skiers would head for White Hills or Eidelweiss in the morning and frequent the casinos at night.

But one man was more successful than all the others. Harvey Gross, a Sacramento butcher, acquired property at Stateline owned by the Galilee Episcopal Church. Gross added a gasoline pump (the

Forty years later, in the 1970s, gambling casinos and commercial development had transformed the same stretch of highway. James Hildinger.

only year-round pump at the south shore) and placed six slot machines and a few gaming tables in a small log building. His wife cooked food at their home and served it at their café. From this beginning came Harvey's Wagon Wheel, which by 1963 served five thousand meals every twenty-four hours and reportedly had more slot machines than any casino in the world. In that year, Gross constructed the first high-rise building on the south shore, an eleven-story hotel-casino extending far above the tops of the surrounding trees.

When William Harrah expanded his casino business to Tahoe's south shore in 1955, he acquired various properties and quickly built a major casino. Operating twenty-four hours a day and providing free bus service from some northern California cities, the casino flourished. The South Shore Room opened in 1959; Red Skelton headlined, and big-name entertainment became the rule.

Twenty years after its opening, Harrah's Tahoe had expanded to a fifty thousand square-foot casino in an eighteen-story structure, with a six-level parking garage, restaurants serving ten thousand meals daily, a convention center, and plans for further growth. The casinos on the north shore, more isolated from motels and hotels, served by relatively poor roads, and accessible to fewer people, played a secondary role at the lake once Harrah had arrived.

The impact of gambling on growth within the basin would be difficult to overestimate. The casinos hired an increasing percentage of persons employed around Tahoe. Most lived on the California side, where housing was more available. Gas stations, motels, laundries, restaurants, liquor stores, and all varieties of service businesses multiplied rapidly. Urbanization was under way.

Urbanization, 1945–1960

Following World War II, urbanization occurred at such a pace that no one fully understood its implications. As time passed, more and more people did express concern about the increasing problems that result from growth of an urban population in the middle of a fragile mountain ecosystem. But attempts to curb the growth or to correct the problems in these years tended to focus on specific problems or communities; no one dealt effectively with the basin as a whole. Not until the late 1950s were serious questions even posed about the environmental consequences of urbanization.

The main problem as perceived in 1945 by the most active leaders in the basin was how to attract tourists and potential residents to an area that had been nearly deserted during the war years. At this time, few if any people understood the potential dangers to the purity of the water or air, and no one foresaw how rapidly the quality of life in the basin could deteriorate. An aerial photograph of the south shore in 1948 reveals only trees. Scattered cabins lay hidden in the woods, but no building broke through the natural canopy of the tree tops.[10]

That year, the basin's population during the peak months of July and August, including weekend and holiday crowds, averaged 27,500. Roughly 8,000 resided on the south shore between Tahoe Valley (junction of Highways 50 and 89) and Stateline; and 5,800 lived on the north shore between Carnelian Bay and the Nevada side of the border. Thus roughly half the basin's summer population was concentrated in two small areas, and a third residential area, between Lake Forest and Tahoma on the northwestern shore, held another 5,400 people. In comparison, the entire population of the Nevada shore was less than 4,200—evidence that large open spaces remained within the basin, even along certain sections of the shoreline.[11]

Boosterism became the order of the day. The Rotary Club, the Lake Tahoe Southside Improvement Association, and other groups formed to encourage the tourist trade. And, most important, business leaders formed a new organization late in 1948 that eventually merged with the old Lake Tahoe Sierra Association to form the Lake Tahoe–Sierra Chamber of Commerce. This group claimed to include nearly all the year-round business interests in the basin; its board of directors represented each of the nineteen post office districts at Tahoe. For a brief time the north and south shores seemed to have common interests and to be ready to cooperate.

These new groups sponsored many activities, including an annual summer festival, highlighted by hydroplane boat races on the lake. An annual Highway 50 Wagon Train between Tahoe and Placerville, the Auburn-to-Tahoe jeep trip, rodeos, and other seasonal events helped create the image of Tahoe as a year-round playground. Tourists could choose from myriad activities, including golf, horseback riding, moonlight boat rides, drive-in theatres, dancing, and floor shows at the casinos, as well as fishing, camping, and hiking. Skiing increased 450 percent during the 1950s alone.

Improving transportation continued to be a high priority. Efforts by the Placerville to Lake Tahoe Resort Owners Association and others contributed to the completion in 1947 of a new all-weather road from Echo Summit to Lake Tahoe and along the south shore. Nevada Governor Vail Pittman, California Congressman Clair

Engle, and others joined in the festivities that opened this new stretch of Highway 50, assuring year-round access to south Tahoe.

Air travel gained support also. Although planes had landed on a dirt strip near Stateline since the 1930s, this so-called airport was short, dangerous, and sometimes occupied by grazing cattle. Nevertheless, twenty-two passengers aboard a Bay City Transport DC-3 in 1946 made the maiden fifty-five-minute commercial flight from Oakland to the newly opened Tahoe Sky Harbor Airport. When Sky Harbor proved unacceptable to federal authorities, Tahoe residents and business interests searched for a new airport site. The tracts considered included one recently acquired by the U.S. Forest Service at Pope Beach. A new airport was finally opened between Tahoe Valley and Meyers in the summer of 1959. It was heavily used almost immediately.

The growth at Tahoe reached new heights in the years following 1955. Spurred by developments like Heavenly Valley and Harrah's Club, and encouraged by employment opportunities in the building trades and the gambling industry, people flocked to Tahoe. Public school enrollment at south Tahoe suggests the magnitude of the change: 47 students in 1945, 460 in 1955, and 4,432 in 1965. A *Sacramento Bee* writer noted in 1957 that forty real estate dealers stayed busy on the south shore alone, and a thousand new motel and hotel units were added there each year. Thousands of people responded to signs advertising small plots in subdivisions, "$15 down, $15 a month," while prices for lake frontage climbed to $300 a front foot in preferred locations.[12]

Before the close of the 1950s, many resorts were staying open all year. Even in midweek, automobiles crowded the limited parking space next to the casinos. Harrah's buses made three free trips a day seven days a week from Stockton and Sacramento to the casino, and the casino planned to double its capacity in 1958.

In 1959 the El Dorado County Planning Commission approved a master plan for the south end of Lake Tahoe that envisioned a population of two hundred thousand by 1984, including fifty-thousand permanent residents, an equal number of summer home residents, and a hundred thousand tourists. Looking at the entire

If the ecological health of Lake Tahoe had been a major concern in the 1950s, Tahoe Keys would not have been built. Tahoe Keys Marina.

basin, members of the engineering committees of the California-Nevada Interstate Compact Commission foresaw a population of four hundred thousand at some future date, which would cause congestion in parts of the basin greater than that of many metropolitan areas in California at that time.

As if in confirmation of these predictions, the Dillingham Corporation, which purchased land from another development company, launched a huge development project called Tahoe Keys. As described in the *Sacramento Bee,* a massive dredger began a four-year operation to dredge some five million cubic yards of decomposed granite from marshland to create a $150-million residential resort. The machine, on a floating platform measuring 30 feet by 120 feet, would dredge a system of 150-foot-wide lagoons, each 14 feet deep, inland from the mouth of the Upper Truckee River just east of Pope Beach. The developers proposed ultimately to provide more than two thousand luxury homesites, as well as a convention site with a multi-story hotel, a large marina with winter storage for two thousand boats, and a thirty-acre regional shopping center.[13] Although not all the plans came to fruition, Tahoe Keys became a major development on the shores of the lake and, in the process, destroyed a significant part of the largest marsh habitat in the Tahoe Basin.

The Lake Tahoe South Shore Chamber of Commerce looked back proudly in the early 1960s at what had been achieved on the south shore. The recreation industry continued to spur development. Motels, supermarkets, restaurants, bars, clothing stores, ski rental shops, and many other businesses flourished. Construction, the Chamber of Commerce noted, had "passed the erratic-spurt stage and has now settled into a pattern of solid, dependable development reflecting a stable real estate trend, a predictable population level, and a firming economy in general." Agriculture had nearly disappeared completely, and it had been replaced by such sources of employment as sheet-metal work, custom furniture manufacturing, automobile sales and service, printing and publishing, advertising art, and public relations. The Chamber of Commerce announced it had launched a carefully planned campaign to attract electronic laboratories, and that south Tahoe would become a prime convention center.[14]

The north shore also felt the pressures of growth. Lakeshore lots that could not be sold for $250 apiece twenty-five years earlier now sold for $400 a front foot. The permanent population had climbed to an estimated six thousand and, as one newspaper put it, real estate offices were "more numerous than gas stations, taco stands, and Dairy Queen stores combined." At perhaps twelve different locations, subdivisions spread into the hills near the lake as forested areas gave way to the bulldozer and subdivider.

Of greatest significance for the north shore, in 1960 the Crystal Bay Development Company purchased nine thousand acres for $25 million. This 14.5-square-mile property, which included Incline Valley at the northeastern corner of the basin, had been acquired by George Whittell in the 1930s from the estate of lumber baron

Walter Hobart. Whittell had sold the property for $5 million to the Nevada Lake Tahoe Investment Company, a syndicate of business interests from Oklahoma, Kansas, and Hawaii, which sold it for a 500-percent profit the following year.

Raymond M. Smith, who presented a preliminary plan for development of the land early in 1960, proposed construction of a new town at Incline. Smith foresaw a fifty-six-acre shopping facility, four or five hotels with two to four hundred rooms each, a casino area of twenty or thirty acres, a civic or community center of about ten acres, a public park of some seventy acres, and space for an apartment and office complex and motels.[15]

By the 1960s the Tahoe Basin had become afflicted with runaway growth. The scattered cabins and summer resorts of the late nineteenth century had given way to high-rise casino-hotels, year-round tourism, and urban sprawl in certain parts of the basin. But at the same time, private citizens and public officials had been taking steps to keep a large part of the basin undeveloped to protect its scenic and recreational values and the quality of the water of Lake Tahoe.

3   Parks and Forests

Early Environmental Concern

Most people accepted as a matter of course the changes in
the Tahoe Basin that resulted from human habitation and development. Not all visitors, however, were unaware or unconcerned
about the inroads of loggers. When John Muir, the Scotsman who
later became America's leading advocate of national parks, passed
through the Tahoe Basin in the years between 1873 and 1875, he
wrote that, of all the glaciated lakes in the Sierra he had seen, "Lake
Tahoe is king of them all, not only in size, but in the surpassing
beauty of its shores and waters." He also commented that logging
"is being pushed so fervently from year to year, almost the entire
basin must be stripped ere long of one of its most attractive
features."[1]

David A. D'Ancona, a visiting businessman from England,
viewed the mountains east of Lake Tahoe in summer 1876. To him
the forest with its bare, broken trunks and scattered stumps
"appeared like a big cemetery, every trunk looking like a tomb-
stone." He asked, "Are they really not tombstones left in memory
of the mighty giants of the forest laid low by man's unceasing love
for gain?" Crossing Spooner Summit to Glenbrook, D'Ancona
noted the thriving sawmills that cut trees into large timbers to prop
up the mines of the Comstock. He also noticed a "huge fire" on the
beach, "disposing of the surplus wood which would be so valuable
if it only could be carried where it is much needed."[2]

Members of the Wheeler Survey visited the basin that summer and called the lake the "gem of the Sierras." From Mount Tallac, they viewed a landscape "at once unique and comprehensive and equalled by few of the many wonderful views of our western region. . . . It would have been well years ago had the General Government reserved the slopes leading to this lake as a permanent pleasure ground, to be regulated for the benefit of all the people, as well as a specially beautiful spot for rest and recreation for travelers from all lands."[3]

Most local people expressed more interest in the acquisition of land for profit than about the basin's protection. The *Truckee Republican* in 1873 complained that sections of timberland owned by railroad companies sold at increasing prices, whereas alternate sections retained by the government were practically unavailable except for agriculture and grazing. The difficulty in obtaining timbered land, the *Republican* remarked, hurt the mining interests (and, it might have added, the local lumber companies); the government policy clearly invited fraud and trespass on government property. The newspaper suggested an orderly system of acquisition based on sale of tracts of land at nominal prices. The Timber and Stone Act of 1878, which allowed for acquisition of 160 acres of timbered and stony land at a low price, met with favorable response.

Yet even among local newspapers, concern for Tahoe's forests and scenic beauty found expression. An article in the *Truckee Tribune* noted that lumber barons would spend thousands of dollars to visit the Alps but not a dollar to save Tahoe, whose scenery, it said, surpassed that of Europe. In fact, to cut Tahoe's forests seemed a sacrilege:

> If in some old cathedral there was a picture painted and framed by an angel, one such as mortal art never could approach in magnificence, the world would be shocked were some man to take off and sell the marvelous frame. But Tahoe is a picture rarer than ever glittered on cathedral walls; older, fresher and fairer than any work by the old masters, and yet they are cutting away her frame and bearing it away. Have we no State pride to stop the work?[4]

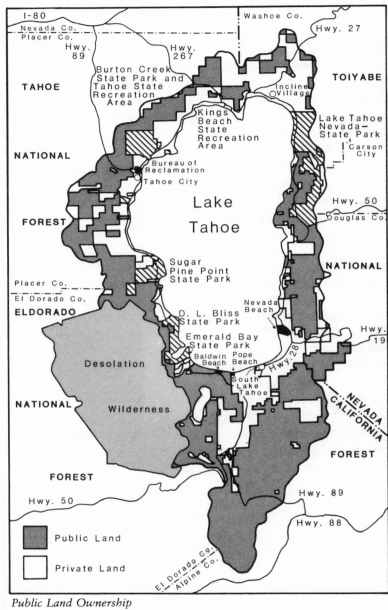

Public Land Ownership

The Lake Bigler Forestry Commission

The state of California did take notice. In 1883 a resolution by Assemblyman James V. Coleman declared that it is the state's duty to preserve natural scenery for the health, pleasure, and recreation of both state residents and tourists. Further, the resolution decried the denudation of forests along the shores of "Lake Bigler" (Lake Tahoe).[5]

On March 8, the governor appointed the Lake Bigler Forestry Commission, headed by Coleman. As the commissioners explained, every aspect of agriculture depended on the water supply, which in turn depended in large part on protection of the state's forest land. The commission's report compared California's forestry problems to those of Switzerland, where destruction of trees had resulted in severe soil erosion, loss of agricultural lands, floods, and the filling of river channels.

Although much of the Nevada side of the basin already had been denuded, the California side remained relatively unspoiled. So the commissioners urged "preservation of this lovely gem," as well as provision for a "perfect resort" for the state's people and thousands of desirable visitors. To accomplish these goals, they recommended that Congress acquire land owned by the Central Pacific Railroad in the northwest part of the basin, allowing the railroad to select lands of equal value outside the basin; and that California request ownership or a trusteeship of all federal land on the California side of the basin "for the purpose of forever holding and preserving it as a state park" or state forest.[6] The commissioners felt confident that the federal government would comply because of conversations with officials of the Department of the Interior and because Congress previously had passed acts setting aside other lands for "public park purposes." With most of the forest land in state hands, it was anticipated that private property owners would no longer have an incentive for investing capital in the railroads, flumes, mills, and wagon roads upon which large-scale logging depended.

The commission thought it advantageous that some of the best land on the lakeshore proper belonged to wealthy citizens, who would value the property more for summer residences and resorts than for the board feet of lumber it might yield. Because the scenic value of privately owned land would be greatly enhanced by preservation of the surrounding area as a great state park or forest, it seemed logical to conclude that these property owners would rally behind the commission's plan. Finally, a map of the California side of the basin revealed large expanses of land, including considerable shoreline, that had not yet passed into private hands. These lands, the commission proposed, should "come into the possession of the State and remain forever open to the free use of travelers for the purposes of pleasure, rest, recreation, and healthful sport."

Assemblyman Coleman introduced the commission's proposal in a concurrent resolution to the state legislature in 1885. It was approved in the Assembly but died in the Senate for reasons never fully explained. Perhaps, as historian C. Raymond Clar has suggested, the alleged mismanagement of Yosemite Valley by a state commission contributed to the Senate's lack of enthusiasm for state control at Tahoe.

The legislature did act on one of the commission's recommendations: it created what was intended as a permanent state forestry commission, the first of its kind in the nation. The State Board of Forestry issued two reports—one on destruction caused by unchecked forest fires and one on wasteful logging practices—before being dissolved in 1892. Not until the 1920s did the state once again take a serious interest in the preservation of the California side of the basin, and by then only small segments of the shoreline remained in public hands.

The Lake Tahoe Forest Reserve

In the meantime, the federal government had taken steps promising to preserve some of the most scenic regions in the Sierra Nevada. As early as 1864, Congress granted Yosemite Valley and the Mariposa Grove of Big Trees (*Sequoiadendron giganteum*) to

Upper and Lower Angora Lakes, overlooking Fallen Leaf Lake and Lake Tahoe, lay within the township proposed for preservation within a federal forest reserve. James Hildinger.

the state of California to be held inalienable for the recreational and scenic enjoyment of the public. Congress further established Sequoia, Yosemite, and General Grant national parks in 1890, well to the south of Lake Tahoe. The next year, a little noticed rider to a public land act provided the backbone for the future forestry program, allowing the president to set aside public lands in forest reserves. Presidents Benjamin Harrison and Grover Cleveland soon proclaimed as public lands the San Gabriel and San Bernardino reserves in southern California, as well as the vast Sierra Forest Reserve of more than four million acres, stretching from Yosemite National Park in the north to a point well south of Sequoia. Although the forest land of the Tahoe Basin remained unprotected, a public campaign was eventually mounted for its preservation.

Late in 1896 word spread that E. J. Baldwin, proprietor of the Tallac hotel on the south shore of Lake Tahoe, aspired to gain control of several beautiful small lakes at the southwest corner of the basin. California's two United States senators, Stephen M. White and George C. Perkins, requested that the township in question be withdrawn from entry, that is, be made unavailable for private acquisition under federal land laws.[7] Although it is not clear who first made the proposal, the idea grew of making the township into a permanent reservation. This beautiful thirty-six-square-mile block of timbered land included Fallen Leaf Lake and many smaller alpine lakes that stretched into the heavily glaciated Desolation Valley.

One of the interested parties, and perhaps the originator of the idea, was Nathan Gilmore, the proprietor of a small hotel at Glen Alpine, located within the disputed township. Gilmore, who brought cattle to Tahoe in 1863, had discovered a mineral spring whose water he bottled and sold as Glen Alpine Tonic Water. He later established a small rustic resort at the site of the spring, advertising accommodations at $10–14 per week. To protect the isolation and scenic beauty of the area, Gilmore expressed willingness to give up his own land claims if the president of the United States would incorporate Glen Alpine and environs into a forest reservation.

Gilmore had substantial allies, including the Sierra Club, a San Francisco-based outing and conservation organization founded by John Muir and others in 1892. Muir had worked actively in support of the Sierra Forest Reserve, and the club wished to see the protection of the Sierra Nevada forests extended north from Yosemite to beyond Tahoe. In a letter to the commissioner of the General Land Office, the club's vice-president, Warren Olney, called attention to the township that bordered the western shore of Lake Tahoe. Olney explained that Gilmore had provided a favorite summer retreat for college professors, teachers, and others who had a fondness for mountain scenery. From Olney's perspective, it was a case in which "everybody is interested in preserving the property for the use of the public on the one side, against a private speculator [Baldwin] on the other."[8]

Enclosed with Olney's letter was a petition from the president of Stanford University, David Starr Jordan, and forty-nine professors requesting protection for the township surrounding Glen Alpine. A second petition, with the signatures of President Martin Kellogg and nearly 150 professors, students, and alumni of the University of California at Berkeley, followed early the next month. The governor of Nevada, as well as several other state officials and prominent citizens from Carson City, submitted a similar petition. These protests against the threatened survey and filing of land claims in this township had the desired results. Local land officers were directed to allow no entry, and the General Land Office ordered an inspection of the suitability of the land for designation as a forest reserve.

By January 1897 three tracts near Tahoe had been suggested for possible reservation: a vast acreage stretching north from Yosemite to the Central Pacific Railroad track at Truckee; the west side of the Tahoe Basin; and the Glen Alpine township. The advocates of a Tahoe reserve continued to focus their energy on Glen Alpine. Jordan wrote to Interior Secretary Cornelius N. Bliss in April 1897 to warn that Baldwin wanted to preempt the township as a "hotel preserve" so that he could "exclude all persons not paying tribute to the Tallac Hotel." Although Jordan desired preservation of the entire Sierra crest south to Yosemite, he believed that Glen Alpine township contained the "finest scenery" in the entire area.[9]

The Sierra Club continued to confer with officials of the General Land Office, urging an examination before the winter snows once again made the region inaccessible. One special forest agent and supervisor, B. F. Allen, in turn reported to his superiors in Washington, D.C., the concern of "prominent citizens" of northern California for securing the Glen Alpine tract as a "Forest Reserva-tion."[10]

The proposal for a Tahoe forest reservation had received suffi-cient publicity in newspapers and through the activities of Special Agent Allen by the end of 1897 that the opposition's forces began to mobilize. William H. Mills, land agent of the Central Pacific Railroad, although not opposed to the reservation of forests still in primal condition, warned against the possibility of corrupt prac-tices in lieu land exchanges where private property existed. Under existing land laws, privately owned land within the boundaries of a forest reservation could be exchanged for an equal acreage of forest land elsewhere. Mills feared that private interests would propose forest reservations in areas where their own self-interests would best be served. He warned that "the whole plan will be transformed into a speculative scheme, and a movement proceeding from es-thetic tastes, the love of nature and the instinctive desire to preserve in their native beauty the coniferous forests of our coast will de-scend to the level of a scramble for illicit personal gain."[11]

In spite of such misgivings, Allen inspected the land and then proposed in December 1897 a large forest reservation to include all of the California side of the Tahoe Basin from Tahoe City to Camp Richardson. He thus proposed protecting well over half of the Cali-fornia shoreline and its backcountry, including acreage to the west and southwest of the basin, and the headwaters of the American River and lesser streams flowing into the Sacramento Valley. Allen then posted public notices in newspapers requesting responses to his recommendation.

Local residents and business interests expressed alarm. They realized that the proposed reservation included twenty-eight town-ships and parts of three others bordering Tahoe's western shore, as well as extensive forested land and some private property. A num-ber of citizens from El Dorado County, in which most of the re-serve would be located, protested in a petition addressed to the commissioner of the General Land Office and the secretary of the interior. The petitioners had no objection to reserving Glen Alpine township, which they viewed as "high, barren, very mountainous and unused except for summer resorts by mountain tourists."[12] But the rest of the land, they believed, would be better left under the care of the county and private citizens.

These citizens expected no benefit from federal control; on the other hand, they considered that the patenting of these lands "increases the taxable property of the Community, adds to its resources, makes room for more people, and does no real injury to the young forests already thriving on every hand." The right of sheepherders to use the high mountain pasturage in summer gained specific support, and the petitioners argued that fruit and potatoes, in addition to lumber, could be produced if the land remained open to private development. The petition, along with a number of other protests, arrived in Washington, D.C., early in 1898.

Lumbermen operating in the Sierra foothills, especially near Placerville, complained about the threat posed by a forest reserve to both investments and jobs on the western slope. The *Auburn Placer Herald* questioned the wisdom of setting aside land at the suggestion of "gentlemen sportsmen" of the Sierra Club, an action regarded as contrary to republican principles. Spurred by such protests, local Congressman Marion DeVries requested that any action in regard to the proposed reserve be postponed pending further investigation.

Warren Olney of the Sierra Club responded that he had no objection to a reduction of the boundaries proposed by Allen. Olney had agreed with Allen's initial proposal only because Allen believed there would be no objections, and because the two men realized it would be much easier to reduce than to increase the boundaries, once proposed. All that mattered, Olney said, was protection of a "reasonable amount of land," including the highest and most picturesque mountains and lakes.

The issue came to a head when Special Agent Allen, numerous letters of protest in hand, returned to the field for a thorough reexamination of the matter. His second report, filed in February 1899, significantly reduced the proposed boundaries, thereby eliminating most of the opposition. He excluded nearly all the timbered lands on the western slope outside the basin, as well as two tiers of townships that bordered the lakeshore, roughly from Meeks Bay to Tahoe City, in which the Central Pacific Railroad owned alternate sections of land. On April 13, 1899, one year after the death of the elderly Nathan Gilmore, President William McKinley signed the proclamation setting aside 136,335 acres in the southwestern part of the basin as the Lake Tahoe Forest Reserve.[13]

The new forest reserve included not only the original Glen Alpine township, but also essentially all of what is now the Desolation Wilderness Area to the east of the Crystal Range—one of the most beautiful and heavily visited wilderness areas in the country. In addition, the reserve incorporated a relatively short but especially beautiful section of Lake Tahoe's shoreline, stretching from Rubicon Bay to Camp Richardson. Those lands already owned or legally claimed by private individuals were excluded. Creation of the Lake Tahoe Forest Reserve marked the origin of federal activity to protect and manage land within the Tahoe Basin.

The Tahoe National Park Proposal

In June 1899, William Mills reversed his earlier position and urged that the forest reservation be extended "over the catchment area of the lake." He argued that the railroad from Truckee to Tahoe City, then under construction, would open new forest areas and lead to the renewal of destructive logging. Mills claimed that the Central Pacific Railroad, which he represented, had sold all its lands of value in the vicinity and thus had no corporate interest in an enlarged Lake Tahoe Forest Reserve. Yet Mills emphasized the importance of protection for the headwaters of the American River and other unprotected forest land on the western slope, where the railroad owned extensive acreage.

Concern for watershed protection in the northern Sierra clearly overshadowed interest in protection of the limited forest lands within the Tahoe Basin. Farmers dependent on irrigation in California's great Central Valley could not survive without protection of the timbered watershed in the Sierra Nevada. In an *Atlantic*

Monthly article, John Muir had complained that the Sierra's forests, whether reserved or unreserved, were "sadly hacked and trampled," except those in the national parks, guarded by soldiers.[14] When George B. Sudworth, a government agent, inspected extensive forest land in the northern Sierra, including the Tahoe Basin, in summer 1899, he reported wasteful lumbering practices and the need to control sheep grazing and fires. He also noted: "Nearly all settlers interested in grazing and wood-consuming industries within this territory are opposed to the maintenance of forest reserves."[15] But elsewhere in California the concern for deforestation was rising. The work of Muir, Theodore P. Lukens, Abbot Kinney, and numerous other champions of watershed protection was having an effect.

Professor Marsden Manson, a well-known civil engineer and conservationist who understood the severity of erosion caused by deforestation in many parts of the world, painted a bleak picture of the conditions in the Sierra:

> Around Lake Tahoe the timbered areas have been entirely swept off, with the exception of a few thousand acres around Tallac, and some at the north end, reserved by the owners for later use. The mountain sides around the Hot Springs [Brockway], and nearly all of the moraines and flats around the south and east side of the lake, have been denuded. These areas, bereft of timber, are now ready to be abandoned to the State, large tracts being for sale at fifty cents per acre. The railroads, which were constructed to carry logs to the lake, have been torn up, and the region, shorn of its wealth and beauty, has been partly burned over to give a few sprouts to hungry hordes of sheep.[16]

Manson suggested a novel remedy: have Congress set aside the entire watershed as a forest reserve and grant it in trust to the regents of the University of California, who would "protect, maintain, develop, and extend the water supply of these areas forever." After all, Manson noted, the government had failed; why not let someone else have an opportunity? A short and loosely worded bill reflecting Manson's proposal was introduced in Congress, but it never gained serious consideration.

Interest in preservation of the lands in the Tahoe Basin remained high, nevertheless, as the last year of the century progressed. Leaders of the California Water and Forest Association, the State Board of Trade, the Sierra Club, and other influential organizations pressed for extension of the Lake Tahoe Forest Reserve. They took advantage of a short visit to California by Binger Hermann, commissioner of the General Land Office, to lobby for their cause. They also encouraged Hermann's efforts to amend legislation relating to lieu land exchanges in order to eliminate the opportunity for fraud and the continued destruction of prime forest lands owned by the federal government.

Charles Walcott, director of the U.S. Geological Survey, in response to a letter from Hermann about possible forest reserves in Nevada, recommended in September 1899 that almost the whole Nevada side of the Tahoe Basin be withdrawn from entry. The idea of a forest reserve on the Nevada shore was not new. Gifford Pinchot, then a special forestry agent and later chief forester of the United States, had noted in 1898 that logged-over areas "are as eligible for forest reserves as though they were covered with trees, because only under Government care can they ever regain the value and usefulness which they have lost."[17] But B. F. Allen discouraged such action, claiming that the denuded lands were owned mainly by large corporations that would only select valuable lieu land elsewhere if their cutover areas were included in a reserve.

Senator William M. Stewart of Nevada, late in 1899, initiated a new proposal: the creation of a Lake Tahoe National Park. Stewart had noticed in the last Nevada election that the platform of the Silver Party included a plank advocating that Tahoe be made into a national park and its waters used for irrigation. Stewart wrote to William Mills of the Central Pacific Railroad for information and suggestions. Mills supported the proposal, although he expressed greater concern for protection of the headwaters of the American River and the western slope of the northern Sierra—presumably to assure hydroelectric power and irrigation water to the Central Valley—than for the Tahoe Basin itself.[18]

Once the Geological Survey, at Stewart's request, had delineated

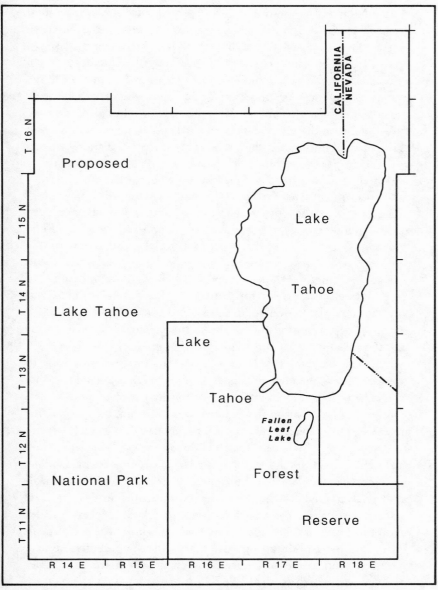

*Lake Tahoe Forest Reserve (1899) and Proposed Lake
Tahoe National Park (January 1900)*

the boundaries for a national park, Stewart introduced S. 2320 in January 1900 to establish a large national park in the northern Sierra. The proposed tracts, incorporating thirty-one townships, were to be "set apart as reserve forest lands and dedicated as a public park or pleasure ground for the benefit and enjoyment of the people, to be known as the Lake Tahoe National Park." The area included not only virtually all of the Tahoe Basin but also extensive forest lands on the western slope, as Mills had advocated. Section three of the bill directed that all surplus waters at Tahoe be dedicated to irrigation purposes. The Geological Survey was to survey and prepare plans for a dam within one year, and the necessary land costs of construction were to be paid by the state of Nevada.

The expected benefits to Nevada obviously would have been great, so the bill gained enthusiastic support there. The *Reno Evening Gazette,* in addition to praising the protection of the scenery in the area, surmised that Tahoe's surplus water could irrigate two hundred thousand acres of Nevada farmland and provide hydroelectric power for homes and industry. Nevada's surveyor general, E. D. Kelley, foresaw almost unlimited potential for farming, depending on the height of the proposed dam at Tahoe and the amount of water available each summer.

But then, on January 27, 1900, Stewart submitted a petition to the secretary of the interior, signed by the governor and all the state officials of Nevada, and another petition signed by several conservation leaders and prominent citizens of California, both asking for an expansion of the Lake Tahoe Forest Reserve to include the entire basin. Because of what he deemed "the emergency" that existed— the threat of additional logging—Stewart asked that his park bill be held in abeyance and that the Department of the Interior immediately proclaim the enlarged forest reservation. Stewart did not draw a sharp distinction between a national park and a forest reserve, except to recognize that a forest reserve did not require the difficult task of pushing a bill through Congress. Also, apparently, he paid little attention to the difference between the proposed boundaries of the park, which would include a large acreage on the western slope, and the forest reserve advocated in the petitions, which would be restricted to the Tahoe Basin.

Support for a national park at Tahoe came from unexpected sources. Duane L. Bliss, general manager of the Carson and Tahoe Lumber and Fluming Company, now pursuing the tourist trade at Tahoe City, corresponded with Stewart and worked actively for the proposal. After all, the greater the natural beauty of the lake, the more prosperous the tourist trade. Bliss also recognized the benefit of the sale or exchange of land still held by CTLFC in the basin. The proprietor of Lakeside House on the state line at the south shore, E. B. Smith, praised Stewart's national park bill and urged extension of the proposed boundary eastward to include the entire watershed on the Nevada side of the basin. Smith was concerned about the effect of prior deforestation and of reduced water supply on his tract of more than a thousand acres of land at what was called Laphams, or Stateline. And William Mills, the Central Pacific land agent, became in effect Stewart's lobbyist in California.

Opposition to the national park proposal increased rapidly, however. Because the park bill incorporated considerable timbered land on the western slope, it encountered the same objections from the same people who had opposed Special Agent Allen's original forest reserve proposal of December 1897. A lengthy and influential article in the *San Francisco Examiner,* run under the headline "Corporations May Gain Valuable Timber Lands in Exchange for Those They Made Worthless," summarized their argument.[19] Accompanied by a map that labeled the west, east, and north shores as "stripped of timber," the article argued that the park bill would make a gift of tens of thousands of acres of the choicest public land to the large property owners who had denuded Tahoe's forests: namely, the Sierra Nevada Wood and Lumber Company, CTLFC, and the El Dorado Wood and Flume Company.

Although the *Examiner* acknowledged that the park bill outwardly would benefit the public through protection of roughly thirteen hundred square miles of timber, and would also aid irrigation in Nevada, it concluded that the bill essentially would mean "payment of nearly $250,000 in cash or the granting of over 50,000 acres of lieu land to men who have already made millions of dollars within that reservation as proposed." To make matters worse, the newspaper continued, Stewart's bill included nearly eighty thousand acres of "barren, rocky, precipitous land" owned by the Central Pacific Railroad and extending twelve miles west of the Tahoe watershed into an area presumably important to the future economy of El Dorado and Placer counties.

In support of this contention, the El Dorado County Board of Supervisors emphasized the threat of the proposed park designation to county dairy and stock-raising interests, and the need for "use of grazing lands in the valleys and mountain sides near the summits, and in the vicinity of the lake and streams that flow therefrom."[20] Numerous letters and petitions of county officials, lumber interests, stockmen, and others flooded the desk of the local congressman, Marion DeVries, who requested that no action be taken by the federal government until a hearing and investigation on the matter could be conducted.

Stewart attempted to alleviate the fears of his opposition. In a letter to the *Examiner,* only parts of which were printed, he stressed the importance of the proposed park to the "agricultural development and prosperity of Western Nevada," as well as the need to protect the forests from the "shameful, deplorable" destruction caused by lumbermen.[21] But Stewart, though he defended the inclusion of the headwaters of the American River on the western slope, had already shifted his strategy from pushing the national park bill, which would require congressional approval, to support for a proclamation to set aside the same acreage in an expanded forest reserve. He now concentrated on convincing the secretary of the interior and the commissioner of the General Land Office of the advisability of such action.

The main stumbling block remained the question of lieu land selection, which federal officials feared could cause a good deal of political embarrassment. Stewart therefore sent a succession of letters to Binger Hermann, commissioner of the General Land Office, outlining various proposals for bills assuring that no one would benefit unduly, at public expense, from any land exchange. Basically, Stewart proposed that the secretary of the interior be given wide discretion, both to induce the expected exchanges and to provide for fair play to both parties.

In the meantime, despite the support of the commissioner of the General Land Office for a national park, government action was blocked pending completion of a new inspection of the disputed area. Forest Superintendent Charles S. Newhall, who had submitted a report in January 1900 in which he supported forest reserve status for Donner Lake, some forty other small lakes, and the numerous branches of the American River, was assigned the task. His report, delayed until December by the press of other business, favored creation of a large forest reserve that would include most of the Tahoe Basin.[22] He noted that although nearly all marketable timber near the lake had been cut, vigorous second growth was already taking its place.

In response to the protests by lumber, livestock, and mining interests on the western slope, Newhall explained that these people did not understand the difference between a national park and a forest reserve. A park would be "prohibitive" in its administration, allowing no commercial development, whereas a forest reserve would be "regulative and protective," allowing careful resource development according to scientific principles. Newhall discovered that the petitions of protest from El Dorado and Placer counties had been circulated in part by mining interests because Stewart's park bill would prevent all prospecting and the filing of new mining claims. One of the petition's circulators, when informed that a forest reserve permitted such activity, volunteered to circulate a new petition in support of the reserve.

Newhall believed that the four main objections offered by critics were valid in regard to a national park but invalid for a forest reserve. These objections were the restriction of livestock grazing; curtailment of the county tax base; the hindrance to enterprise, particularly to a railroad into the timber belt on the western slope;

and the exchange of prime timbered areas for valueless cutover land. In regard to the last point, Newhall suggested that if the lands in range 18, along the eastern shore of Tahoe, could be excluded for the present, most denuded forest land at Tahoe would be removed as a point of contention. In other words, he suggested restricting the forest reserve primarily to the California side of the basin. In conclusion, Newhall stated, "I do not favor making of this large territory a Park, with a prohibition policy; but I do strongly recommend the extension of the Tahoe Reserve."

In spite of this favorable report, there had been so much confusion and conflict over the entire issue that the government was loath to take any action. Even John Muir had written to Newhall, fearing the "grossest frauds" by the lumber companies against the public interest. As Muir concluded, "Not even for a much desired extension of a reservation should such injustice be for a moment considered."[23] Federal administrators and state officials, fearing trouble in an election year, became increasingly cautious. Thus, despite the continued support of Stewart, the Sierra Club, Bliss, and others, the national park bill languished and died.

Although the proposal for a national park had received widespread support among prominent California and Nevada officials, environmental organizations, and citizens, it was defeated by persistent problems. Stewart would have been well advised to exclude the western slope from a Lake Tahoe National Park proposal, but he acceded to the wishes of Mills. Stewart also could have eliminated much opposition had he both understood and explained at the beginning the difference between a park and a forest reserve. His proposal might have had a better chance if he had offered it in the first place as an extension of the Lake Tahoe Forest Reserve. But perhaps not. Throughout the west there was much confusion about the difference, if any, between parks and reserves.

Stewart did not succeed in convincing opponents that the Lake Tahoe Basin would soon recover from its denudation and regain its remarkable beauty. He failed, too, in convincing others that land exchanges could be conducted equitably—a failure perhaps inevitable in the atmosphere of rising distrust of monopolies, both in and beyond California. The land exchange issue proved decisive, and it ultimately brought about the defeat of the bill for a Lake Tahoe National Park.

National Forest Enlargement

The demise of the national park proposal did not end interest in expansion of the Lake Tahoe Forest Reserve. Inspection of the land proposed for an expanded Tahoe reserve continued. According to Charles H. Shinn, who investigated the area in 1902, the basin suffered from a half-century of careless land use. Yet now, he said, both the scattered resorts, catering to a growing tourist trade, and the few camps of other seasonal residents were abandoned by October each year. The cutover timberlands lay open to fire, especially on the California side of the lake. In fact, Shinn reported coming across many small, smoldering fires.[24] To protect against forest fires and to prevent rampant overgrazing by livestock, Shinn favored expanding the existing 136,335-acre reserve to more than 900,000 acres, including some forested land in the Truckee Basin to the north, as well as land on the western slope and within the drainage area of the Carson Valley, to the east.

The proposal to enlarge the forest reserve gained continued active support from several groups, especially the California Water and Forest Association. Concerned about the impact of improper use of the Sierra watershed on the farmlands below, the association concluded: "The question is a matter of life and death to the Sacramento Valley. There is not enough lumber in all the Sierras to pay for the destruction of the fertility of the valley land."[25]

At its annual convention in 1901, the association endorsed President Theodore Roosevelt's message on forestry, especially the portion stressing the relation between forests and irrigation. Through its quarterly journal, *Water and Forest,* the association urged the creation of forest reserves from Yosemite north to the Oregon border. Together with the Sierra Club and others, the association alerted the Department of the Interior and President Roosevelt about the magnitude of the problems.

Based largely on an urgent appeal from the association, Binger Hermann temporarily withdrew from settlement, entry, or sale eighty-six townships of land in the northern Sierra, pending determination of the "advisability of including said lands within a forest reserve." Hermann explained that, prior to any recommendation, a "searching examination" into the status of all lands proposed for the reserve would be necessary. But because portions of the land in question were rapidly being claimed under the Timber and Stone Act and other land laws, he requested their temporary withdrawal. He omitted the lands on the Nevada side of the basin, however, as well as the lands lying immediately north and south of the lake, because they were "almost wholly covered by adverse holdings."[26]

Despite the obvious caution of the Department of the Interior toward proposed expansion of the forest reserve at Tahoe, Roosevelt offered encouragement. While visiting Carson City on a western tour in May 1903 he remarked: "Your interest and the interest of irrigation in California imperatively demand the extension of the forest reserve system, so that the source of supply for the great reservoirs and irrigation works may be safe from fire, from overgrazing and from destructive lumbering."[27] In Roosevelt's opinion, the problem of forestry was in many ways the most vital internal problem in the country because lumbering, the fourth-ranked industry, was tied indirectly to transportation, manufacturing, and commerce and directly to agriculture, grazing, and mining.

At the time of Roosevelt's trip, an article, "The Question of Forest Reserves," in the *Sacramento Evening Bee* argued strongly that the temporary withdrawal of land should be made permanent.[28] The article acknowledged the problems of lieu land exchange that earlier had defeated Senator Stewart's national park bill, yet concluded that lieu land for private landowners was fair because good timber would soon grow again on cutover land in the Tahoe Basin. In any case, the author noted, "it becomes a question of either holding the forests for the public benefit or allowing them to pass absolutely and irrevocably, in the course of a very few years, into the hands of private owners."

Clearly the chief concern in California was economic and practical; how to protect the lumber industry, provide for irrigation, maintain navigation on interior waterways, and promote other vital economic interests related directly to the Sierra watershed. Despite the obvious importance of the forests of the northern Sierra, only three forest reserves existed north of the Tehachapi Mountains in California: the Sierra (6,400 square miles), the Stanislaus (1,080 square miles), and the Lake Tahoe (213 square miles).

Between May and July 1903, Albert F. Potter of the U.S. Bureau of Forestry met with representatives of the California Water and Forest Association, the Sierra Club, the Central Pacific Railroad, the California Gas and Electric Company, the California Chamber of Commerce, state and local governments, and many other groups. Potter concluded that there was widespread support for expansion of the forest reserves, except by local people. He also reinforced the conclusion that the Tahoe Basin was recovering rapidly from the destruction caused by earlier logging.[29]

In the meantime, Stewart, Bliss, and friends continued their active campaign for an enlarged Lake Tahoe Forest Reserve. In October 1903, Stewart wrote directly to President Roosevelt urging preservation of the basin. His primary motive, however, was probably expressed in the following statement: "Since it has been determined to begin the first irrigation scheme in Nevada on Lake Tahoe, which will make it necessary to raise the Lake about twelve feet, I consider the present an opportune time to consider the advisability of including the Lake and lands within the present Forest Reservation."[30] Stewart defended acquisition by the government of privately owned lands within the basin through the controversial lieu land exchange, and he compared inclusion of

Lake Tahoe within a national forest reserve to the prior setting aside of Yellowstone Lake in Yellowstone National Park. The bottleneck at this point, according to Stewart, was the unwillingness of the Department of the Interior to act.

Nevertheless, early in 1904, as a result of a request directed by Stewart originally to the Department of Agriculture, the Department of the Interior temporarily withdrew from entry extensive acreage in the Tahoe Basin. Included were selected sections on the higher slopes near the lake.[31]

Then Congress passed two bills, early in 1905, that had considerable effect on Tahoe's future. First, administration of the forest reserves was transferred from the General Land Office in the Department of the Interior to the Bureau of Forestry in the Department of Agriculture, where the reserves came under the charge of Gifford Pinchot. And the lieu land law was repealed, removing the most troublesome obstacle to the creation of forest reserves.

Following the passage of these acts, opposition to new forest reserves seems to have declined markedly, at least for the time being. Of course it helped a great deal to have a president who actively supported conservation. Within the next three years, Roosevelt doubled the amount of land in forest reserves. Between March and June 1905, he established four new reserves in northern California: Plumas, Trinity, Klamath, and Lassen Peak. By the end of the year he had added Shasta and Yuba, and on October 3, 1905, Roosevelt proclaimed the long-awaited major extension of the Lake Tahoe Forest Reserve.[32]

The enlarged boundaries of what became the Tahoe National Forest included essentially all of the California side of the Lake Tahoe Basin, except for most of township 12, range 18. This area, once known as Lake Valley, today includes the urbanized zone between Meyers and Stateline at the south shore. Because all privately owned lands and valid land claims were excluded from the enlarged reserve, most of the Lake Tahoe shoreline in California remained unprotected. And nearly all the Nevada side of the basin, except the northwest corner, was excluded because the land was already largely in private hands. Nevertheless, by 1905 the foundation had been established for the substantial federal holdings that exist today at Tahoe.

Later National Park Proposals

Although the U.S. Forest Service administered a growing expanse of forest lands in the Tahoe Basin after 1905, interest in making Tahoe into a national park recurred from time to time. According to one account, in 1910 the Native Sons of the Golden West adopted resolutions in favor of establishing a Frémont national park from the existing national forests at Tahoe. The Sierra Club soon lent its support to the proposal.[33]

Probably as a result of the efforts of the Native Sons and the Sierra Club, in March 1912 Congressman Joseph R. Knowland of California asked Secretary of the Interior Walter Fisher for a description of the land surrounding Tahoe, for "an effort is to be put forth to make of this a national park."[34] On April 3, Knowland introduced H.R. 22832, a bill to establish a Lake Tahoe national park in the area surrounding the lake in California and Nevada. The boundaries included all of the Tahoe Basin except for existing land claims.

This bill avoided many of the pitfalls of earlier proposals. It omitted large tracts of timber accessible from Placerville and Folsom in the Sierra foothills on the western slope; it included the most scenic as well as the most sparsely settled mountain region bordering the Tahoe Basin to the south; and it defined the borders so as to reduce future administrative problems.

Knowland incorporated several provisions that allowed or left open the possibility of economic benefit from use of the park. For example, he recognized the right of the Bureau of Reclamation to enter and develop any area within the park as a government reclamation project. Also, the secretary of the interior was given complete authority to provide for regulation of the preserved area, including the discretion to allow leases for "summer homes or cottages." Such legislation was not uncommon prior to the establishment of the National Park Service in 1916, for until that time there was no accepted policy for administration of national parks. Indeed, in the bill establishing Glacier National Park in 1910, Congress had included wording allowing precisely such uses.

Knowland's national park bill did not attract much support in California, Nevada, or the nation's capitol. The General Land Office reported that nearly 122,000 acres of land had been patented within the area of 492,160 acres (exclusive of Lake Tahoe) affected by the bill. When Knowland asked for information about the lake, the Department of the Interior declared that it had no publications and that Knowland should contact the Southern Pacific Railroad for information.

Knowland reintroduced his bill in 1913, and Congressman John A. Elston introduced an identical bill in 1918, but without success. Later, C. T. Bliss, vice-president and general manager of the Lake Tahoe Railway and Transportation Company, wrote to Stephen T. Mather, director of the National Park Service, requesting that Tahoe be listed with Muir Woods and other "natural monuments" that received Park Service publicity in printed circulars. Bliss, the son of lumberman Duane L. Bliss, obviously wanted to promote tourism.

Horace M. Albright of the Park Service responded that national monuments could be created only by presidential proclamation, and that Tahoe already rested within the boundaries of a national forest. Albright added that he hoped Congress might give the Park Service complete authority over all national monuments; if this should happen, "the establishment of a national monument to include Lake Tahoe would be a project that we could seriously consider."[35]

By the late 1920s, the idea of a Lake Tahoe national park seemed dead. Mather, a longtime California resident, had visited Lake Tahoe on several occasions and observed the events that were moving the basin toward further despoliation. On one such visit, in 1921, he accompanied Secretary of the Interior Albert B. Fall to help block the proposed cutting of the rim of the lake to provide more water for a Nevada reclamation project. But Mather did not support the national park proposals. For one thing, Congress was in no mood to authorize new parks, and it was difficult enough to establish Mount McKinley and Grand Canyon national parks, which were in relatively pristine condition. Second, and most important, so much of the lakeshore and adjacent lands had passed into private hands that protection of a national park seemed impossible. Finally, Congress did not appropriate funds to purchase land for parks in those days, a practice that became common only after the Cape Cod National Seashore had been established in 1961.

Nevertheless, interest in a park continued. Charles E. Townsend, an old college friend of Mather and a homeowner at Tahoe, wrote Albright in April 1931 expressing his concern about public pressure to pump water from Tahoe during the drought then imperiling agriculture in Nevada. He asked why the entire lake area then owned and controlled by the government could not be made into a national park. Albright responded, "Unfortunately there is nothing we can do in the Lake Tahoe situation."[36] Later the same year, Roger Toll of the Park Service visited the "proposed Lake Tahoe National Park area." Toll described the lake as well forested and a "popular summer resort." But because the original wilderness conditions had been "extensively altered" and private ownership was widespread, and because Toll did not believe that Tahoe compared scenically to Crater Lake and some other lakes in the west, he concluded that "this project may be considered closed."

William Penn Mott, Jr., of the National Park Service, later director of recreation and parks in California, filed a report in 1935 entitled "Proposed Lake Tahoe National Park." The report became the last serious assessment by the agency of the potential of the entire Tahoe Basin as a national park. According to Mott, "private enterprise and extensive development around the entire border of the lake has destroyed the possibility of conserving and preserving on a national scale the natural beauty, character, flora, and fauna of this area."[37]

Mott noted that the extensive private lands were distributed among perhaps two thousand individual owners, and that speculative prices of $10 and more per acre made the purchase of large tracts impossible. Most of these developments, in his opinion, had been "ruthless commercial enterprises" that had largely destroyed the charm and natural character of the land most vital to the proposed park—"the land immediately adjacent to the lake." No one foresaw that in a relatively few years prices for forest land in the basin would rise a hundredfold, and that the price for lake frontage would reach astronomical figures. But it would have made no difference, for in 1935 no money was available for purchase of park lands. However, Mott did advise that U.S. Forest Service and state and local government officials should made every effort "to preserve and conserve all that remains of this once gem of natural beauty."

National Forest Land Acquisition

President Roosevelt consolidated the Tahoe and Yuba forest reserves into the Tahoe National Forest in 1906, and President Taft created the Eldorado National Forest in 1910 from parts of the Tahoe and Stanislaus national forests. In 1945, national forest land on the Nevada side of the basin was transferred to the Toiyabe National Forest. The Forest Service established the Lake Tahoe Basin Management Unit in 1973 to administer all three national forests within the basin as a single unit.

Partly because of the difficulties of administering land which contained many tracts of privately owned property, particularly at the northern end of the lake where the Central Pacific Railroad owned alternate sections of land, the Forest Service attempted for many years to acquire additional property.[38] In 1936, for example, the Forest Service attempted unsuccessfully to acquire the extensive cutover lands still held by the Carson and Tahoe Lumber and Fluming Company and the Hobart Estate (Sierra Nevada Wood and

Lumber Company), offered for sale for a reported $325,000. Unfortunately, no federal funds were made available.

Shortly thereafter, much of the land on the Nevada side of the lake was sold to George Whittell, a multimillionaire real estate promoter from California, for a price reportedly in excess of a million dollars. Part of this property later became the site of today's major land development at Incline Village. Another missed opportunity occurred in the 1950s, when the Forest Service reportedly turned down a chance to purchase 750 swampy acres at the mouth of the Upper Truckee River for $75,000. This area soon became Tahoe Keys, a multimillion-dollar commercial development that destroyed prime swamp and marshland habitat in the basin.

Fortunately, the Forest Service had better success at other times. In 1950 and 1951, for example, it acquired more than 3,500 acres of excellent recreational land at the south shore—the Pope and Baldwin estates—in exchange for allowing timber valued at $946,464 to be cut on national forest land outside the basin. Through the exchange, the government acquired nearly 10,000 feet of lakefront property, including the Pope and Baldwin beaches, as well as extensive shoreline on Fallen Leaf Lake.

With the passage of time, the Forest Service had to turn increasingly to direct purchase of land, and in the 1970s the agency launched an active program to acquire land in the basin wherever it was voluntarily offered for sale. In 1970, under the Land and Water Conservation Fund Act, the federal government purchased 4,732 acres of the former Whittell Estate in Nevada for $1.5 million. Although the tract included no shoreline, it made a handsome addition to Toiyabe National Forest. Two years later the Forest Service purchased more than 10,000 acres of former Whittell land, mostly in the Tahoe Basin, from banker Jack Dreyfus, Jr., thus preventing probable development along several miles of shoreline. Through prior acquisition of the Lake Tahoe Nevada State Park and the more recent purchase of a smaller Bliss property at Glenbrook, the public fell heir to the bulk of the Nevada side of the lake, which helps explain that area's relatively pristine condition between the two highly developed zones at each end of the lake.

The Forest Service also pursued an active land acquisition program on the California side, although much of the prized shoreline had already been developed. In 1974 the Fibreboard Corporation sold 10,121 acres in the mountainous northwest section of the basin for $9,925,000. Smaller tracts on the lake naturally cost considerably more per acre. The Meeks Bay Resort, for example, had fallen into the hands of the Macco Corporation, a subsidiary of the Pennsylvania Railroad, which planned to develop a resort complex with seventeen hundred condominium units. But when the railroad fell on financial hard times, it sold its prized 645-acre property to industrialist William R. Hewlett, who generously held the property until the government could accumulate the $3.1 million necessary to purchase it. Although expensive, this land provides public access to a fine beach, as well as to the rugged Desolation Wilderness to the west.

Between 1965 and 1980, the Forest Service acquired slightly more than 36,000 acres for approximately $60 million. As of 1980, the Forest Service held 65 percent of the land area in the basin, although only 16 percent of the lake's seventy-one miles of shoreline. Further, over the years the states of California and Nevada had set aside approximately 6 percent of the basin's land in state parks, including several stretches of shoreline property of exceptional beauty.

California State Parks

Yosemite Valley and the Mariposa Grove were granted to California in 1864 for "public use, resort and recreation." Other states also established parks in the nineteenth century. In 1885, for example, the New York legislature established the Adirondack Forest Preserve (subsequently redefined and enlarged into Adirondack Park) and the Niagara State Reservation. These preserves have remained under state control; Yosemite reverted to federal control.

The California legislature first appropriated state funds to purchase park land—redwood forest land near Santa Cruz—in 1902. In subsequent years many other states established parks of their own, but not until the 1920s, after Stephen Mather helped sponsor a national conference on state parks, did organized state park movements appear.

The California state park movement originated in 1927. In that year the legislature approved three bills that created the State Park Commission to oversee existing state parks (directing it to give special attention to the coastal redwoods); provided funds for a survey of lands suitable for new state parks; and approved a constitutional amendment for the sale of $6 million worth of state park bonds, to be matched by private contributions, for acquisition of properties to be added to the new state park system. In 1928 California voters approved the bond issue by an overwhelming margin.[39]

The newly established State Park Commission appointed Frederick Law Olmsted, Jr., son of the famed landscape architect, to undertake the survey. Olmsted's report, published in 1929, provided the framework for state park acquisition for years to come. Olmsted noted the danger of destruction to some of California's finest recreational land as some 1,880,000 automobiles took to the state's highways. He also observed that in many areas "cabin-site subdivisions" had been developed for private speculation in such an unsatisfactory and crowded manner that the natural beauty was largely destroyed. Although Olmsted did not devote much of his report to the Tahoe Basin, he did mention several small tracts of land in El Dorado County on the western shore that had state park potential, including Rubicon Point and the Baldwin-Brigham property where the outlet from Fallen Leaf Lake enters Lake Tahoe.[40]

The first land set aside for state park purposes at Tahoe was a small tract of thirteen acres next to Tahoe City that had been the site of a fish hatchery since before the turn of the century. The state had obtained the property for $1,000 in 1899, and the legislature approved a campground on the property in 1919. The State Park Commission acquired the land in 1927 and called it Tahoe State

Park. Since that time the campground (Tahoe State Recreational Area) has had heavy use, partly because of its strategic location near the crossroads at the north end of the lake.[41]

The next California park at Tahoe, variously called Rubicon Point, Bliss, or Bliss-Rubicon, both aided and benefited from passage of the state park bond issue. In June 1928 the children of Duane L. Bliss offered a gift of scenic land along the shores of Tahoe, subject to approval of the bond issue. Immediately after voter approval of the matching funds, the State Park Commission under William E. Colby approved Rubicon Point as the first project on which state bond money would be spent. After four years of negotiations, the state acquired more than nine hundred acres of scenic land, including 14,840 feet of Tahoe lakeshore and 3,500 feet on Emerald Bay, valued at $265,000, half of which was generously donated by the Bliss family.

With the growing popularity of Bliss Park after World War II (visitation doubled between 1946 and 1948), camping had to be limited to two weeks per family. The first full-time resident ranger was appointed, as well as the first seasonal naturalist. The Placerville *Mountain Democrat* complained that Bliss Park was not developed to its capacity, and that prospective campers had to arrive early in the morning and wait to have any chance of finding a vacant campsite.

Nearly all of the $15 million appropriation for park land acquisition that was approved by the California legislature in 1945 had been spent by 1953, when the Division of Beaches and Parks heard that the property at the head of Emerald Bay, including Fannette Island and the Vikingsholm, was for sale. The Vikingsholm, considered by many to be the finest example of Scandinavian architecture in the Western Hemisphere, was a carefully crafted reproduction of a Norse mansion of about A.D. 800. A wealthy widow from Chicago, Mrs. Lora J. Knight, had spared no expense to build this thirty-eight-room house. It was completed in 1929, and Mrs. Knight spent her summers there until her death in 1945.

Desirable as this property appeared, the state still had to find matching private donations of land or cash before any public funds could be used. Fortunately, the owner of the property, Harvey West, agreed to hold the land off the market for the state. West, a Placerville lumberman who had owned a mill at Tahoe Valley during World War II, had purchased the land in 1949. He donated half the value of the 177-acre property to the state, and the balance was purchased for approximately $150,000, including $25,000 from the Save-the-Redwoods League to pay for the furnishings at Vikingsholm. A grateful State Park Commission agreed to name a unit of the newly christened Emerald Bay State Park after West.

Acquiring other tracts of privately owned land adjoining West's property proved more difficult. These properties varied from one-third of an acre, part of an old subdivision called Emerald Bay Vista, to the 288-acre Clarence S. Kempff estate. Also included were two old Emerald Bay resorts. By 1954 the state had acquired extensive acreage around the shores of Emerald Bay, which, together with D. L. Bliss State Park to which it was contiguous, constituted one of the most beautiful parks in the nation. The El Dorado County Chamber of Commerce and only a few others disapproved of these purchases, on grounds that the land should be left to private development and should not be taken off the county's tax rolls.

Newton B. Drury, chief of the California Division of Beaches and Parks, defended the state park system, comparing it in quality of scenic beauty to the national parks, which he had also administered. Drury could point with pride to such state park lands as those in the coastal redwoods, the Calaveras Big Trees, Point Lobos, the extensive Anza Borrego Desert, and, of course, the D. L. Bliss–Emerald Bay state parks. Yet, he warned, "year by year the bloom is being rubbed off the California landscape." The state park system contained only six-tenths of 1 percent of California's hundred million acres in 1958, and much of this was in the desert, so that, to Drury, an active acquisition program was entirely appropriate.

Little of the Tahoe shoreline was left in public ownership by the late 1950s, even with the acquisition of the Emerald Bay property. One outstanding site, the Ehrman Estate at Sugar Pine Point on the west shore of the lake, had remained in the hands of a single family for several decades. Because the owners had cared so well for their elegant, three-story summer home and had protected the natural condition of the neighboring land, the State Park Commission took a special interest in it. When the Department of Parks and Recreation issued the *Lake Tahoe Region Study* in 1965 on the feasibility of establishing several new state parks and recreation areas in the basin, Sugar Pine Point headed the list. Acquisition of the land was recommended under the Cameron-Unruh Beach, Park, Recreational and Historical Bond Act of 1964, a $150-million measure approved by the voters at the general election in November. One reason was that other nearby state parks were overcrowded: nearly twenty thousand people in search of campsites were turned away from Bliss and Emerald Bay state parks each season in the early 1960s.

With a growing population of more than eleven million people within a day's drive of Lake Tahoe, there seemed to be no question of the importance of acquiring the new park land. In December 1965 the state purchased 1,975 acres, including 7,700 feet of lake frontage, for $8.3 million, then added a tract of 36 acres the following year. Sugar Pine Point State Park spanned roughly three and a half miles west of Lake Tahoe along the General Creek watershed, leading toward the Desolation Wilderness Area.

Of the remaining four areas considered in the regional study, only Burton Creek has been acquired subsequently. Burton Creek State Park, established in 1978, is located about a mile northeast of Tahoe City. The area purchased, considerably smaller than originally proposed, consisted of approximately 1,900 acres, including about 300 acres in Antone Meadows and along Burton Creek that was set aside in two natural preserves. The remaining land will be developed for park purposes in the 1980s. Also in the 1970s, James McClatchy and others donated half the appraised value of a 173-acre tract on Ward Creek west of Highway 89—an area perhaps to be developed for day use. It is not known whether any other land will be added to the California state parks at Tahoe, but land of particular interest includes the beach area just north of D. L. Bliss State Park and the Cascade Lake area just south of Emerald Bay.

Lake Tahoe Nevada State Park

Nevada's parks program lagged far behind California's. Moreover, when Nevada officials first tried to acquire land in the Lake Tahoe area, they found themselves hampered by the fact that nearly all of the Nevada side of the basin was privately owned and by the small budget of the state government. Land acquisition on the Nevada side was thus doubly difficult and was not accomplished until recently.

As early as 1923, an archaeological site (Lost City) in Clark County, Nevada, was set aside as a state reservation. But Governor Jack Scrugham, who had pushed this and other acquisitions, was not reelected, and activity in behalf of parks waned. Throughout the 1920s Nevada periodically set aside small areas as state recreation grounds and game refuges under the Fish and Game Commission. The state also acquired several valuable tracts of property through land exchanges with the federal government, but they remained undeveloped until the 1930s, when workers of the Civilian Conservation Corps helped improve these areas of scenic, historic, and archaeologic interest.

In 1935 the Nevada State Legislature finally created a State Park Commission and formally set aside four areas as state parks. But because of insufficient funding the parks remained neglected, and appropriations ended with the advent of World War II. Not until 1955, with the reactivation of the State Park Commission, did the legislature provide funds for hiring personnel to begin effective administration of state parks. In 1957 the legislature enlarged and strengthened the commission and gave the governor power to proclaim areas as state parks upon recommendation of the commission.[42]

In the meantime, interest in establishing state parks at Tahoe had arisen. In 1935 and again in 1937, the Nevada legislature passed a joint resolution asking Congress to purchase certain lands at Tahoe for "recreational purposes" and for construction of an "emergency aviation field." The resolution noted Tahoe's great scenic beauty and the rapid purchase of land for commercial purposes, and it called on the Nevada congressional delegation to act in support of the resolution. Again in 1941, Nevada forwarded a joint resolution to Congress. This time the proposal did not mention an airport but instead requested that Congress set aside, under Forest Service supervision, a suitable area along the eastern shoreline of the lake "for the health and recreation of the people of the State of Nevada." But once again nothing resulted.[43]

In 1938 the Nevada State Planning Board and the State Park Commission, in cooperation with the National Park Service, had completed a study of Nevada's recreational needs under a federal recreational study act. Because one-third of the population of the state, an estimated 103,000 people, lived within fifty miles of Lake Tahoe, the basin had a particular attraction as a recreation area. Recognizing that Tahoe was still in its infancy as a summer and winter playground, the study noted: "The National Park Service, the Forest Service, and the State Park Commission are hopeful that some part of this marvelous area will be set aside and designated as a State park or monument in order that future travelers to the West as well as natives may enjoy the charm of this area."[44]

It is not surprising that Nevada looked to the federal government for assistance in establishing parks; the federal government owned 88 percent of the state. The State Planning Board and the State Park Commission recommended additional study, in cooperation with federal agencies, of a Lake Tahoe interstate recreational area. They wished to determine what land at Tahoe could be acquired and what policy of administration could be developed with California officials. But the advent of the war, plus an apparent shortage of funds for both the National Park Service and the Forest Service, discouraged any action.

Much of the cutover timberlands on the Nevada side of the basin had passed into the hands of George Whittell. Eventually his property included more than twenty thousand acres, stretching many miles along the shoreline from Crystal Bay in the north to Zephyr Cove in the south, excluding Glenbrook and a few areas in other private hands. Proponents of a park on the Nevada shore had to consider the whims of Whittell, who was both an eccentric and a recluse.

The Forest Service developed a small but popular campground at Nevada Beach, not far north of Stateline, in about 1950; but interest in a Nevada state park revived only after 1955, when the legislature reactivated the State Park Commission. In August 1957 the commission discussed the possibility of obtaining a lease from Whittell on some of Tahoe's beach property. By May of the next year, the south portion of Sand Harbor had been surveyed and mapped, and Nevada Governor Charles H. Russell negotiated an agreement with Whittell for state use of the land. The beach, fewer than nine acres in area, was christened Sand Harbor State Park, the first state park on the Nevada shore.

The tenuous condition of the lease, as well as the inadequate size of the beach property, led to renewed efforts to establish a large state park on the Nevada shore. William C. Yeomans, in his *Report to the Nevada State Park Commission* (1961), urged that Nevada "develop and maintain the best possible park system" to attract tourists. When Governor Grant Sawyer toured the Tahoe Basin in July 1961, he was surprised at how little of the shoreline remained in public control. An editorial in the *Reno Evening Gazette* supported Sawyer's plea for a Tahoe park, arguing that Tahoe "belongs to all the people" and not just to the property owners at the lake. Sawyer proposed negotiations with Whittell to obtain lakeshore for public use before the land was lost completely to development.

Leslie Gould, chairman of the Nevada State Park Commission, and Joseph C. Houghteling, chairman of the California State Park Commission, discussed the possibility of interstate cooperation for a park at Tahoe when they met at the dedication ceremonies of the Plumas-Eureka State Park in California.[45] The idea of such an interstate park had a precedent in the cooperation of New York and New Jersey over the Palisades Park along the Hudson River; for that park, New Jersey had land and New York had funds. Houghteling responded enthusiastically to Nevada's interest in the Whittell property. The possibility of cooperation seemed to everyone's advantage, as Nevada had the only large expanse of undeveloped shoreline, whereas Californians would be the ones to make heaviest use of any recreational facilities developed. Also, the California government had the resources to help finance such a project.

Once they had discussed the situation and had gained the support of their respective governors, Gould and Houghteling arranged a meeting of the new Interstate Park Commission on November 18, 1961.[46] The Interstate Commission, composed of members of each state's park commission, discussed the need to move rapidly as property values skyrocketed. Because the Sand Harbor lease from Whittell could be terminated at any time on thirty days' notice, there was an obvious need to acquire land on a permanent basis.

Before the close of its first meeting, the Interstate Commission passed various resolutions calling for a bi-state approach to acquisition of Whittell's and other private properties at Tahoe. It established a joint committee to consider including all state parks at Tahoe under the administration of a single authority. Further, the two state park commissions were directed to formulate "an overall park and recreation plan for the Lake Tahoe area," in full consultation with local and other interested public agencies.

The Interstate Commission met a second time in February 1962 and recommended drafting a compact. In California, responsibility passed to the California Commission on Interstate Cooperation, which recommended that a Lake Tahoe park authority be established by interstate compact with the state of Nevada to acquire, operate, and maintain public parks. The Nevada Legislative Commission, a counterpart, agreed to discussions with California, and a subcommittee soon approved a draft of a compact. But when Governor Sawyer, in his message to the Nevada legislature in 1963, urged creation of a bi-state park, his proposal created heated debate. The draft compact, introduced with identical bills in both state legislatures, died in committee in Nevada. As a result, the California legislature took no further action on the bill.

In the meantime, the Sierra Club organized a Lake Tahoe Park Committee, of three members each from the club's Toiyabe Chapter in Nevada and the Mother Lode Chapter in California, to publicize the bi-state proposal. An article in the *Sierra Club Bulletin* envisaged an interstate park of 35,000 acres with 5,000 campsites. The Nature Conservancy, another environmental organization, offered its services to enlist funds from private foundations and to aid negotiations for the purchase of land.

The Nevada legislature refused to approve the interstate compact. The lawmakers did provide a $500,000 fund to buy options on desirable tracts and to survey and appraise proposed park lands, though the fund was not part of any bi-state proposal. Gould thought it disgraceful that the Nevada legislature had defeated the proposed bi-state park, and he blamed Lieutenant Governor Paul Laxalt for killing the bill. Governor Sawyer sharply criticized the legislature's action.

Sawyer, in calling a special session of the legislature for January 1964, listed the need to take action on Tahoe as one of the reasons. A Nevada park bill, incorporating the right of eminent domain and an appropriation of $1.5 million for land acquisition and park planning, became law, though a second bill for a bi-state park failed. The park act authorized acquisition of a 13,500-acre tract with 7.5 miles of shoreline between Incline Village and a line approximately parallel to the route of Highway 50 across Spooner Summit. In April 1964 a group of public officials and private citizens met in Carson City to advise the governor and assist in planning the new park. Time was critical; private investors continued to covet the Whittell property.

There were further delays, and negotiations to acquire land from Whittell failed. Finally the state of Nevada commenced condemnation proceedings on part of the property. With the aid of a $50,000 grant from the Max C. Fleischmann Foundation that was matched by the Nevada legislature, the state hired expert counsel and started legal action in July 1966. A jury verdict in November 1967 favored the state, resulting in the acquisition of roughly 5,000 acres from Whittell for about $3 million. Other lands were added, and the Lake Tahoe Nevada State Park soon encompassed more than 13,000 acres, including some of the most beautiful vistas of the lake.[47]

By the 1970s the combined acreage set aside in state parks and national forests surpassed 70 percent of the land area in the Lake Tahoe Basin. The state parks—Bliss, Emerald Bay, Sugar Pine Point, Tahoe State Recreational Area, and Lake Tahoe Nevada— offered swimming, camping, and more. The U.S. Forest Service administered several fine beaches, including Pope, Baldwin, Kiva, and Nevada, as well as extensive areas incorporating most of the mountainous terrain surrounding the lake. Clearly, parks and forests had come to play a vital role in the life at Tahoe, both for recreation and in the efforts to retain portions of the land and lakeshore in a natural and largely undeveloped condition.

4 Water Use and Quality

Dams and Aqueducts

The most precious resource in the American west is neither gold nor oil, but water. In the second half of the nineteenth century, farmers downstream from the northern Sierra Nevada in the Central Valley of California and the valleys fed by the Truckee, Carson, and Walker rivers in Nevada looked for a reliable source of water to irrigate their crops. Miners in both states needed water, particularly for Virginia City's Comstock Lode and for hydraulic mining in California's Mother Lode. Further afield, San Francisco, the metropolis of the west coast, threatened to outgrow its local water supply and looked to the Sierra for potential reservoir sites.

One man, Alexis von Schmidt, played the dominant early role in attempts to utilize the water of Lake Tahoe. Schmidt arrived in California with the forty-niners at the age of twenty-eight. There he became a civil engineer, a career at which he was both highly imaginative and successful. After designing an effective local water supply system for San Francisco and completing other projects, he turned his attention to the Sierra Nevada. In 1863 he proposed that water be piped from Tahoe to Virginia City. When the Board of Aldermen of Virginia City balked at the expense and questioned the feasibility of the project, Schmidt helped establish the Lake Tahoe and San Francisco Water Works Company in 1865 to bring Tahoe water to the Bay Area.

Schmidt's proposed mammoth project drew a mixed response. Many found the proposal exciting; others complained about the cost involved and cautioned that the project could not be completed within the century. The main opposition came from Nevadans who argued that California had no legal right to appropriate the water. The state boundary runs through the lake—the outlet is on the California side, though the water eventually flows into Nevada.

Although the opposition stalled his proposal initially, Schmidt took the offensive in 1870 and made an offer to San Francisco: he would provide twenty million gallons of water daily; in return the city would submit a $10-million bond issue to the voters and allow the Lake Tahoe and San Francisco Water Works Company to buy out the existing water company, assuring monopoly control. At the same time, a bill introduced to Congress promised to provide the company with building materials, a right-of-way across federal land, and a land grant of alternate sections of land for twenty miles on each side of the proposed aqueduct.

Nevada newspapers, especially the Virginia City *Daily Territorial Enterprise,* led a sharp attack on what it perceived as the continuation of robbery by a "gang of San Francisco speculators." As its editorial of March 2, 1870, put it: "They may take the gold and silver from our hills, and bind us in vassalage to the caprices of their stock boards, but the pure water that comes to us from Lake Tahoe, that drives our mills and makes glad our waste places, is God's exhaustless gift, and the hand of man cannot deprive us of it."

Actually, sufficient opposition existed within San Francisco itself to kill the proposal, at least temporarily, for citizens anticipated corruption and feared that high taxes would be levied to finance the scheme. Elsewhere in California public response was mixed: those who stood to gain were enthusiastic, others found the idea impractical and suspect. Downstream from Tahoe, citizens of Truckee predicted the ruin of their lumber business if Tahoe water were diverted to San Francisco.

Schmidt argued that the lake had sufficient water for both states and that his company would use Tahoe water for only a few months each year, when runoff from the Western slope of the Sierra proved insufficient. By the end of 1870 he had acquired land at the lake's outlet at Tahoe City for $3 per acre and constructed a small dam.

The following year, Schmidt made a generous offer to the San Francisco Board of Supervisors, to whom he promised water within four years. Water would be diverted from the Truckee River to Squaw Valley, flow five miles through a tunnel to the north fork of the American River, and then proceed through an aqueduct, a reservoir, and a pipeline to San Francisco. Along the way from the mountains to the coast, the system would provide water to mining, farming, and municipal customers. Schmidt considered the estimated cost of roughly $10 million dollars a sound investment. Although the supervisors accepted Schmidt's proposal in 1871, the mayor of San Francisco vetoed the project, fearing monopoly control by a private corporation and possible legal suits over water rights. Schmidt pursued his plan, entering into an agreement with the Central Pacific Railroad for joint construction of a tunnel through the Sierra for both water and railroad tracks. But problems arose, and the contract was canceled.

Because water remained scarce and the extensive supply at Tahoe continued to be attractive, reconsideration by residents of both states was only a matter of time. One group that called itself the Nevada and Lake Tahoe Water and Manufacturing Company proposed in 1887 a four-mile tunnel through the Carson Range to connect Lake Tahoe and Carson Valley. But rivalries between potential water users in Nevada prevented any effective cooperative efforts. In 1890 Francis J. Newlands, later a United States Senator, proposed a network of reservoirs in the Sierra to serve the future development of Nevada. According to Newlands, Tahoe afforded the "cheapest reservoir space known in the west."

Newlands noted also that the lake was then controlled by a dam operated by the Donner Boom and Logging Company. This company, essentially a subsidiary of the Central Pacific Railroad, had acquired control of Schmidt's dam and, under a twenty-year permit granted by the California legislature, controlled the flow of water to float logs downstream to mills at Truckee. Newlands failed to acquire the dam from the Central Pacific, but he purchased 160 acres nearby at the lake's outlet as a possible alternative site for a dam of his own.

In the 1890s, Californians expressed renewed interest in a Tahoe water supply, which might now be combined with hydroelectric power generation. An inspection party from San Francisco visited Tahoe in 1900 but concluded that a more accessible water supply could be obtained on the western slope of the Sierra. Continued opposition by Nevadans provided an additional deterrent to any California proposal to tap the supply at Tahoe. So San Francisco refused Schmidt's offer to sell, for $50,000, the water and property rights still held by his company. These rights passed to San Francisco attorney James A. Waymire after Schmidt died in 1906. Waymire's death soon thereafter ended his own grandiose scheme for the development of Tahoe water for hydroelectric and domestic use. By this time, San Francisco had launched its campaign to acquire water from the Tuolumne River, a plan that led eventually to the infamous Hetch Hetchy dam in Yosemite National Park.

The defeat of these early proposals to use Lake Tahoe as a mammoth storage reservoir marked only the beginning of a heated controversy. Schmidt and others had the engineering skill to carry their plans to completion. What they did not have was adequate financial and political support. Also, the continuing rivalry between Nevada and California discouraged citizens in either state from risking unilateral action; any such activity would have been challenged in the courts, if not by armed force.

The Tahoe Water Controversy

In 1902, President Theodore Roosevelt signed the Reclamation Act, a measure through which the federal government provided water for irrigation in the arid and semi-arid areas of the American west. Because the author of the act, Senator Newlands, represented Nevada, it is not surprising that the nation's first reclamation project was completed in that state. In June 1905, water began to flow through a thirty-one mile canal from the Truckee River to the Carson River and on to the desert of the Carson Sink, some sixty miles east of Reno. The Newlands Project, later called the Truckee-Carson Irrigation Project, was intended to open extensive acreage in western Nevada to agriculture, providing the basis for a stable and prosperous economy.

The project depended on an extensive and presumably reliable source of water in the Sierra Nevada, as well as successful application of this water to crops. Unfortunately for the farmers, the Bureau of Reclamation made serious errors, underestimating the cost that farmers would have to repay, miscalculating the value of the crops that could be produced in the alkaline soil, and overestimating the acreage that could be brought under cultivation. Perhaps most serious, the bureau proceeded without acquiring clear title to the resource upon which the project depended: the water of the Lake Tahoe Basin. The bureau apparently believed it could easily gain control of the Tahoe dam and the surplus water that it impounded. In 1903, an agent of the Department of the Interior posted a notice of the government's right to the water flowing into Tahoe and of the right to control and use at will the water stored in the lake behind the dam.

Other parties, however, had a vital interest in Tahoe and objected strongly. Farmers on irrigated lands naturally wanted a cheap, dependable, and plentiful supply of water at the season when maximum crop production required it. Power companies wanted a steady flow of water for generating hydroelectricity throughout the year. Tahoe property owners wanted to maintain the beauty of the lakeshore and to protect their property values and the use of their piers, boathouses, and beaches. The needs of all groups could not be met simultaneously.

The small dam at the outlet of the lake had passed into the hands of the Fleischackers, a wealthy San Francisco family that had bought several small hydroelectric power plants along the banks of the Truckee River and formed the Truckee General Electric Company. The company controlled the dam in spite of a questionable

The timber dam at the outlet of Lake Tahoe became a focal point of controversy in the early twentieth century. Special Collections, University of Nevada–Reno Library.

legal right to do so, regulating the water supply to provide a steady source for power generation. Based on this energy source, flour mills, saw mills, and smelting and reduction works, as well as paper, box, and furniture manufacturers, located along the banks of the Truckee.

The first effort by the federal government to purchase the dam from the Fleischackers was fruitless, as the government thought the asking price too high. By 1905 federal officials had proposed that the government build a dam of its own, a short distance downstream from the lake. But the power company and wealthy property owners of the area used the courts to block this project, as well as later ploys to bypass the existing dam. William Thomas, chairman of the powerful California Water and Forest Association and also a property owner at Tahoe, spearheaded the defense by Tahoe summer residents against what was perceived as a dire threat. They feared that a government-controlled dam, operated to aid Nevada farmers, would result in wide fluctuation in the level of the lake, flooding valuable property in the spring and exposing stumps and rocks during periods of low water in the fall. The potential damage to private property would be compounded by the negative impact on the tourist trade. Such prominent and wealthy property owners as John D. Spreckels and Adolph Sutro joined Thomas and several others in sending a petition to the governor of California urging protection of the state's water rights and of individual property rights at Tahoe.

The controversy came to a head in 1908–1909. An eastern syndicate, Stone-Webster and Company, perhaps inspired by a rumor that the Southern Pacific Railroad would soon convert from steam to electric power, acquired an option to purchase the Truckee River General Electric Company. Then it began extended negotiations with the Bureau of Reclamation to gain an assured flow of water for hydroelectric power development. By summer 1909, under the threat of a condemnation suit by the federal government to get control of the Tahoe dam, Stone-Webster entered into an agreement with the Department of the Interior. The agreement provided for government control over the dam, which would be rebuilt by the power company, and over the water of Lake Tahoe. In return, Stone-Webster would receive the guarantee of a certain amount of water throughout the year for power generation, as well as the rights to build a tunnel to divert water directly from Tahoe and to construct reservoirs, power lines, and roads on public lands. Because the Truckee-Carson Irrigation Project verged on collapse unless it received additional water soon, the government willingly negotiated a bargain favorable to Stone-Webster, which looked forward to a monopoly of power development and profits in the area it served.

Gifford Pinchot, chief of the U.S. Forest Service, opposed the policy at Tahoe of Secretary of the Interior Richard Ballinger; Pinchot objected that the contract with Stone-Webster was not in the public interest, partly because it granted power development rights in perpetuity. With support of the Department of the Interior, however, Stone-Webster proceeded to construct a new dam at Tahoe's outlet, and it also acquired smaller, competing companies in western Nevada and northeastern California. When the terms of the proposed contract leaked to newspapers, the *San Francisco Examiner* exclaimed, "Secret Deal With U.S. Puts Tahoe In Syndicate's Clutch."

Tahoe property owners, led by William Kent, rallied in opposition to the pending contract. Kent claimed it would ruin Lake Tahoe and cost the American people millions of dollars in water power rights. He warned President William Howard Taft and high-ranking administration officials of a potential scandal. The combined opposition of the property owners, the Forest Service, and assorted California newspapers and legislators led that year to the defeat of the proposed agreement.

In spite of Department of the Interior efforts to meet some of the objections leveled against the contract, the negotiations dragged on. In 1911, Californians rose up in opposition to a renewed effort by the Bureau of Reclamation and the power syndicate to reach agreement. The state of California, which had not been consulted by the bureau, argued that Tahoe's water belonged to California, not to the federal government or the power company. As in the past, California and Nevada found themselves on opposite sides of the fence, and the legislature of each state sent a resolution to Washington appealing for federal cooperation in the Tahoe controversy. Faced with constant criticism, the power company finally withdrew from negotiations.

Yet the importance of Tahoe water, both for hydroelectric power development and irrigation, could not be ignored. A severe water shortage in summer 1912 threatened both the crops of farmers served by the Truckee-Carson Irrigation Project and the people of Reno and other communities dependent on electrical power generated by the water of the Truckee River. In October, a crew of men sent by the power company and the Bureau of Reclamation arrived at the lake's outlet with the intention of cutting a deeper channel through the natural rim of the lake to release more water. Irate property owners at Tahoe blocked the threatened action with an injunction.

Thoroughly distrusting the intentions of both the Bureau of Reclamation and Stone-Webster, a group of prominent Tahoe property owners filed articles of incorporation of the Lake Tahoe Protection Association on January 23, 1913. This organization, which had existed informally for several years, was the first environmental group created specifically to preserve the lake's beauty. The association hoped to prevent any serious lowering of the lake level. Its objectives also included the protection of fish and game in the basin, prevention of fires, enactment and enforcement of laws preventing pollution of the lake by sewage and garbage, improvement of navigation safety on the lake, construction of better roads and trails, and other measures to keep Tahoe an attractive and enjoyable summer resort area. Will S. Bliss and other members of the association kept a wary eye on all negotiations that might affect the future of Tahoe.

Following public hearings on the Lake Tahoe controversy, dispute revolved increasingly around the issue of how much the level of the lake should be allowed to fluctuate. The Bureau of Reclamation held out for a six-foot fluctuation between high and low water levels, whereas the Lake Tahoe Protection Association favored a four-foot range. The association argued that the bureau could provide for the needs of Nevada's farmers by developing dams in the Truckee River Basin, and that the bureau needed only limited use of Tahoe water.

Although the legal question of who ultimately held water rights at Tahoe remained unsettled, the contesting parties at last reached a temporary settlement. All agreed that the federal government should control the recently completed dam at the outlet of the lake. The property owners agreed that some water could be taken from Tahoe; the government in turn agreed not to consider cutting the rim of the lake for the time being. And the power company agreed to a "friendly" condemnation suit, which in 1915 resulted in the government's acquisition of the dam and adjoining property for $139,500. The government also gained ownership of four feet of Tahoe water—that between 6,225 and 6,229 feet in elevation above sea level, stored behind the dam. The power company gained assurance from the government that it would receive a specified amount of Tahoe's water each month throughout the year.

The truce did not last long, however: each of the parties pursued its own interest. After a three-year period of abundant precipitation, the lake often fell dangerously low for two decades. Complicated negotiations seemed to follow each ebb and flow of the lake level.

Conflict arose in 1919 and 1920, dry years in which the lake fell to its lowest point thus far in the twentieth century. The Bureau of Reclamation asked owners of Tahoe shoreline property to sign quitclaims that would release the government from legal penalties for any property damage resulting from use of the lake as a storage reservoir. Alarmed Californians, fearing some nefarious plot by the bureau and perhaps others, met at Tahoe on August 9, 1919, in a "mass meeting" to discuss the situation and to plan strategy. Representatives appeared from various state and local governmental agencies, including the office of the California attorney general, local business groups, automobile associations, chambers of commerce, and environmental groups such as the Lake Tahoe Protection Association and the Sierra Club. Obviously, California intended to defend its recreational interests in the Tahoe Basin against the bureau.

Colonel E. E. Winslow of the U.S. Army Corps of Engineers conducted an investigation into the Tahoe controversy the following year. Winslow placed much of the blame on poor communication by the bureau and on its concessions to power company interests. He opposed any proposal to cut the rim of the lake, and he suggested that California revive a 1912 suit against the power company to test its claim to water from Tahoe. Finally, Winslow approved of bureau regulation of the lake level within a six-foot range, especially in order to provide Nevada farmers with water when they most needed it.

Drought conditions recurred, and Nevada farmers had to plead with Californians for a small amount of additional Tahoe water to avert disaster. In 1924, when the lake level actually fell below the outlet, and no water whatsoever flowed into the Truckee River, the desperate farmers threatened to blow an outlet through the rim with dynamite. Californians argued that the farmers and the bureau had not taken corrective measures to provide for alternative reservoir sites in the Truckee watershed and elsewhere.

In 1929, not only did the stock market crash, but several years of drought began that plagued the western United States. When the Truckee River east of Reno dwindled to a dry river bed in summer 1930, Nevada farmers sent a crew of men with a steam shovel in the middle of the night to the outlet of the lake. Apparently the men began cutting a diversion ditch on the property of the Sierra Pacific Power Company (the successor to the Truckee River General Electric Company) to tap the lake below the rim and release some 75,000 acre-feet of water claimed by the farmers. A direct confrontation between the crew and Tahoe residents was narrowly averted when a deputy sheriff used a temporary warrant to stop the steam shovel operator, whom he accused of disturbing the peace.

Tahoe residents rallied in defense of the lake, guarding the rim and the dam after rumors spread that they might be dynamited. On the second night, a group of the Tahoe "vigilantes" stole the magneto from the steam shovel and tried to fill the diversion ditch. Cooler heads prevailed, and a court injunction put a stop to all excavation. The dispute ended temporarily with Nevada allowed to pump a small amount of water from the lake, and California and Nevada agreeing to form an interstate committee to study all problems related to Tahoe water.

Negotiators from the two states reached a compromise known as the Truckee River agreement in 1934. The agreement provided for

> a prohibition on cutting the rim of Tahoe or diverting water through a tunnel or by other means from the lake;
> regulation of the lake level within a six-foot limit, between 6,223.0 and 6,229.1 feet;
> permission for construction of the Boca Reservoir on the Little Truckee River, reducing dependence of Nevada farmers on Lake Tahoe;
> permission for the Sierra Pacific Power Company to build a smaller reservoir, on condition that it reduce its winter use of Tahoe water;

control of the Tahoe dam by the Truckee-Carson Irrigation District as an agent for the United States, with the provision that
the district avoid high-water damage to private property on the
lakeshore.

With the return of wet years in the late 1930s, the Tahoe water
controversy faded, at least temporarily.

A court decision in 1944, commonly called the Truckee River
Final Decree, adjudicated the water rights of the Truckee River
water users in Nevada. The decree reaffirmed the 1915 and 1934
decisions and recognized that the United States had the right,
dating from 1903, to store and use at will the water behind the
Tahoe dam. It also stated that Truckee River water could be
used for irrigating 232,800 acres of the Truckee-Carson Irrigation
Project and 5,875 acres of land held by the Paiute Indians at
Pyramid Lake, as well as for the generation of power and for
domestic uses. The decree, unfortunately, took no account of the
future needs of water users within the basin itself.

The California-Nevada Interstate Compact

California and Nevada formed the Lake Tahoe Interstate
Water Conference Committee in 1931. The committee functioned
intermittently, acting more as a forum for discussion than as a body
with legislative or police powers. Members of the committee from
both states, mainly lawyers and engineers who represented special
interests, agreed to continue to meet after 1934 in order to administer the Truckee River agreement.

Signs of conflict soon appeared within the committee. A large
group of property owners at Lake Tahoe, who had organized as the
Save Lake Tahoe Association in July 1934 under the leadership of
Louis Bartlett, complained that they had not been party to the
agreement of 1934 allowing a high-water level of 6,229.1 feet.
Bartlett had argued that such high water could cause serious
flooding and property loss at the south shore. He also believed that
preservation of the beauty of Tahoe and its use as a recreation area

was incompatible with use of the lake's water primarily for the benefit of power companies and irrigators.

As fate would have it, heavy snowfall in 1937 brought the lake level up rapidly, adding to the concern of property owners. Various proposals were discussed to establish reservoirs downstream for storing excess water from Tahoe. At the same time, the Bureau of Reclamation revived a proposal by a bureau engineer to divert some Tahoe water to Washoe Lake in Nevada via a long tunnel. But because the Truckee River agreement prohibited such development, and neither California nor Nevada wished to renew the controversy, the proposal died quickly.

Nevertheless, the problem of the water level at Tahoe continued during World War II. After the war ended, suspicions and self-interest undermined proposals for compromise between Nevada and California. With rapid population growth in each state and the beginning of a remarkable postwar economic boom at Tahoe, the demands on the water from the lake became greater than ever. Thus the California delegation to the Lake Tahoe Interstate Water Conference Committee reacted with alarm when it appeared that Nevada might pursue separate planning to meet its own water needs. The Lake Tahoe Sierra Association, representing business and property interests in the basin, appointed a committee to study the possible impact of Nevada reclamation projects on the lake. In 1948, when the water sank to its lowest level since 1934, rumors circulated that Nevada farmers would request that water be pumped from Tahoe.

A joint report by the California and Nevada state engineers on water use in the Tahoe Basin, published in 1950, revealed that future inhabitants of the Tahoe area would use little more water than in the past, partly because water once used for agriculture in the basin could be converted to domestic use. Also, much of the water used would find its way back into the lake, where it would be available for reuse downstream in Nevada. This conclusion, however, did not take into account the amount of water subsequently pumped from the basin as effluent in order to maintain water quality.

During the early 1950s, the Interstate Committee again encountered Tahoe's high-water problem, which increased in significance as Tahoe's beaches and shoreline attracted growing numbers of users. Legislative action on earlier proposals by the Army Corps of Engineers had been stymied by lack of interstate and local cooperation. Whereas the main concern of the corps was flood control, the Bureau of Reclamation once again had its own plans for development of irrigation and hydroelectric power projects, including proposals for new reservoirs in Hope and Carson valleys. As proposals and counterproposals proliferated, including the idea of tunnels to carry water directly from Tahoe to both Nevada and California, chances of conciliation between the special interest groups declined. In an attempt to find a way out of the deadlock, Congress passed a bill in 1955 establishing the California-Nevada Interstate Compact Commission.

The commission seemed to promise success; neither California nor Nevada wished to have the controversial water problems settled in a lengthy court battle. California wanted assurance that a dependable supply of Tahoe water, as well as some water from the Truckee, Carson, and Walker rivers, would be reserved for its future needs. Nevada recognized that congressional support for development of a comprehensive water plan, especially proposed Bureau of Reclamation dams desired by Nevadans, depended on compromise with California. Because neither the states nor the lakeshore property owners at Tahoe had been party to previous agreements or court decisions on the rights of downstream water users, their water rights remained undetermined. The compact provided an opportunity to apportion water rights, including rights to Lake Tahoe and the Truckee River—at least for that water not previously claimed—through negotiation.

Although the Compact Commission first met in 1956, it spent two and a half years gathering and studying data before beginning serious negotiations. In 1963 the commission published a report. Californians had argued that domestic water use at Tahoe should have priority over irrigation in Nevada. They had pointed out that in the absence of a compact, development on the California side of the basin would proceed unchecked, to the ultimate disadvantage of downstream water users. Nevadans, seeing court litigation as both risky and expensive, tried to make the best of a negotiated settlement. The commission recommended allocating thirty-four thousand acre-feet of water for use in the basin, an amount expected to be ample for all foreseeable needs. Of this amount, California received twenty-three thousand acre-feet and Nevada eleven thousand.

Other provisions of the proposed compact included construction of an overflow weir at the outlet, as first suggested by the Army Corps of Engineers. The compact also allowed pumping of water from Tahoe for essential purposes in times of drought, when no other water was available downstream. Furthermore, the federal government retained its right to store water between the levels of 6,223.0 and 6,229.1 feet.

Although the commissioners agreed on the division of water supplies in the Tahoe Basin, they failed in an effort to expand the responsibilities of the commission to provide for comprehensive planning. Joseph F. McDonald, head of the Nevada-California Lake Tahoe Association, which was founded in 1957, noted the need for coordination between the five basin counties to survey and seek solutions to Tahoe's problems. In fact, McDonald proposed a Lake Tahoe authority, similar to the New York Port Authority, and looked to the Compact Commission as the most likely candidate to fill that role. But Placer and El Dorado county officials, fearful of federal control in the basin, blocked the proposal.

As a result, the question of water quality was separated from the question of dividing the surplus water of Tahoe. The compact, if approved, would encourage development at the lake: there would be essentially no limit to the water supply available for urban use—and no controls on growth. In brief, the commission avoided suggestions of regional planning, guarded local interests, and protected established water rights.

A formal compact was not completed until 1968, thirteen years after Congress had established the commission. The delay resulted in part from the complexity of settling differences in three separate river basins, as well as an interstate lake. Most members of the Compact Commission represented local rather than state interests and were ill-equipped to deal with the larger issues raised in the course of the commission's work.

The compact had gained the approval of both state legislatures by 1971. California acquired a guarantee of the water needed at Tahoe for large-scale development of the lucrative recreation industry, and Nevada gained a favorable position in regard to surplus water for irrigation from the three rivers. Because the compact allotted to Nevada all surplus water not specifically granted to California, Nevadans would benefit in wet years.

Many problems remained for future settlement by a permanent commission. Of course, the entire compact depended on final ratification by Congress. A Department of the Interior representative had presided at the commission's meetings and obviously understood the terms of the compact; thus it was a surprise to both California and Nevada when Secretary of the Interior Walter Hickel announced that he could not support the compact. He objected to limitations placed on federal authority over water use in the area and, most serious, he argued that the compact neglected the rights of the Paiute Indians at Pyramid Lake, the ultimate destination of the Truckee River.

The Paiute, whose rights antedated the rights of everyone else, had lived in abject poverty for decades while the level of Pyramid Lake in the middle of their land fell more than eighty feet. The loss of water through evaporation greatly exceeded the inflow from the Truckee River—especially once the Truckee-Carson Irrigation Project had diverted about half the river. The lowering of the lake threatened the Indians' economy, which was based on fishing. In addition, any expansion of agriculture and hope for a thriving tourist trade in the future depended on restoration of Pyramid Lake. Although some Nevadans argued that a choice had to be made between Lake Tahoe and Pyramid Lake, as there was insufficient water to save both, many Californians suggested an alternative: conservation. They believed that elimination of waste from

Nevada's irrigation system could provide most if not all the water necessary to save Pyramid Lake.

Resolution of the conflict, which continues today, depends in part on the court settlement of Indian water rights cases. A district court ruled in 1972 that an additional 135,000 acre-feet of water should flow into Pyramid Lake annually, but the Supreme Court ruled against the Indians in 1983.

Water Quality and Sewage until 1960

A new and more serious issue arose in the decades following World War II: water quality. In earlier days, the purity and clarity of Tahoe's water had been legendary. Visitors marveled at the beauty of the lake, and resort owners advertised the health and vitality of the air and water in the basin. John LeConte, a scientist who visited the lake in 1873, confirmed what everyone assumed: the water of Lake Tahoe was very clear and contained no noticeable suspended matter. LeConte could clearly see a white dinner plate more than a hundred feet below the surface of the lake.

Even though the extensive logging in the two decades after LeConte visited must have created considerable erosion and a temporary decline in water quality, few people bothered to comment on pollution problems at the time. In 1906, Chancey Juday noted while investigating the lake's fisheries that sediment from swollen streams could be traced far into the lake. But logging had virtually ceased by the turn of the century, and no one had much reason to be concerned about water quality for many years thereafter. Then, with the rapid influx of people and the construction boom of the late 1940s, it became apparent that the people of the Tahoe Basin could no longer avoid consideration of the immediate and long-term consequences of a growing city along the shores of the lake. Dependence on the proliferating septic tanks, with inevitable seepage into the lake and nearby streams, bode ill for the future.

Water pollution at Lake Tahoe posed problems beyond those encountered by most communities. The normal American waste disposal method, dumping material into a nearby stream to be carried out of sight and out of mind, simply does not work in a basin where the pollutants remain on one's doorstep. The lake has only a limited ability to purify itself. For one thing, the retention and flushing time for Tahoe is roughly 675 years; in other words, if the basin were empty, with its natural inflow it would fill in about 675 years. Thus nonbiodegradable pollutants that flow into the lake remain there to the detriment of more than twenty future generations. The accumulation of matter and chemicals might seem harmless to many people, but few could seriously question that it constitutes a pollution problem if the supply of drinking water were to become unsafe.

Water clarity was also a concern, especially because the beauty of the lake attracted tourists, the backbone of the basin's economy. As nutrients, especially nitrogen and phosphorous, enter the lake in ever-increasing amounts, the danger of eutrophication increases—a process by which added nutrients increase plant growth and result in deterioration of water quality. And nutrients did enter Tahoe, not only from sewage wastes, but from the runoff generated by increased disturbance of the mountain slopes, caused by land clearance for buildings and by cutting and filling for roads.

In the summer of 1946, Wallace W. White, the Nevada state health engineer, said that construction at Tahoe should be curtailed, if not prohibited, until local communities could provide adequate sewage systems to prevent "serious contamination" of the water supply. Although White noted that no sewage then emptied directly into the lake, and that water samples disclosed no contamination to date, he also explained that some disposal of sewage into Tahoe had been discovered from time to time. Also, several resorts on the Nevada side of the lake were having difficulty resolving their sewage problems. And in the following summer, White predicted the spread of disease and the destruction of Tahoe's beaches unless modern sewage disposal systems were constructed. Noting that "sewerage is critical and needs attention immediately," he advocated sewer districts for both the north and south ends of the lake.[1] Dr. Fred Loe, head of Nevada's Department of Health, agreed and noted that the concentration of some fifty or sixty thousand people in the Tahoe Basin in summer caused the problem. The day of separate sewage disposal by individual property owners had to end.

The discovery in 1948 of raw sewage running into the lake from land owned by George Whittell probably did not surprise White and Loe. Whittell claimed, with apparent justification, that the problem resulted from crowds of illegal campers and picknickers who ignored "no trespassing" signs. The next year the Nevada legislature passed a law prohibiting discharge of wastes directly into the lake or within a hundred feet of a stream or spring in the basin. The law also required a written permit from the Department of Health for construction that required domestic water or sewage disposal in areas draining into the lake.

The California State Department of Public Health expressed a similar concern about the deterioration of water quality, and public health officials in both states conferred in the hope of finding a solution. Because sanitation and health constituted just one of several emerging problems in the basin, Reno attorney Lester Summerfield, who owned a summer home at Tahoe, suggested to the governors of both states that the legislatures appoint committees to study the problems of Tahoe. He argued that the counties bordering the lake could not effectively handle the situation, and he noted that the problems were "too big for any one county or any combination of counties with their limited delegated governmental powers." Summerfield hoped for some sort of compact under which an interstate commission could be formed with the power to tax property and to promote such services as police and fire protection. "Above all else," he said, the commission "should be empowered to impose and enforce sanitary regulations to prevent the pollution of the lake."[2]

Although California and Nevada did appoint a Commission on Intergovernmental Relations, which met in August 1949 and discussed a wide range of topics, nothing of consequence resulted. Sewage disposal clearly ranked as the most serious problem, but the question of who would finance construction of the sewage-treatment plants necessary to serve the summer crowds remained unresolved. Also, no agreement could be reached on such important issues as the regulation of development in the basin or the acceptance of a basinwide standard for sewage disposal. Under California's Water Pollution Control Act of 1949 (the Dickey Act), the primary responsibility for pollution control passed from the Department of Public Health to several regional boards under the State Water Pollution Control Board (today's State Water Resources Control Board). The Lahontan Regional Water Quality Control Board acquired responsibility for the Tahoe Basin. This board forbade the discharge of sewage into water sources in the basin that failed to meet federal standards for drinking water.

Local action was taken in California, too. In the 1950s the public utility districts of Tahoe City, North Tahoe, and South Tahoe constructed sewage treatment facilities. And in Nevada, Douglas and Washoe counties formed small sewer districts to serve the gambling industry at each end of the lake. Voters reluctantly approved bond issues or special assessments to finance the proposed sewer systems. But the rapid increase in numbers of both people and buildings soon overwhelmed the capacities of the treatment plants. Disposal of effluent also posed a problem because disposal sites within the basin were limited. In addition, most residences still depended on individual septic tanks.

An engineering study completed for the South Tahoe Public Utility District in 1959 reviewed four possible methods for sewage disposal, including the export of effluent from the basin. Because of the problems of finding and gaining approval to use disposal sites and of meeting water-quality standards in other districts, this idea was set aside for the time being. Two other methods, direct discharge into the lake and injection of effluent into deep wells in the basin, were rejected because of the danger of eutrophication at the lake. So the study recommended expansion of the existing disposal method, spraying effluent onto land sites within the basin, until some better solution could be achieved. The report did mark an important break with the past in its recognition of an ultimate solution: removal of sewage entirely from the basin.

The report also marked a shift in emphasis from discussion of water quality as essentially a problem of public health to discussion of the health of the lake itself. Events of 1959 made this shift timely. On November 26, the *Tahoe Sierra Tribune* reported that "a heavy infestation of submerged water weeds has become established along the south shore of Lake Tahoe, and much of the recreational value of the beaches could be lost if these weeds continue their spread and growth." This species of aquatic plants, first observed in 1952, had spread rapidly since 1958. They interfered with swimming and boating and drifted onto beaches, leaving them "untidy, foul-smelling and attractive to flies and other insects." A report on the infestation by the El Dorado County agricultural commissioner placed no blame on anyone for the situation. Because the plants thrived on a muddy or silty bottom in shallow water, the low lake level and high summer temperatures may have caused the problem; yet, he noted, erosion from ground disturbed by construction undoubtedly added to it. Under the circumstances, it was not surprising that some people cast a suspicious eye on a mammoth dredging operation at Tahoe Keys—a $150,000,000 residential complex under construction in the marsh at the mouth of the Upper Truckee River, in the midst of the plant-infested area.

In the early 1970s, efforts to protect water quality dominated environmental activities within the basin. But by this time environmentalists could no longer afford to consider a single issue in isolation from the host of other problems caused by urbanization.

5 Planning and Conflict

Local Response to Urban Problems

Explosive growth following World War II converted the Tahoe Basin from a relatively quiet summer resort area to a bustling "all-year playground." With the expansion came new dangers to the ecological stability and health of the natural environment. Efforts to achieve some degree of control over growth gave rise to continuing heated debate.

Because people were scattered throughout the basin, each community attempted to meet its own needs, including fire and police protection, schools, water supply, and sewage disposal. Fire had always been a concern, particularly during the summer months when the forest became dry and highly flammable. The absence of uniform building codes to assure proper electrical wiring and safe fireplaces and heating units compounded the problem, and the heavy traffic of visitors to the basin increased risks further. Tahoe residents expanded their fire districts or established new ones; the success of these ventures depended in large part on the local community's willingness to pay higher taxes.

In the postwar years, theft increased, and protection by county sheriffs was inadequate. County governments that traditionally had focused on residential areas outside the basin, like Placerville, Auburn, Reno, and Carson City, responded slowly to the pleas for better police protection in the lake district. Vacation homes left vacant in winter proved a tempting target for burglars and vandals.

By 1947 the El Dorado County Board of Supervisors had authorized a full-time deputy for the south shore, and the Placer County supervisors had gradually expanded the police force on the north shore. On the Nevada side, residents established a Citizens' Committee that appointed its own deputy sheriffs.

At both ends of the lake, the influx of people quickly led to crowded schools. Several small school districts on the north shore eventually joined the Tahoe-Truckee School District and benefited from a bond issue to construct new facilities. At the south shore, the Lake Valley School District provided schooling only through the eighth grade; older students attended the high schools in Gardnerville and Placerville. Then in 1952 a four-year high school opened at the south Tahoe American Legion hall, which was soon replaced by a new $450,000 high school. But almost immediately the new school proved inadequate.

Both water supply and sewage disposal also underwent change. With growing but scattered communities, enterprising individuals had developed small water systems to serve summer homes. These privately operated water franchises normally depended on a nearby creek or well, although on occasion they pumped water directly from the lake. With the spread of new housing and the threat of pollution, individual outhouses or septic tanks increasingly became inadequate for sewage disposal.

The lack of adequate zoning and building codes also plagued the basin. Longtime residents, who had built their homes and businesses without restrictions, became increasingly anxious about indiscriminate new construction in their communities. Others, such as realtors and developers at south Tahoe, argued that a uniform code would reduce property values and halt almost all construction. Although the fastest growing counties had established limited controls by the early 1950s, these quickly became inadequate to curb the sprawl and the eyesores.

A survey of planning problems at Tahoe in 1960 revealed the severity of the situation on the south shore. The County Planning Department estimated that five thousand new lots had been processed during the previous year and estimated the eventual "holding capacity" of the area to be fifty thousand people. County planners were essentially giving business interests the zoning codes they requested. South Tahoe had no control over billboards, trailer courts, and the like; Placer County, though somewhat more advanced, had a zoning ordinance badly in need of revision; and much of the basin remained in an open-use category, subject to speculative activity and considerable subdivision. In brief, county planning and zoning remained minimal and largely ineffective. In addition, contractors often failed to obtain building permits and thus avoided inspection altogether.

A Nevada planner, Raymond M. Smith, who had described the Lake Tahoe area as a "fast growing city with a big hole in the middle of it," argued that the Nevada side of the basin was on the whole "cleaner, better and more vigorously controlled" and that it faced a brighter future than its California counterpart. Consequently, he urged, "California must put her own house in order" as soon as possible. Much of the decline in environmental quality was attributed by Smith to a conflict in values: the older residents and the visitors who sought the quiet, beauty, and peace of Tahoe were overrun by "hordes" of new residents seeking to establish businesses, raise families, and live life reminiscent of the urban areas from which they had come.[1]

Smith succinctly summarized the impact of growth at Tahoe and the need for some kind of control beyond the level of county government:

> A surprisingly large amount of new development is taking place within the Tahoe Basin, apparently, with no relationship to desirable land use patterns, future road locations, future utility of community facility needs; merely, it seems at random. This is, and will result, in faulty community patterns, uneconomic use of the land and other resources and a jumble of attitudes and actions bordering on the chaotic. There is at present no State policy, either in California or Nevada, regarding a regional approach to the problem, although many individual state agencies are concerned and performing valuable work within their fields.[2]

Such criticism of the impact of development in the basin appeared more and more often. Even proposals for improved roads, so long a goal of Tahoe residents, no longer met with unqualified support. When California highway crews started to resurface and widen the highway between Al Tahoe and Stateline to four lanes in 1957, some argued that the added road capacity would only attract more people to the casinos and add to the congestion. The editor of the *Lake Tahoe News* retorted that roads were built in response to existing needs, not to attract additional traffic; but he clearly understood the importance of the casinos to the entire business community. If Stateline closed down, he argued, "those few who would be left in business here would be running roadside hot-dog stands and selling only to an occasional sightseer."[3] The road construction proceeded on schedule. But another and more controversial proposal for road construction encountered far stiffer resistance, signaling that environmentalists would play an increasing role in decisions affecting Tahoe's future.

The Emerald Bay Bridge Controversy

One of the most heated issues of the 1950s and 1960s involved a proposal to construct a year-round highway along the western side of Lake Tahoe. Business interests complained that the narrow two-lane road from Tahoe City to Tahoe Valley via Emerald Bay was slow and dangerous. Worst of all, in their opinion, winter snows blocked the road for several months every year. Following their success in urging the improvement of Highway 50 following World War II, casino and other interests made an improved year-round west-side highway their top priority.

State Senator Swift Berry of El Dorado County argued that development of Tahoe as a year-round resort and of Squaw Valley for the 1960 Winter Olympics made it imperative to have a good all-year road. Together with the Lake Tahoe Chamber of Commerce, the El Dorado County Board of Supervisors, and others, Berry advocated a low-level route close to the lake with a bridge across the mouth of Emerald Bay. As if to add fuel to their argument, a mammoth earth slide at the head of Emerald Bay in the winter of 1955–56 closed the existing road throughout the following summer. Irate resort owners appealed to the California Highway Commission for action.

Because the proposed road and bridge would cut through both the D. L. Bliss and Emerald Bay state parks, the only state parks in the basin at that time, the California State Park Commission had a vital interest in the matter. Newton Drury, chief of the California Division of Beaches and Parks, led a small but vocal group of environmentalists who opposed what they regarded as a desecration of Tahoe's scenic jewel, Emerald Bay. Homeowners on the west shore —largely residents of the San Francisco Bay Area—and the Sierra Club, the Save-the-Redwoods League, and others joined to defend the integrity of the parks. As an alternative to the low-level bridge route, the State Park Commission suggested a high-level route around the upper end of Emerald Bay, making use of tunnels or snowsheds to cross the slide area. This route would closely follow the existing road, minimizing the need for cuts or fills, as well as eliminating the controversial bridge.

Studies by engineers and geologists revealed that both high- and low-level routes were feasible, but the Highway Commission and Tahoe business interests continued to favor a bridge, arguing that it would be faster, safer, and more reliable. At a time when the commission commanded great power, and freeway construction was proceeding essentially unchecked, construction of a low-level route seemed only a matter of time. Yet a bill introduced in the state legislature by Berry and Harold T. "Bizz" Johnson to promote the bridge route was defeated in April 1958, in the face of rising sympathy for the preservation of the Tahoe state parks.

With the battle lines drawn, the controversy came to a head. State Highway Engineer George T. McCoy recommended an all-weather low-level route, but the state park commissioners refused to grant a right-of-way for a road through the park. Senator Berry argued that a bridge would enhance the beauty of Emerald Bay, and that embankments could be planted to blend with the surrounding scenery, but his opponents disagreed. In building a low-level road, earth fill 50 feet deep and 210 feet wide would be

Advocates of a low-level road argued that a bridge across the mouth of Emerald Bay would enhance its beauty. James Hildinger.

dumped across the north point of D. L. Bliss State Park at the entrance to Emerald Bay. The right-of-way would eliminate sixty-eight acres from the two parks, almost all of which was shoreline and virgin timberland, cut directly through existing and proposed campgrounds, and destroy the integrity of each park as a planned unit.

Assemblyman Jesse Unruh, who reportedly had camped in both

parks, requested that Berry's bill be referred to the Ways and Means Committee. Because considerable funds had been spent on improvements in the state parks, Unruh argued that the matter needed considerable study before the Assembly acted. Sacramento Assemblyman Thomas MacBridge supported Unruh's motion, explaining that gambling interests at Tahoe spearheaded the efforts to build a low-level route. By an overwhelming vote of 55–19, the Assembly sent the measure for a low-level route back to committee, effectively killing it. As the 1950s ended, the Emerald Bay bridge controversy receded, at least temporarily.

But business interests and many permanent residents at both ends of the lake continued to press for a west-side "freeway" with a bridge across Emerald Bay. In 1962, renewed proposals to build a four-lane freeway along the west shore once again brought the Emerald Bay bridge issue to the forefront of attention. The California Division of Beaches and Parks and many concerned visitors to Tahoe joined west-shore homeowners in opposing the proposal. Late in 1963 a group of citizens and landowners organized the Committee to Save the West Shore of Lake Tahoe and lobbied actively to block the proposed multilane freeway, which the committee argued was intended primarily to connect the casinos at the north and south shores. The committee claimed that the freeway would inevitably hasten commercialization within the basin and lead to construction of an Emerald Bay bridge.

During three public hearings held by the Tahoe Regional Planning Commission in June 1963, the idea of a parkway system circling the lake dominated discussion. With the Highway Commission insisting on a four-lane freeway along the west shore, however, the two commissions could not agree. The controversy dragged into the following years, and critics warned against vesting the Highway Commission with the power to determine the future of Tahoe's landscape through its decisions on road construction.

At a public hearing of the California Assembly Committee on Natural Resources, Planning and Public Works, held in September 1964, David C. Dunlap of the Sierra Club and Howard F. Fletcher of Friends of Emerald Bay Parks led the opposition to an Emerald

Bay bridge. Dunlap summarized their argument: "The damage to the State Parks from being cut in two by this two- or four-lane low-level speedway would be incalculable. The highway cuts and fills along the steep Tahoe shoreline both north and south of Emerald Bay would be an eyesore for the whole lake. The causeway and bridge at Emerald Bay would ruin the most spectacular area of natural beauty which remains at Lake Tahoe."[4]

Robert Bradford, chairman of the Highway Commission, stated that a four-lane scenic highway would be needed "in the foreseeable future"; but he added that no final decision would be made pending further study. As it turned out, time was on the side of those opposing the west-shore freeway. Pressure subsequently mounted in San Francisco and elsewhere in the state against excessive and inappropriate freeway construction that would split neighborhoods and mar the landscape. Although complaints have continued about the narrow, winding road around Emerald Bay, and although the parkway proposal has been studied further, no construction has taken place. Nevertheless, proposals for a major west-shore freeway continue to appear.

Growth in the Mid-1960s

The trends at Lake Tahoe in the mid-1960s were ominous. The total population on a busy summer weekend rose to an estimated 150,000, and some people thought this figure would double by 1980. As increasing numbers of affluent and mobile visitors flocked to the lake, the demand increased for second homes, including condominiums, and for rental property. Gambling remained the largest single attraction in the basin. Casinos accounted for more than one-third of the visitor-days and, by 1970, yielded annual revenues estimated at $89 million. The increase in tourist visitation was especially rapid during the winter months, largely because of the improved and expanded ski facilities and the easy north-shore access via Interstate 80.

Clearly, Tahoe was the beneficiary or victim, depending on one's point of view, of the population boom sweeping California and the west. Nearly fifteen hundred people entered the state each day in the mid-1960s to take up residence. Such an explosive growth rate obviously could not be sustained for long, but meanwhile the state seemed incapable of coping with its growth-induced problems. California had no master plan for the state or for Tahoe and simply tried to accommodate the growth as best it could in piecemeal fashion. The only enforceable plan for the basin, the Forest Service's multiple-use management plan for 1962, applied only to publicly owned forest lands, 48 percent of the acreage within the basin.

Responses to the growth varied widely. At the south shore, a Chamber of Commerce report noted that the next decade would be a period of rapid growth and development, and that "unlimited opportunities will be available for profitable operation to light in-dustrial and commercial service type organizations." The chamber proudly listed signs of progress, including: "six full-service banks; eight large supermarkets; four insurance agencies; a proposed con-vention and recreation center; two radio stations; branches of Bay Area and Sacramento department and clothing stores, as well as many of our own; a 6500-foot airport runway with 2 major airlines servicing our area; our own saving and loan association; top enter-tainment and dining facilities . . . which add together to make Tahoe 'a great place to live.'"[5]

Harvey Gross, founder and owner of Harvey's Wagon Wheel Resort Hotel and Casino at Stateline, when interviewed for a televi-sion broadcast on Tahoe's environmental problems, stated that he was "real pleased" with the growth and expected development to continue. From his perspective, gambling was a "very great asset" to the basin because it provided many jobs, as well as entertainment for tourists. The commentator of the telecast expressed a different point of view: "The states of California and Nevada have not, for all their brave words, cooperated effectively, and time is running short. Traffic congestion, building congestion, pollution conges-tion and political congestion all meet on the South Shore of Lake Tahoe."[6]

Others also criticized development of the basin. An article in *Holiday* described Harvey's casino: "Like an incredible tower of tropical fruit, it looms over Highway 50—eleven turquoise stories tall, trimmed with marble and golden aluminum, studded with yellow-railed balconies. A vast wheel-and-longhorn skull device sprawls three stories high across its face; above the hotel roof the emblem appears again, topped by a colossal red neon Harvey's sign."[7] This single casino offered 3 restaurants, 9 bars, employment for 1,600 summer employees, parking for 1,000 cars, and gambling at 1,115 slot machines, 37 blackjack tables, 11 crap tables, 3 roulette wheels, and 2 keno lounges. Across the street, Harrah's Tahoe provided what was purported to be at that time the largest building in the world devoted to gambling and entertainment.

Such developments stimulated formation of the League to Save Lake Tahoe in December 1965. The league, an outgrowth of the Tahoe Resource Conservation Society, founded in 1957, quickly became and has remained the most active environmental organization dedicated to "preserving the environmental balance, scenic beauty and recreational opportunities of the Lake Tahoe Basin." The membership, composed mainly of Tahoe residents and homeowners and of concerned citizens from elsewhere in northern California and western Nevada, came together to promote several objectives: to limit expansion of casinos and other developments considered unsuited to the natural environment, curtail proposals for new highways (especially the west-shore freeway), promote research related to the decline in water quality, and create an effective regional government for the basin. Because a number of league members owned lakeshore property, the league was lax in protecting public access to the lakeshore and in controlling the construction of piers.

In the same year, the voters of the California communities of Tahoe Valley, Al Tahoe, Bijou, and Stateline decided overwhelmingly to unite as the city of South Lake Tahoe. For too long, as one resident explained, "we were run by the board of supervisors of El Dorado County, 60 miles away, and nobody down there seemed to give a damn what was happening up here."[8] Now, local residents concerned about the quality of their environment looked forward to control of growth by a city council. William A. "Wink" Ames, an insurance agent who had helped lead the lengthy campaign to incorporate, hoped that some of the beauty and alpine quality of the area could still be saved. The first mayor of the new city, W. Brad Murphy, pledged himself to block further "hodgepodge" urbanization. Although some changes did take place, including control of the size of billboards, South Lake Tahoe continued to grow more rapidly than the first city fathers desired, and soon land developers and realtors dominated the city council. The local government failed to curb urban growth.

Some residents of the city of South Lake Tahoe argued that creating a new county would solve the problems of pollution and overdevelopment. The proposed county would encompass the entire west side of the lake within the basin. Similar proposals appeared from time to time for the Nevada shore—to form new counties in the basin in order to separate their control from county seats and population centers far removed from there. Though county officials opposed proposals for any kind of regional control that would supersede their own authority, a movement was well advanced by the mid-1960s to resolve Tahoe's environmental problem by instituting some sort of regional authority.

Regional Planning: A Beginning

An organization calling for regional planning of the Tahoe Basin arose in 1956 as a response to the issues of declining water quality and other deleterious effects of urban growth. In that year, Lester Summerfield, president of the Max C. Fleischmann Foundation in Nevada, asked Joseph F. McDonald, retiring chief of Reno Newspapers, Incorporated, to form a nonprofit organization for Lake Tahoe's protection and "orderly development." Both Summerfield and the late Max Fleischmann had owned homes at Tahoe and had shown a special interest in its future. The foundation promised McDonald at least $50,000 a year for three to five years, no strings attached, for the organization to pursue its objectives.

Early in 1957 articles of incorporation were filed for the Nevada-California Lake Tahoe Association in the hope of providing a coordinated approach to the myriad of worsening problems in the basin. Response to the organization seemed positive. The *Nevada State Journal* of Reno called on the residents of the five counties bordering the lake to lend their cooperation, and the *Reno Evening Gazette* stated that the new association "should have the solid support of the states of Nevada and California" and the cooperation of everyone concerned about Tahoe's preservation.[9]

As soon as the association began to study the basin and propose regional controls, however, local interests expressed concern. Fearing conversion of the association into a "Lake Tahoe authority," an editorialist in the *Lake Tahoe News* warned against any action by the state governments without full consultation with local people. The South Shore Chamber of Commerce protested a bill, supported by McDonald, that would allow the California-Nevada Interstate Compact Commission to make a planning survey of the basin. The director of the chamber called the "McDonald plan" vicious, and tantamount to the kind of political control pursued in the Soviet Union.

After attending many civic gatherings and public meetings, McDonald concluded that factionalism ran rampant, with south shore interests concerned more about promoting business than about cooperating to protect the lake. He remarked, "The south-end boys are still dubious about everything pertaining to the lake except flooding it with tourists."[10] In an attempt to promote cooperation and unity, McDonald met with representatives of the three Tahoe chambers of commerce, who eventually agreed that a council organization similar to the San Francisco Bay Area Council should be established to benefit the entire Lake Tahoe region.

McDonald and the Nevada-California Lake Tahoe Association provided a $10,000 grant to initiate the Lake Tahoe Area Council. The council, incorporated in Nevada, represented all basin interests and acted as a nonprofit clearinghouse for ideas and problems. It enlisted public support and coordinated efforts to solve problems through existing public and private agencies. Clearly, the council did not replace any existing agencies or threaten local government. It functioned primarily to encourage research and education related to the lake and to facilitate cooperation in resolving issues.

After extensive debate about its purpose, the council held its first public meeting on November 28, 1958, at the Nevada Lodge in Crystal Bay. More than three hundred civic and business leaders attended, including people from throughout northern California and northwestern Nevada. They listed the issues to be dealt with: formulation of a master plan for orderly development, a solution to sewage and waste disposal problems, establishment of zoning and building codes, and provision of safe, dependable water. After four additional public meetings, the Lake Tahoe Area Council was formally organized on April 17, 1959. The organization received the support of the governors of California and Nevada and many legislators, and donations of $5,000 each from William Harrah and McDonald.

McDonald himself—having encountered resistance to proposed state legislation for a planning survey of the basin to be carried out by the California-Nevada Interstate Compact Commission—tried working directly with county officials to obtain the survey. Largely through his efforts, regional planning commissions were established on each side of the basin: the Bi-County Planning Commission of Placer and El Dorado counties in California and the Tri-County Planning Commission of Washoe, Ormsby, and Douglas counties on the Nevada shore. Such organization was necessary before the council could request federal funds for a comprehensive planning survey. McDonald hoped for both a master plan and a regional authority to administer it.

In 1959, Raymond M. Smith, regional planning director for Reno, Sparks, and Washoe County, accepted the position of executive director of the Lake Tahoe Area Council. Smith stated the goal of the council: "to assure that the Lake Tahoe of tomorrow reflects a continuing economy in an even more desirable environment than it has today."[11] Working with the planning commissions of the five counties bordering the lake, Smith said he hoped to complete a master plan in a few months. It was therefore a surprise when he suddenly resigned, effective July 1, 1960, to become planning director of the Crystal Bay Development Company's mammoth Incline Village project.

The Incline project became a major point of contention between the developers and those concerned about environmental quality in the basin, including the Lake Tahoe Area Council. Critics of Incline argued that it would hasten the rate of pollution of the lake. Regardless of pleas for further study, development at Incline progressed rapidly with the approval of the Washoe County Commissioners. The sheer bulk of an estimated half-million tree stumps, left from prior logging and from new development, alone caused a disposal problem of major proportions.

In the same period, the planning directors and representatives from each of the five county planning commissions met with the Lake Tahoe Area Council planning committee and formed the Tahoe Regional Planning Commission. The commission was composed of three people from each of the two California counties in the basin and two each from the three Nevada counties—a total of twelve members. Its Technical Advisory Committee was composed of the planning directors from each of the five counties.

The commission, whose powers were only advisory, supported a master plan. McDonald provided seed money, and the Lake Tahoe Area Council agreed to provide administrative support. The planning survey was assured when the federal government's Urban Renewal Administration gave $45,000 for half the cost of the project, and the Fleischmann Foundation and local counties divided the remaining cost. The commission hired Wilsey, Ham and Blair, an engineering consulting firm, to complete the master plan, and work on the study began in 1962.

The Lake Tahoe Area Council urged the counties to defer any major land re-zoning until publication of the master plan, and in 1963 the council led efforts to publicize a preliminary draft. The final version, the *Lake Tahoe 1980 Regional Plan,* was issued early in 1964. Using 1980 as a base, the report predicted a large population increase, including tourists, of from 126,300 on a summer weekend in 1962 to 313,000 in 1980—a figure above the actual weekend population that year. This projection depended on adequate sewage disposal; otherwise, Tahoe's population could not increase much beyond its figure then. The report, in the 1960s spirit of growth, allowed for major development within the basin, including dual and in some areas triple bands of roads around the lake. According to a later transportation study, the 1980 plan "was based on the political premise that building a strongly interlinked urban economy was the most desirable future outcome for the region."[12]

The 1980 plan did not adequately consider the ecological consequences of continued growth. In addition, no single agency existed with enforcement powers, so the regional authority that the California-Nevada Interstate Compact Commission might have brought about never came to pass. No way existed to assure that all five counties in the basin would adopt uniform zoning ordinances and act in concert, nor was there a way to control independent agencies like the California Highway Commission, whose actions could have major consequences for Tahoe land use and growth. In fact, the 1980 plan did not legally bind anyone.

A Douglas County plan, issued later in 1964, indicated the magnitude of the problem. It noted that the "urban core" at Stateline, Nevada, would accommodate as many as 65,000–95,000 cars daily by 1985 and suggested that "an estimated saturation population of 76,000 at year 2010 can be accommodated by adjustments to the densities proposed."[13]

Carl R. Pagter and Cameron Wolfe, Jr., in the *California Law Review* in 1964, suggested forming an autonomous federal agency similar to the Tennessee Valley Authority for regional administration of the basin if other efforts failed. They noted that no agency or group except the Lake Tahoe Area Council had consistently advocated a preservation program for Lake Tahoe: "Strong limitations are as appropriate at Tahoe as in any national park. A thriving metropolis characterized by towering skyscrapers and blazing neon signs is no more appropriate at Tahoe than at Crater Lake, Yellowstone, Yosemite, or other of the nation's exceptional physical assets."[14]

A later assessment of the 1980 plan by two political scientists concluded that it was "largely an extrapolation and extension of existing trends into the future rather than a goal-oriented guide for integrating man into a very fragile environment."[15] The authors noted that the efforts to reach a regional solution were inspired by nonlocal interests as much as by residents of the basin. Local governments might not have participated at all in the efforts of the Tahoe Regional Planning Commission without the incentive of federal assistance for sewage disposal and other practical purposes. In fact, the effort to cope with the problem of water quality led to the most notable environmental achievement of the decade for the area, a solution to the problem of sewage.

Waste Disposal and Water Quality

At the same time the Lake Tahoe Area Council pursued development of a basin master plan, it also affirmed the need for a feasibility study of sewage effluent disposal for the Tahoe Basin. The rapid development of Incline had brought both issues to a head; now the council, with funding from the Fleischmann Foundation, promoted both the master plan and a survey that would "determine the ways and means of constructing, financing and operating a bistate sewage disposal system for the entire Lake Tahoe Basin."[16]

Various strategies for solving the sewage disposal problem had been suggested in the late 1950s, but the method current then—spraying effluent onto land within the basin—had been allowed to continue. Severe sewage problems clearly were developing, however, at the north and south shores and at the burgeoning community of Incline Village, and the spray method was inadequate for Tahoe's growing population. Spraying the effluent could not protect against contamination of water supplies within the basin, or prevent the ultimate degradation of the lake through pollution. And spraying killed trees on the sites used.

In November 1960, officials dedicated a new $1,575,000 sewage treatment plant at Al Tahoe, one step in a major expansion of the system. Yet no adequate solution appeared to exist. Early in September 1961, some two million gallons of sewage overflowed from the south shore treatment plant and into the lake. Officials of the Lahontan Regional Water Quality Control Board and the State Department of Public Health protested. Before long the Lahontan board had ordered the utility district to stop the release of effluent into the lake. This order threatened an end to the current monthly rate of sixty new connections, or added customers. Months passed, and the inability of local officials to resolve the sewage disposal problem without outside assistance became increasingly apparent.

The situation at the north shore was not much better. Although population growth there was slower, fewer good sites existed for the disposal of sewage effluent, and nearly all the streams provided water for local domestic use. Inevitably, the sewage treatment plant of the North Tahoe Public Utility District, heavily used by the north Tahoe casinos in Nevada, reached its capacity, and a proposal that sewage effluent be dumped into the Truckee River elicited outrage from the residents of Reno and Sparks, who used Truckee water for their domestic supply.

A grant of $125,000 from the Fleischmann Foundation to the Lake Tahoe Area Council in 1961 enabled the council to hire Engineering-Science, Incorporated, to complete a study of the sewage disposal problem throughout the basin. After eighteen months of intensive study, a five-member blue ribbon team offered its recommendations in a 160-page report, one of the most important and influential publications ever issued on Tahoe. The report, entitled *Comprehensive Study on Protection of Water Resources of Lake Tahoe Basin through Controlled Waste Disposal*, and issued in June 1963, concluded that "increasing human activities in the Lake Tahoe basin, and the associated increase in waste production and disposal within the basin, pose a serious threat to maintenance and preservation of the clarity and beauty of the lake waters."[17]

The study predicted that the amount of nutrients produced by human activity would soon reach levels several times that produced by natural conditions. By far the best method of effluent disposal, it noted, was removal from the basin entirely, "either by export or by discharge to the Truckee River." Five agencies then providing sewage services within the basin became nuclei for the formation of larger and more comprehensive districts to carry out the proposed sewage export.

But the Nevadans of Reno and Sparks continued to fear that Tahoe sewage would contaminate their drinking water. Similarly, California state agencies rejected the idea of disposal in the American River and thus into the Central Valley. A proposal to construct a dual-purpose highway and sewage effluent tunnel under Daggett Pass, between south Tahoe and Carson Valley, attracted interest, especially because Carson Valley farmers needed the reclaimed water for irrigation. But the pressing sewage problems required faster solution than was possible through that project, which would have taken considerable time to finance and complete.

The Lake Tahoe Area Council lost no time in publicizing its study, and in August it invited the President's Water Pollution Control Advisory Board to visit Tahoe and review the situation firsthand. When board members suggested that federal intervention might be necessary to protect Lake Tahoe, which was an interstate body of water, both Governor Edmund Brown of California and Governor Grant Sawyer of Nevada visited the lake (on November 11, 1963) and issued a "Governors' Program for Progress." In it, they recognized the council's study as a basis for future actions and recommended cooperative efforts among state and local authorities to export treated sewage from the basin.

Several public utility districts in the basin took steps in 1964 to expand their facilities. Placer County received a grant from the Fleischmann Foundation to study the export of effluent from the north shore, and the South Tahoe Public Utility District (STPUD) started work on a tertiary treatment plant.

The Federal Water Pollution Control Administration held a

conference at Tahoe in 1966 to help mobilize support for water pollution control. The conferees warned that contamination of the lake would result from continued entry of nutrients from municipal sewage treatment plants, septic tanks, and other sources via surface runoff and subsurface seepage. They recommended that all waste water receive at least secondary treatment and be exported from the basin by 1970; that all solid waste be exported by the same year; and that a regional agency be established with effective power to control land development.

A report in 1966, published by the same agency, noted that the phosphorous level in the lake had reached a critical level, and that a substantial increase in nitrogen could destroy the clarity of the lake and greatly accelerate the growth of noxious algae near the shore. Sewage, unfortunately, was not the only cause of the problem; nutrients from land altered by people also contributed heavily to it. The report concluded: "It is imperative that the man-associated nutrients not be permitted to enter the lake if Lake Tahoe is to remain clear and beautiful."[18]

Despite such testimony, debate continued over the seriousness of water pollution at Tahoe. John T. Leggett, executive officer of the Lahontan Regional Water Quality Control Board, and Fred R. McLaren, its senior engineer, stressed that Tahoe's water met acceptable standards for drinking water. In 1968 they asserted that there is "no major lake in all the world which has water more crystal clear, pristine pure, unpolluted, and uncontaminated as that which now exists in Lake Tahoe." They continued, "It can be conclusively stated that the clarity of Lake Tahoe has not decreased since the lake was first sampled in 1873—nearly 100 years ago."[19]

On the other hand, Charles R. Goldman, a limnologist at the University of California at Davis, stressed in several publications that Tahoe suffered from steadily increasing fertility from nutrients entering the lake, a process that would result eventually in eutrophication, turning the lake from "clear blue to turbid green." Evidence revealed that the lake's fertility had increased 50 percent in the 1960s. Goldman noted that aerial photographs showed

Silt accumulates where the Upper Truckee River enters Lake Tahoe,
evidence of soil erosion upstream. James Hildinger.

"spectacular local increases in turbidity due to the inflow of sediments and nutrients from tributaries of disturbed watersheds."[20]

The implementation of proposals to protect the quality of Tahoe water took several years. As late as summer 1966, an estimated two-thirds of the summertime population still was not served by the existing municipal sewage systems but depended on septic tanks and privies. By 1968 California and Nevada gained federal approval for their plans to implement and enforce water quality standards in interstate waters as required by the Federal Water Pollution Control Act of 1965. Also in 1968, the federal government provided $6,500,000 in grants for sewage projects in the basin.

The export of sewage also began in 1968, with the aid of an Economic Development Administration loan to the STPUD of $3,253,000. Highly treated effluent was pumped twenty-seven miles from south Tahoe to a manmade reservoir in Alpine County.

According to Russell L. Culp, general manager of STPUD, the new facility was the "most advanced full-scale wastewater treatment plant in the world" at that time. Not only did it provide the normal processes of removal of solids and biological oxidation, but it also provided "chemical treatment and phosphate removal, nitrogen removal, mixed-media filtration, activated carbon adsorption, and disinfection."[21] The completion of the sewage export system, although delayed well into the 1970s, received national attention and was hailed as a major accomplishment.

This advancement came none too soon. Five years after the spraying of effluent next to Heavenly Valley Creek had been discontinued, the creek carried about sixty times more nitrate-nitrogen into Lake Tahoe than did Ward Creek, which flowed from unsprayed watershed. There was no way to tell how long excessive amounts of nutrients would continue to enter the lake from the abandoned effluent disposal sites and septic tank leach fields, legacies of the era when water quality was not a major concern.

The improved and expanded sewer systems in the basin, despite their distinct advantages, had the secondary effect of encouraging further development. As a study sponsored by the Environmental Protection Agency explains, a strong correlation exists between expansion of sewage treatment facilities and increases in land use densities. Specifically, the number of lots in subdivisions and high-density residential and commercial land uses increase rapidly. The study concludes that the construction of extensive advanced sewage treatment and export facilities has a "significant and direct influence on the location, type, and intensity of land development."[22]

Although the expanded sewage facilities attracted new customers who helped defray the expense of the costly systems, some environmentalists questioned whether the capital expended, especially the federal funds, might not have been spent more wisely on purchasing recreational lands. These lands would have reduced the land available for development and the pressure for an ever-enlarging sewer system.

As the 1960s came to a close, the California legislature passed the Porter-Cologne Water Quality Control Act of 1969, which replaced the Dickey Water Pollution Act of 1949. Under the new legislation, the State Water Resources Control Board and nine regional boards shared responsibility for formulating and adopting water quality control plans within the state. The act directed that state water policy include long-range planning for protection of groundwaters and surface waters, and it provided enforcement provisions in case of noncompliance with state policy. The Lahontan Regional Water Quality Control Board, with responsibility for the Tahoe Basin, established a goal of maintaining or enhancing the water quality of Lake Tahoe and prohibited the discharge of sewage and waste material into the lake from California sources.

Federal involvement with Tahoe's water quality also increased at the end of the 1960s, with passage of the National Environmental Policy Act (NEPA) of 1969. This act established a mechanism by which the public and various government agencies would provide information and criticism to those federal agencies with authority to grant approval for major development projects. The process was formalized in an environmental impact statement that was circulated for public comment prior to a final decision. The process incorporated a discussion of significant environmental effects and consideration of alternatives. The California Environmental Quality Act of 1970, modeled largely after NEPA, established similar procedures at the state level.

This legislation raised hopes that corrective measures to assure the quality of water in Lake Tahoe would be forthcoming. In the meantime, the water quality problem of the 1960s had sparked tremendous controversy. More than any other issue, the dispute provided impetus at last to create a regional authority for the entire basin.

Establishment of the Tahoe Regional Planning Agency

Alfred E. Heller, director of California Tomorrow (a nonprofit educational organization concerned about the quality of

California's environment), has stated emphatically that "if the purity and beauty of Tahoe are to be saved, we must have an agency powerful enough to knock heads together and get the job done."[23] What Heller had in mind was action by the federal government and its agencies. But the federal agencies in the basin continued to concentrate primarily on the issues of water quality and water rights. They left resolution of the other environmental problems, including the central issue of uncontrolled growth, to state and local governments.

Following publication of the *Comprehensive Study,* the Lake Tahoe Area Council analyzed government activity in the basin. Its report, issued in December 1963, recommended formation of a regional agency with limited functions to solve problems that local governments could not resolve. In the following year, the council approved a resolution requesting that the governors of California and Nevada form a Lake Tahoe basin advisory committee to help bring about planning and controls for the entire basin. The council's report, as well as mounting criticism of the ineffectiveness of the powerless Tahoe Regional Planning Commission, came to the attention of California Assemblyman Edwin L. Z'Berg, chairman of the Assembly Committee on Natural Resources, Planning and Public Works.

Z'Berg, who played an integral role in planning efforts in the following years, called a meeting of his committee at Lake Tahoe in September 1964. According to the committee report, the impact of development had been "serious"; without controls on growth, the basin faced the "possibility of general and irreversible overexploitation." There was "a clear need for the creation of some kind of bi-state regional authority to govern basin development," an authority with broad powers to develop and enforce a regional master plan. A regional authority thus empowered would ensure "optimum development and maximum preservation of the values which are unique to the Lake Tahoe Basin."[24] Z'Berg urged immediate legislation in both California and Nevada to strengthen the Tahoe Regional Planning Commission.

Uncontrolled growth at Stateline (1966) provided strong evidence of the need for an effective regional authority to regulate growth. California Department of Transportation.

Partly as a result of the extensive hearings on Tahoe's problems held by the Z'Berg committee, the legislators of both states agreed to establish a Lake Tahoe Joint Study Committee. The committee was charged to study, develop, and present recommendations "concerning an area-wide agency to provide for the orderly development of the Lake Tahoe Basin."[25]

The committee appointed Albert Lepawsky, a University of California political scientist, to the key position of coordinator of the study. With Lepawsky at the helm, the committee carefully examined the considerable data already available on Tahoe, held several public hearings, and studied major alternative approaches to regional problems that had been adopted elsewhere in the United States. The committee early decided to reject two alternatives that it considered extreme: giving over direct control of major functions in the basin to a federal authority, and continuing the current dispersed pattern of planning without any formal regional implementation authority whatsoever. The first proposal was politically unacceptable at state and local levels; regarding the second, the existing system of sixty-one overlapping governments at Tahoe had proved ineffective.

In March 1967, after sixteen months of intensive study and discussion, the Lake Tahoe Joint Study Committee presented its final report. The most important of its seven major recommendations was for "creation, by concurrent legislation of the States of California and Nevada, of a Tahoe Regional Agency possessing region-wide and bi-state jurisdiction." According to the committee, the agency's primary responsibility should be to "preserve and maintain the physical environment of the Lake Tahoe Region, including its natural endowment for recreational and residential purposes, and thus to encourage the economic stability of the region."[26] In addition, the agency would be designed to "supplement and coordinate, not to supplant or duplicate" local governments. Thus the agency should formulate land use plans and standards according to their effect on the region as a whole, and it should enforce such standards.

Z'Berg immediately introduced a bill largely based on the recommendations of the Joint Study Committee. The bill (AB 1362) recognized the inability of local government to control development within the basin and declared that creation of a regional government was necessary "to prevent irreparable injury to Lake Tahoe as a unique national treasure." Under this legislation the governing board would receive extensive powers and would enforce a comprehensive, long-term regional plan. The board would also have the power to tax the local counties and to implement its own capital and public works improvements.

To arrange immediate protection for the California side of the basin, the authors of the bill added an important provision not included in the committee recommendations: creation of the California Tahoe Regional Planning Agency (CTRPA). This state agency, with membership identical to the California membership on the proposed bi-state governing board, was to function only in the interim before the bi-state agency became effective.

The bill to create a bi-state regional agency received broad support in California from the news media, from many legislators, and from such organizations as the League to Save Lake Tahoe and the Planning and Conservation League. Advocates recognized that a regional agency could evaluate the effects of future land use on the entire basin and then regulate use to maintain environmental quality. Critics argued that it would curtail the decision-making power of local government and prevent private interests from utilizing the basin's natural resources as they wished.

The city of South Lake Tahoe led a spirited attack on the Z'Berg bill, arguing that the Tahoe Regional Planning Commission should be the agency to arbitrate regional problems at Tahoe. But the commission had proven unable to elicit voluntary compliance with its 1980 plan and lacked the power to enforce it. The city council of South Lake Tahoe, for example, adopted a zoning ordinance allowing high-rise development on both sides of Highway 50 near Stateline in opposition to a forty-five-foot limitation recommended by the commission.

The Greater North Lake Tahoe Chamber of Commerce appealed directly to Governor Ronald Reagan to defeat the Z'Berg bill, arguing that the legislation would establish an unrepresentative government at Tahoe in violation of local rights. The chamber board of directors gave a vote of confidence to the existing situation at Tahoe, stating that the local governments and the Tahoe Regional Planning Commission "are doing a commendable job solving the problems at Lake Tahoe."[27] On the next day, officials of El Dorado and Placer counties and the city of South Lake Tahoe proposed forming their own Tahoe regional agency; in theory, this agency would have worked cooperatively with a similar organization on the Nevada shore.

The Z'Berg bill passed in the Assembly in August 1967 by a vote of 58–19. It then encountered serious difficulty. The Senate Governmental Efficiency Committee delayed action: the *San Francisco Examiner* laid part of the blame on Governor Reagan for his "embarrassing silence" on the Tahoe issue, calling his attitude a "disappointment." Apparently Reagan was philosophically opposed to the state's intervention in what he considered a local problem. The *Examiner,* however, insisted that Tahoe was not a local concern and was more than merely a state problem. The newspaper advocated federal intervention if the bill to establish a regional agency failed.[28]

The state Senate finally approved a much amended bill, resulting in the establishment of a considerably weaker regional agency than that originally proposed. In its final form, the legislation treated Tahoe mainly as a local concern. The bill neither mentioned the interest of citizens outside the Tahoe Basin in its future nor incorporated the sense of urgency and need for regional control that was expressed in the Lake Tahoe Joint Study Committee report. Of more direct effect, as a result of lobbying by local governmental officials, the Governing Body of the bi-state agency was reduced to ten members, predominantly local representatives; and its authority was reduced in significant ways. In the final version of the bill, although the agency was allowed to prosecute for violations of its plan as misdemeanors, it lost the power to use legal measures to prevent violations before they occurred. The agency no longer had the express power to review local decision, and it lost the direct power to tax, thus increasing financial dependence on local support. Further, creation of a technical advisory committee provided another avenue of local control. In brief, the California legislature amended the Z'Berg bill so as to establish local dominance of a regional supervisory agency that was given neither financial independence nor authority to enforce its decisions.

In February 1968 the Nevada legislature adopted a comparable proposal, although Nevada gave even greater power to local governments and thus promoted an even weaker regional authority. Nevada counties had full discretion in selecting agency members. Action on any matter required a dual majority vote of the members present from each state. One provision stated that any proposed development on which the governing body of the agency failed to take final action within sixty days would be automatically approved. This left the door open for approval of new casinos in the decade ahead. Further, Nevada inserted a "grandfather clause" to protect existing businesses, particularly the casino-hotels, from new restrictions, and the state put a $150,000 annual limit on the budget of the new agency. In brief, the Nevada legislature proposed a regional agency with authority to engage in general planning and to review land use but with little enforcement powers.

In response, Z'Berg argued that California would be better off trying to control development on its own side of the lake through the CTRPA than accepting an ineffective regional agency. He warned: "If in the short run Nevada chooses not to join in this effort by creating a meaningful regional agency of its own, it will then be clear that failure of local and state government to responsibly manage this great national treasure will lead inevitably and properly to intervention by the federal government."[29]

When Z'Berg's Natural Resources Committee voted 4–2 against the bi-state compact as proposed by Nevada, Z'Berg found himself the target of sharp criticism from governors Reagan and Laxalt, among others. Reagan called on Z'Berg "to reconsider this ill-thought-out and petty action and begin to act responsibly for the benefit of all concerned."[30] Z'Berg responded: "The committee was simply unwilling to accept the substitution of an ineffectual, watered down bistate regional agency—such as the Nevada legislation would establish—for the very effective California Tahoe Regional Agency created by our 1967 legislature, which is now operative within the two thirds of the Lake Tahoe Basin lying in California."[31] In particular, he criticized the provisions introduced by Nevada which, he stated, "would be tantamount to bowing to

the same monied gambling interests and wealthy land speculators"
who had worked against his bill in California the year before.
At this juncture, Michael McCloskey, legislative advocate for the
Sierra Club, offered a compromise solution: allow two agencies to
exist on the California side of the basin. McCloskey recommended
that the California legislature maintain the CTRPA, with power of
approval and disapproval over such public works as highways,
after the bi-state agency had gained congressional approval.
Through this provision, California could both establish and enforce its own higher standards on the California side and also have
an agency to enforce decisions by the bi-state group. This compromise was accepted, and the legislation gained the approval of
the Z'Berg committee and was signed by Reagan on August 2,
1968. In brief, although California accepted the Nevada legislation
for a relatively weak bi-state agency, it retained the CTRPA under
its own control. Finally, on December 18, 1969, after Congress
had added minor amendments, President Richard Nixon signed the
bill that created the Tahoe Regional Planning Agency (TRPA).
Under the enabling legislation, the Advisory Planning Commission, a group dominated by local representatives, was to prepare a
regional plan. The plan would be presented to a separate group, the
Governing Body—representing various political entities interested
in the basin—which could develop any plan it wished and alone
had authority to make decisions. In addition to these two groups,
the compact called for appointment of an executive officer by the
Governing Body and the hiring of whatever agency staff was
deemed necessary.

TRPA, CTRPA, and NTRPA

As in most political matters, the TRPA legislation represented a compromise that did not entirely please anyone. But the
very nature of the compromise itself led to concern, as revealed in
one of the earliest assessments of the act:

The conservationists got in the TRPA one of the first regional governments in the United States established for the purpose of environmental control—a bistate agency which sets a precedent for governing the environment. They also got a state agency with comparatively strong powers to regulate the growth in the Lake Tahoe area. On the other hand, the local interests substantially altered the powers originally intended for the state and bistate agencies, gained control of their financing, and acquired firm authority over representation of both agencies.[32]

The author, Raymond G. Davis, questioned the integrity of those governments that had created two regional agencies and then selected people to represent the agencies "who opposed their creation and who opposed the use of the power with which they were endowed." Another early appraisal noted that the priorities of a region financially dependent on tourism and tourist-related businesses and dominated by short-range local interests were in conflict with the goal of protecting the basin from overuse: "This is an inherent defect in the operation of TRPA; Lake Tahoe cannot be effectively preserved as a national treasure for the people of California and Nevada if decisions concerning its future are based on local priorities."[33]

Immediate local opposition to the CTRPA indicated what was to be expected in the decade ahead. Placer County supervisors withheld financial support and opposed a proposal that review and approval by the agency be required for any development project. In summer 1968, the CTRPA placed a moratorium on all subdivisions that had not yet received approval for sewage and garbage export facilities. El Dorado supervisors responded by withholding their county's share of the agency budget. In October 1969, just before final approval of the TRPA compact by Congress, El Dorado and Placer counties filed suit against the CTRPA, claiming that its statutes and ordinances were unconstitutional because its members were not elected by vote of the people over whom the agency had authority.

When the Nevada Tahoe Regional Planning Agency (NTRPA), the Nevada counterpart of the CTRPA, unveiled its master plan in

1969, it encountered similar criticism. Faced with a 400-percent increase in resident population between 1960 and 1968, NTRPA hoped to limit population on the Nevada shore to fifty thousand. This number, half that allowed by established zoning, would be concentrated at Stateline and Incline Village. But clearly the NTRPA would encounter resistance to any attempt to curtail development. For example, the Douglas County commissioners granted a permit to Oliver Kahle to build a $250,000 "fun ride" on Highway 50 near the Kingsbury Grade junction, about a mile north of Stateline. The proposed structure, a 206-foot steel tower shaped something like an oil derrick and supporting a rocket-shaped cone, would rise well above the treetops. On this simulated moon launch, "you climb aboard, listen to a taped countdown, then to a soundtrack blast off, away you soar" to a view of lake Tahoe.[34] Kahle believed the structure would be a "joy to behold"; the NTRPA viewed the project with dismay. Such were the confrontations looming on the horizon.

Early in 1970, the NTRPA adopted its master plan and several ordinances designed to regulate population densities and land use. But because the agency was scheduled to cease operation once governors Reagan and Laxalt had convened the bi-state regional agency, and because no effective means of enforcing its master plan existed, the agency's ability to regulate growth on the Nevada shore was limited.

Raymond M. Smith, author of the Nevada general plan, supported commercial development. As he explained it, "The scenic quality of the environment is only a function of profit and greater weight may be given to economic growth than to aesthetic conservation." He did admit that preservation of at least "some semblance" of an aesthetic and natural environment "would be necessary to attract the tourist and his recreational dollar."[35]

By the time the TRPA officially began operating in 1970, the environment of the Tahoe Basin had deteriorated still further. The planning efforts of the 1960s nevertheless should not be dismissed as a complete failure. Research on Tahoe had advanced significantly, especially through the efforts of the Lake Tahoe Area Council, which acted as a clearinghouse for funds made available by the National Science Foundation and other groups. Publication of its 1963 study provided well-publicized evidence of the deleterious impact of development on the water quality of Lake Tahoe. The formation of the Tahoe Regional Planning Commission, however limited in power, at least provided an agency that could consider the basin as a whole; and its 1980 plan, despite shortcomings, was the first general plan for the basin and a guide to later local planning. Finally, the Lake Tahoe Joint Study Committee report made clear the necessity of effective regional government—and the decade ended with the creation of the TRPA, CTRPA, and NTRPA.

6   The Tahoe Regional Planning Agency: The Emperor's New Clothes

The First Eighteen Months

Nothing captured the hopes and aroused the suspicions of people concerned with Lake Tahoe in the 1970s as much as the newly created Tahoe Regional Planning Agency. The agency convened officially on March 19, 1970, following a joint proclamation of its founding by California and Nevada governors Reagan and Laxalt. Reagan called it a "milestone" that the two states "now have the means of working together to assure the beauty of Tahoe," and Laxalt cautioned that "no other single area in the country will be subject to more severe economic and ecologic pressure."[1]

The TRPA inherited an unenviable set of circumstances. In the period between congressional approval of the agency in 1969 and its first meeting, growth at Tahoe had continued at a dizzying rate. During the 1960s, assessed property values in the basin had tripled, and opportunities for profits in Tahoe real estate and land development remained substantial. A single-family lake-front lot at Incline Village that sold for $17,500 in 1960, for example, now cost $85,000. The resident population had doubled in the decade, a peak summer population now exceeded 130,000, and state and federal recreation land use had multiplied eightfold. A guidebook to Lake Tahoe published in 1971 noted that south Tahoe, once an abandoned logging area where land sold for $1.50 per acre, now had numerous motels, as well as "40 gas stations, 52 restaurants, 2 newspapers, 2 radio stations, 7 banks, 8 schools, 16 churches, a hospital, and 69 real estate offices."[2]

The TRPA needed to act quickly to impose some order on growth. The task fell to Justus K. Smith, director of the Denver Regional Council of Governments, who was selected from more than seven hundred applicants for the post of the agency's executive director. Smith clearly lacked sufficient personnel for the task assigned him: his initial staff consisted of one planner, one drafts-man, an engineer, and two secretaries. Few foresaw the magnitude of the job ahead or the bold manner in which Smith would ap-proach it. Under the enabling legislation, he had ninety days to prepare and have adopted an interim plan for the entire basin, and he had only eighteen months to develop a regional plan for the long-term development and conservation of the basin. As they set about accomplishing these tasks, Smith and his staff also had to review a continuous flow of proposals for private land development and the construction of roads, utilities, recreation facilities, shore-line development, and outdoor advertising signs. The review pro-cess alone reportedly took three-fourths of the time available to the staff.

Further, the agency suffered from a shortage of funds almost immediately; the two California counties in the basin, El Dorado and Placer, refused to contribute their share of the first year's fund-ing. The two counties, supported by the city of South Lake Tahoe, already had filed a suit in which they challenged the constitutional-ity of the bi-state compact and the obligation of local government to abide by its rules. The El Dorado County supervisors claimed that the restrictive densities proposed in the interim plan con-stituted "inverse condemnation" for which property owners should be compensated.

Smith's idea of the mission of the TRPA differed considerably from that of many people of influence both within and outside the basin. He believed he had been hired to save Lake Tahoe from the unchecked forces of urbanization, and that a principal task would be preservation of the water and air quality of the basin. Many of his critics assumed that the legal objectives of the agency, "conservation" and "orderly development," meant at most planned growth. In their opinion, the TRPA should not act except in compliance with local wishes and should not supersede local control. In fact, the bi-state compact called for the TRPA to handle "general and regional matters," and to let the state, county, and city governments involved in the basin enact specific rules that conformed to the regional plan.

In developing the interim plan, the small staff had time only to paste together a composite of existing maps and plans from local governments. The local plans reflected local needs, did not consider the basin as a whole, and did not specify clear limits to population growth. So the loosely structured interim plan satisfied no one, providing little guidance to local developers on what to expect or help to environmentalists intent on preserving the region. As one environmentalist commented, the interim plan "can be looked upon either as a nonplan or as a blueprint for catastrophe."[3]

What lay ahead, however, was the central task—development of the regional plan. With the inadequate resources at his command, Smith turned for help to Jack W. Deinema, the regional forester. Deinema's unusual position as the nonvoting federal representative to the TRPA gave him considerable power to integrate the planning effort, coordinate federal funding, and work with state and local officials. He had already established a Forest Service team in the basin with expertise in ecology, hydrology, geology, forestry landscape, and recreational planning. This team worked closely with the TRPA staff and even shared the same building. A Federal Coordinating Committee, composed of regional representatives of all federal agencies with special interests at Tahoe, also met regularly. The federal government clearly had an important stake in the planning process: roughly 50 percent of the land in the basin remained under federal administration and ownership. In addition to this federal assistance, more than two hundred consultants, mainly from academia, provided substantial aid.[4]

Together, the Forest Service team, the TRPA staff, and consultants developed the Smith Plan, based in part on ideas popularized by Ian McHarg in his book *Design With Nature*. This was, in brief, a regional plan to regulate the size and distribution of the future population of the basin, based on levels of use that the land was capable of tolerating without sustaining such permanent damage as erosion and water degradation.

Robert G. Bailey, a Forest Service geomorphologist, devised a two-step process to measure the land's tolerance of human use. First he ranked the basin's acreage in seven classes according to the frequency and magnitude of such hazards as "floods, landslides, high water tables, poorly drained soils, fragile flora and fauna, and easily erodible soils."[5] Class one land represented areas of greatest hazard, and class seven land had essentially no hazards. Next he evaluated each unit of land on the basis of its ability to tolerate alteration by people. Bailey placed limits on disturbance of the ground surface in terms of a percentage of each area that could be used for impervious cover, that is, could be covered by buildings, parking lots, and the like.

In this classification system, 76 percent of all land in the Tahoe Basin was listed as "high hazard," 10 percent "moderate hazard," and 14 percent "low hazard." When applied to proposed development, this meant that little or no construction should take place on slopes that were subject to erosion or were in marsh and meadowland. Accordingly, under this classification, Tahoe Keys, built at the mouth of the Upper Truckee River, was most hazardous and should never have been built. And Incline Village, with its steep hillsides and construction beside streams, was already overbuilt.

The land-capability approach departed from earlier zoning practices and caused considerable controversy. Normally, planners specify tracts of land according to such designations as C (commercial), R (residential), M (industrial), and A (agricultural). This scheme has worked reasonably well in most urban and suburban areas of the country, where a major concern might be, for example, to situate homes away from factories. But Smith's chief concern was protection of Tahoe's environmental quality. His approach ran

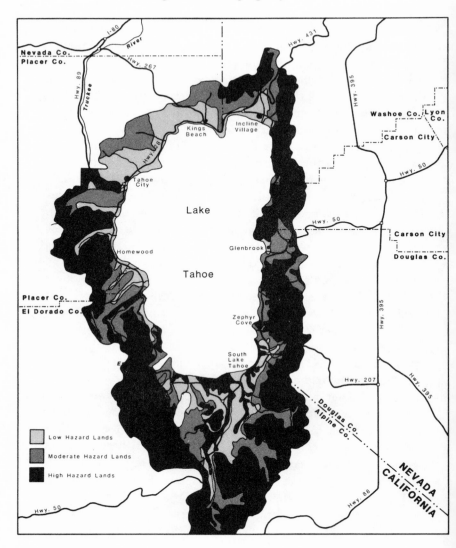

Robert G. Bailey's Land Capability Classification

counter to that of people who believed that planners, through human ingenuity, could keep pollution and soil erosion within workable limits. Many local authorities at Tahoe held that belief. They saw no need to delay development while scientists worked on a land-capability map. Instead, they concentrated on such immediate questions as where to place sewer lines to accommodate the anticipated influx of people.

Despite its usefulness as a planning tool, the land-capability map was no substitute for a regional plan that would include consideration of prior developments, zoning decisions, and the like. Yet Smith, pressed by an impending deadline, used the land-capability map as the basis for his plan. In the process he paid little attention to past zoning decisions, to property lines, or to who might stand to lose by application of the plan.

Increasingly, in 1970 and 1971, public interest groups that would be affected by the TRPA plan complained that their concerns were receiving little attention. Many people felt uninformed and unable to influence the work of the planning team. The lack of alternative plans also restricted discussion and a sense of public participation in the decision-making process.

Local people felt alienated. They did not trust the influx of outside experts, the use of a computer in Berkeley to quantify data, the threat of federal involvement, and what they perceived as neglect of home rule. The agency staff, busy with the scientific aspects of its planning duties, failed to acquire political support in the basin and thus became increasingly isolated. As one staff member commented: "The name of the game was persuasion. J. K. [Smith] never understood what that meant. He thought it was below his dignity to get involved in local politics and pressure groups. He shunned the political aspect and shut himself off from the public and the press."[6] As a result, Smith lost any chance of support from the TRPA Governing Body and the twenty-one-member Advisory Planning Commission.

When the staff finally unveiled its proposed regional plan to an overflow crowd at the Sahara Tahoe Hotel in May 1971, critics labeled it illogical, opinionated, utopian, and unjust. In particular, they attacked a proposal to restrict resident and visitor population to 134,000 at any given time—no more people than would already visit Tahoe on a busy summer weekend.[7] In comparison, the recently approved master plan of the city council of South Lake Tahoe would allow an ultimate population of 151,000 in that city alone, with a density two-thirds that of San Francisco.

From this point forward, the Smith Plan encountered rough sledding. At two well-attended public hearings in June, property owners, developers, and local officials complained about the impact of the plan on property rights and values, existing zoning, and sewer and other utility bonds. The TRPA Governing Body, influenced by the avid denunciation of the plan by the Advisory Planning Commission, voted unanimously to form a special subcommittee under Richard Heikka, the planning director of Placer County, to draw up an alternate plan that would be more acceptable to local interests. Smith, ordered into silence by the Governing Body, lost all hope of success and subsequently resigned.

The Governing Body hired Heikka to replace Smith. Heikka seemed better suited to work out some kind of compromise, and he and a small team of local planners worked quickly and largely in seclusion during the summer months. Perhaps to the surprise of many, Heikka incorporated much of the Smith Plan into his own proposal, adapting the land-capability system to a more conventional land-use approach. The Heikka Plan called for a maximum population of 280,000, well above the 134,000 Smith had proposed yet well below the 800,000 suggested by combination of the local plans. Of course, all population figures were only projections and had little to do with what actually might happen. Population would be concentrated at two urban cores, the north and south ends of the lake, where development already existed. In addition, the plan called for the establishment of green belts and for limits on the expansion of casinos.

After considerable debate, the Governing Body finally adopted Heikka's regional plan in December 1971. The plan gained national recognition, partly because it incorporated the innovative

An encircling forest softens the visual impact of a housing development at Glenbrook. James Hildinger.

land-capability concept. Its implementation, however, depended on adoption of the various ordinances ordered in the original bi-state compact.

An assessment of TRPA performance before adoption of the regional plan gave reason for concern. The staff failed to halt or even seriously delay most proposed projects that it believed were destructive to Tahoe's environmental quality. Time and again it was overruled by the Advisory Planning Commission and the Governing Body, which were dominated by local members sympathetic to development. The information generated by the staff was often disregarded, and the Advisory Planning Commission increasingly based its reviews on standards set by county and city planning agencies.

Two political scientists at the University of California, Davis, provided a critical evaluation. Their conclusion was that "the expert Planning Commission proved unable to plan, the representative Governing Body acquired a clear local bias, and the neutral staff turned increasingly, if somewhat reluctantly, to advocacy."[8] As a result, the initial TRPA planning and regulatory efforts proved largely ineffective. In fact, the TRPA plan was vitiated before its approval. The Governing Body approved so many new developments during the period of preparation of the plan—reportedly 95 percent of the projects brought before it—that rapid growth was assured for years to come.

In an attempt to explain what had gone wrong, John D. Ayer, professor of law at the University of California, Davis, argued that Tahoe was engulfed in public policies that encouraged the misuse of the basin. The key problem, urbanization, exacerbated a host of related problems, such as air and water pollution, that had to be solved at public expense. Replying to the argument that events at Tahoe were simply a response to "market" conditions of what individual buyers and sellers wanted, Ayer pointed out that public policies heavily influenced these conditions.[9] For example, the real property tax made developing privately owned tracts of land especially attractive. Special assessments, such as for modern sewage disposal, also encouraged development, partly to attract more people who would help pay for the bonded indebtedness. County governments certainly encouraged such growth; they gained more in revenue than they lost in providing public service.

Ironically, the federal government also contributed to environmental problems. Despite its concern and responsibility for helping to attain and maintain air and water quality standards, federal agencies fostered growth in two important ways. First, they provided grants to facilitate construction. For example, the expenditure of federal funds for campgrounds, roads, airports, waste disposal, and other purposes contributed to further growth. Second, the agencies issued permits, such as for the Heavenly Valley ski resort, allowing construction financed by private capital on public lands.

Although federal financial grants and the issuance of permits were responses to perceived problems, such as crowded highways and overloaded sewage systems, they encouraged urban development. Each time the government acted to provide additional recreational facilities or expanded highways, it opened the door to more people. Since state and local governments, as well as the private sector, acted similarly, a downward spiral of environmental quality continued. As a federal task force later concluded, "Nowhere in the decision-making process were the interactions among responses or the cumulative environmental effects they caused considered."[10] As long as economic incentives pushed toward development of the basin and no governmental agency stood in the way, urbanization continued.

Although the federal government contributed to the problem, many people looked to it for a solution. Lloyd Krause, senior analyst at the Stanford Research Institute, argued that protection of the Tahoe Basin required national supervision. He asserted that local and county officials were unable to preserve a national asset— and that expecting them to do so was unreasonable. They were elected to serve the short-term interests of their local constituents and could not cope with the "massive financial, legal, and technical resources of powerful corporations and syndicates pursuing profits through urbanizing the Tahoe Basin."[11] These large commercial ventures used advertising to create demand for their services. Krause found it "totally unsatisfactory" that two gubernatorial appointees to the TRPA Governing Body, representing twenty million Californians, could be outvoted by three local officials representing less than .5 percent of that population. Of course, it did not help that the state had approved such misrepresentation in the first place in adopting the bi-state compact.

The Federal Response and the BOR Report

The concern for deforestation and the equitable division of Tahoe water, in particular, had already led to significant federal activities in the area. The U.S. Forest Service alone administered nearly half the land in the basin by the 1960s, although it owned little of the strategic land along the shoreline of the lake that needed protection the most. Many other federal agencies also had some kind of active interest in the basin. But the government remained reluctant to increase its involvement at Tahoe and tried to allow state and local governments to settle most of the problems.

The record of the Forest Service in managing basin lands to protect their scenic qualities and curb excessive development had been mixed. For example, encouragement of such ski resorts as Heavenly Valley in the national forests greatly facilitated growth of the all-year economy and increased urbanization. Of course, the Forest Service operated under the directive of "multiple use"—a concept vaguely defined as management of resources so they are utilized in that combination which will best meet the present and future needs of the American people. Such definition leaves great latitude for interpretation, but tends to encourage maximization of use.

Following a visit to the basin by Secretary of the Interior Stewart Udall, the Lake Tahoe Area Council announced that Tahoe would receive high priority among several areas to be studied as possible sites for "national lakeshore designation."[12] Nevada Senator Alan Bible cited Cape Cod National Seashore in Massachusetts as an area where problems similar to those at Tahoe were being overcome. In brief, existing residential and commercial land use could be integrated with a scenic public recreation area. Bible stated that he hoped the National Park Service would look into the possibility of taking action, particularly on the Nevada shore, where park land might still be acquired relatively cheaply.

In January 1969, Bible initiated consideration of a national lakeshore or recreation area at Lake Tahoe. Under the proposed legislation, the Secretary of the Interior, in close cooperation with the TRPA and other concerned governmental agencies, would determine which lands should be converted to public ownership and how they should be managed. Questions of possible joint federal and state responsibility, and whether the best designation would be a national lakeshore under the National Park Service or a national recreation area under the Forest Service, remained open.[13]

Under this act, signed September 26, 1970, Congress authorized $50,000 for the study and directed the secretary of the interior to submit a report to the president and Congress within one year.[14] Bible regarded the legislation as the logical followup to the bi-state TRPA compact. Next, he urged more rapid federal land acquisition at the lake. This flurry of congressional interest promised a more active role by federal agencies in protecting the basin from misuse.

In September 1971, the Bureau of Outdoor Recreation (BOR) submitted a report to the Department of the Interior in compliance with the directive from Congress. The draft, not yet approved for release to Congress and the public, recommended bold changes at Tahoe to restore and preserve the natural landscape and its scenic and recreational values. The TRPA came under sharp attack: it had approved twelve thousand residential units by July 1971, units sufficient to house thirty-six thousand people, and had denied applications for only five hundred units. The report also criticized the uncoordinated federal expenditures at Tahoe, including grants to help finance and maintain condominiums, the airport, highways, and sewage systems.

The BOR study team recommended that a Tahoe national lakeshore be established to encompass the entire basin and that $70 million be spent there, primarily to purchase land and easements. To reflect the state and national significance of Tahoe, the team favored restructuring the TRPA to end dominance by local members. Specific objectives included increasing public access to the shoreline of the lake, improving scenic quality, providing outdoor recreation compatible with maintaining environmental quality, and retaining the natural landscape and open space on a large scale. The team warned: "Only through across the board organizational-legal-fiscal action will Tahoe be saved, and further public spending justified."[15]

The BOR study recommended significant changes. Especially portentous were the following: no more construction in extensive "landscape conservation" zones, pedestrian access every half-mile of lakeshore, provision for bus transportation and no expansion of the highway system in the basin, height standards on all new buildings in urban zones, no construction that would block a view of the lake from the highway around its borders, and burial of all new utility and transmission lines.

More than six months after the BOR report had been scheduled to be made public, Senator John Tunney of California demanded to know what had become of the final draft. The BOR failed to respond, and rumors reached Tunney that "substantial revisions" were being made. Actually the original study team had been asked by Department of the Interior officials to completely rewrite the report, and the job had been turned over to a small Department of the Interior task force. The final BOR report bore little resemblance to the original draft, copies of which quickly disappeared, and in March 1973 Secretary of the Interior Rogers C. B. Morton recommended against a national lakeshore. Concluding that a lakeshore "would be counter to the desires and interests of the local and regional governments," the final report stated that the TRPA as presently constituted could effectively control Tahoe's environmental problems. Curiously, Morton contended that a national lakeshore would attract too many people and thus endanger the environment. The *Los Angeles Times* and the *Sacramento Bee* ran editorials critical of Morton and the timidity of the federal government. Such failure to act, the *Bee* noted, would never have saved Yosemite, Grand Canyon, or other scenic areas of national significance.

Despite the ineffectiveness of the final BOR report, the federal role at Tahoe became more overt. Jack Deinema of the U.S. Forest Service told the TRPA Governing Body that Tahoe was an area of "national significance" where the public interest should be recognized and fully protected. The Forest Service deferred development on national forest land; the Army Corps of Engineers placed a moratorium on issuance of permits for piers and other structures along the shoreline; and the Department of Housing and Urban Development imposed a moratorium on Federal Housing Administration mortgage-insurance programs in the basin pending effective control of environmental problems by the TRPA. Thus, although Congress never articulated a specific policy for Tahoe, several agencies took action on an ad hoc basis. In addition, Senator Tunney presided at a hearing of the Senate Air and Water Pollution Subcommittee at the Cal-Neva Hotel in 1972 and called attention to the severity of Tahoe's problems. He favored greater authority for the Environmental Protection Agency to control excessive development. It appeared that federal agencies would be playing an increasingly important role in protecting the environmental quality at Tahoe.

The Forest Service in particular took steps to improve its administrative effectiveness. In April 1973 it established the Lake Tahoe Basin Management Unit (LTBMU) to administer all three national forests within the basin (Tahoe, Eldorado, and Toiyabe) as a single unit. This arrangement allowed for coordination of policies on the three forests and more expert decision making. Starting with a budget of $600,000 and a staff of eighteen full-time employees, the LTBMU administered more than half the land in the basin, an area increased yearly through an active land acquisition program.

Only one part of the basin remained unaffected by both development and the government's land acquisition program: the Desolation Wilderness. In 1931, the Forest Service had classified 41,383 acres as a roadless "primitive area," designating it the Desolation Valley Wild Area. In 1969, when the tract was enlarged to more than 63,000 acres and made part of the nation's wilderness system, it became the Desolation Wilderness. The main crest of the Sierra Nevada bisects the wilderness area; actually, only its eastern part rests within the Tahoe Basin. Just to the west of the crest lies a deep glacial trench that extends from Rockbound Valley in the north to Desolation Valley in the south. This rugged mountain area, sprinkled with alpine lakes, became so popular that visitation doubled within three years in the late 1960s, threatening to exceed the carrying capacity of the land. By 1971, the Forest Service required wilderness permits for anyone camping overnight. Proximity to large population centers in California as well as to Lake Tahoe made the Desolation Wilderness one of the most popular hiking areas in the country—and also unusually difficult to protect from overuse.

Casinos and Legal Suits

Gambling remained the most important single activity at Tahoe at the start of the 1970s and undoubtedly had greater impact on life in the basin than did any other factor. People visited the lake in record-breaking numbers, and the summer population of the basin reached an estimated 133,000, including about 26,000 permanent residents.[16] California had 4,500 motel rooms within a half-mile of Stateline; occupancy rates rose with proximity to the casinos.

With gambling revenues rising annually regardless of fluctuations in the national economy, pressure for both new and expanded casinos became a major environmental issue. If the casinos expanded, so would traffic, noise, air and water pollution, and all other aspects of a largely uncontrolled urban development. Even before the first meeting of the TRPA, William Harrah had garnered unanimous support from the Douglas County commissioners for construction of a 31-story 1,600-room hotel adjacent to his club at Stateline. Following TRPA approval of a scaled-down 18-story building, Harrah remarked, "We believe that what we plan to build is precisely what Tahoe needs. . . . The hotel will stand out no more than the vapor of a jet plane or the silhouette of a ship on the ocean."[17] At least the narrow facade of the new hotel faced the lake, and its dark brown coloring helped lessen the visual impact.

There was every indication that the north shore, though not yet as crowded, would soon be much like the south shore. As seen through the eyes of environmentalist William Bronson, north

Pyramid Peak in the Desolation Wilderness, readily accessible from the Tahoe Basin, attracts many hikers. James Hildinger.

Tahoe already left much to be desired: "Five miles east of the northern state boundary lies the 500-room King's Castle, a $20 million gift to the people of the night from Sir Nathan of Jacobson, as he is called over his paging system, the same gentleman who created Caesar's Palace in Las Vegas. Above lies Incline Village, Boise Cascade's huge, mountain-scarring desecration, beyond which a wall of condominium apartments blocks the view almost all the way to Crystal Bay, where half a dozen, more or less, scruffy casinos crowd the road."[18]

In June 1973, the TRPA took no action within the sixty-day limit on consideration of a proposed 446-room 14-story $30-million

Park Cattle Company hotel on the south shore. Under the bi-state compact, this ensured automatic approval, for only a dual majority of California and Nevada members could block the proposed project. The actual vote had been 6–4 in opposition to construction, with all California members casting negative votes. The nonvoting federal appointee, Doug Leisz, of the Forest Service, had "great reservations" about approval because of the lack of a regional transportation plan. Steven Brandt, executive director of the League to Save Lake Tahoe, called the TRPA a "failure."

The following year, the vote of the three local Nevada members prevailed over that of the other seven members to provide automatic approval for two new hotel-casinos, Ted Jennings' Tahoe Palace and Oliver Kahle's Hotel Oliver. Between them, Jennings and Kahle planned more than 80,000 square feet of floor space for gambling, 1,520 rooms, more than 3,400 parking spaces, many restaurants, swimming pools, tennis courts, bowling alleys, show rooms, and bars—all at a cost of close to $100 million. Douglas County commissioners had unanimously approved the proposals in April 1973. The NTRPA, however, had rejected the proposed projects; the two state representatives and two of the three local representatives believed that traffic problems precluded construction at that time. By May 1974, the two recalcitrant local members had been removed from office and replaced by people more responsive to casino interests. The NTRPA then approved the proposed casinos, 3–2, with all local members voting for them.[19]

Adding to the concerns of environmentalists, the Tahoe Palace and the Hotel Oliver were to be built about three-fourths of a mile from Stateline, past the junction of Highway 50 and Kingsbury Grade, creating a second hub for gambling spots at the south shore. If these two new casinos prospered, they could induce investors to build on any of several potential sites nearby. In the thirteen-month period ending in July 1974, the TRPA approved by default under the sixty-day rule three major casino-hotels at the south shore and a major expansion of Harvey's Resort Casino.

A TRPA staff report noted that if all four approved casino-hotels were constructed, the results would include at least twenty-four thousand new residents, the demand for more than eight thousand new housing units, and the need for ten additional traffic lanes on the California side of the border. But because the sewage capacity of existing treatment facilities was nearing its limit, and because contractors tended to cater to the wealthiest clientele, housing in the basin would not exist for most new employees, and they would have to find accommodations outside the basin, probably in Carson Valley. As Richard Heikka explained, "What this means is that California is no longer going to be a bedroom for Nevada employees."[20] The new casinos would also demand more of the already extended water supply and would cause both air and water quality to further deteriorate. Under these circumstances, and because of the growing disillusionment with the TRPA, California Attorney General Evelle Younger brought suit in federal court to block construction of the Hotel Oliver and the Tahoe Palace.

In August 1974, however, U.S. District Judge Bruce Thompson in Reno rejected a California bid for a temporary injunction against construction of the Jennings and Kahle casino-hotels. California argued that the 7–3 vote against the proposed projects was sufficient to defeat them. But Judge Thompson said the court could not change the unequivocal language of the bi-state compact that required a dual majority of members present to take action on any matter. Because no action had been taken on the Jennings-Kahle proposals, the sixty-day rule would allow automatic approval of the casinos. Thompson added that the proliferation of casinos at Tahoe was an "abomination," but that his personal feelings had little to do with the matter. Any changes in the compact depended on legislative agreement between California and Nevada.

Arguing in support of the new casinos, Kahle stated that he had lived up to all the rules, spent a small fortune in legal fees and planning, and now wanted to get his project under way. He reminded California that it had approved the dual-majority rule, and claimed that changing the rules in the middle of the game would be unfair. Besides, he believed his hotel-casino would be beneficial, taking care of upward of half a million people a year. As for housing his two thousand employees, Kahle predicted that they would find places to live. In any case, he stated, "It's not my responsibility." He also argued that the multimillion-dollar casinos are the "back-bone that started this lake to what it is today."[21]

Judge Thompson's decision stood: the U.S. Supreme Court refused to hear the dispute. Nevada's Attorney General Robert List happily reacted, "This decision by the Supreme Court should end the hassle with those who would deprive Nevada of its right to a voice in the future of the Nevada side of the Lake Tahoe Basin."[22] Younger announced his "deep disappointment" at the court's action, and James Bruner, Jr., the new executive director of the League to Save Lake Tahoe, stated that the decision had rendered the TRPA ineffective in dealing with bi-state problems. The league's own legal suit against construction of the two casinos, contending that they would violate TRPA building height limitations, had been dismissed in District Court in Minden, Nevada. The league next turned to federal authorities in an attempt to halt the construction because of the violations of federal air and water quality standards the casinos would engender. Legal battles continued.

This reliance on the courts in the Jennings and Kahle challenge did not set a precedent at Tahoe, for court action characterized the entire decade of the 1970s. Property owners earlier had instituted numerous suits against the TRPA, claiming that restrictions on development under the regional plan and ordinances constituted condemnation without compensation, and that members of the Governing Body were personally liable for millions of dollars. The property owners believed they had a right to do with their land as they pleased, and they objected to the use of government police powers to restrict their activities.

But in fact, land-use regulations by government had been upheld in American courts for decades. For example, the California Supreme Court ruled in 1925 in *Miller* v. *Board of Public Works* that "as a commonwealth develops politically, economically, and socially, the police power likewise develops, within reason, to meet the changed and changing conditions."[23] A 1964 opinion of the California attorney general upheld the legality of a moratorium by the Association of Bay Area Governments on filling and development of the San Francisco Bay. In 1975, a federal court upheld the right of the California city of Petaluma to impose a plan that restricted urban sprawl and slowed the rate of growth. These and many other decisions supported the right of a public agency to restrict the use of privately owned land.

The expansion of the casinos despite concerted legal action to block them epitomized for environmentalists the frustration of trying to control growth at Tahoe. California turned for help to its own agency, the California Tahoe Regional Planning Agency, which had been comparatively dormant since the end of 1971.

The Controversial CTRPA

Like the TRPA, the CTRPA provoked a great deal of controversy, both within and outside the Tahoe Basin. But, unlike the TRPA, criticism of the CTRPA came not primarily from California and environmentalists, but from Nevada and local Tahoe residents and officials. Except for some local people who opposed any outside agency at all in the basin, the CTRPA stepped on a different set of toes.

The California legislature reconstituted the CTRPA in 1973 in response to the ineffectiveness of the TRPA. The last straw, perhaps, had been approval of the large Raley shopping center at Tahoe Vista, on the California side of the lake. On the governing board of the CTRPA were the designee of the secretary of the Resources Agency of California, an appointee of the governor to represent the citizens of northern California and another for southern California, and local representatives from El Dorado and Placer counties and the city of South Lake Tahoe. These six people then chose a seventh to serve as chairperson.

By spring 1974 the agency had resolved earlier problems of lack of legal representation, funds, and staff and was ready for action. In its new organization, the CTRPA could avoid both local control and stalemates in decision making; and legal representation from the state office of the attorney general gave the agency more clout.

In addition, the legislature gave the CTRPA unusual powers, including approval or disapproval of all state public works projects. Control over transportation into and within the basin allowed the agency considerable leverage in future development plans for the basin. Because it was directly funded by the state legislature, the CTRPA did not have to worry about financial support from county governments.

The "new" agency was directed to develop its own regional plan; unlike the TRPA, it was bound by the procedural and substantive requirements of the California Environmental Quality Act. The CTRPA acted, in brief, as an additional line of defense for the California side of the basin, reviewing public and private projects before consideration by the TRPA.

The CTRPA encountered a storm of protest in June 1974, when it proposed an interim plan restricting construction on the California side of the lake to single-family dwellings until the agency had completed its master plan. A crowd of several hundred people, watched by plainclothesmen, roundly booed agency members at a south Tahoe hearing at the local high school. Jim Norton, president of the Lake Tahoe Insurance Agents Association, expressed local sentiment when he stated, "We don't need people who don't live or pay taxes here to tell us how to deal with our problems." Lloyd Krause, co-chairman of a Sierra Club task force for Tahoe, countered that Tahoe belongs to all twenty-one million Californians, not just the people who live in El Dorado and Placer counties. Amid loud catcalls, he stated, "The pursuit of gain by urbanizing Tahoe is not a right. It's a privilege and is revokable at any time."[24]

Developers claimed that the CTRPA plan would require a moratorium on construction, and local business interests claimed that the agency, controlled by nonresidents, was bent on destroying Tahoe as a tourist attraction. The Lake Tahoe Economic Crisis Committee, with representatives from local trade unions and from real estate and other business interests, joined forces to form the Council for Logic, which opposed the building slowdown. The council advocated protection of the rights of private property owners through decisions by locally elected officials and vehemently opposed the CTRPA interim plan. It also argued that the CTRPA policy would be inflationary, driving the price of existing housing in the basin well beyond the reach of low- and medium-income people.

Despite the protests, the CTRPA approved tough interim building controls in July by a 5–2 vote. Any construction other than single-family homes on individual lots and commercial projects on less than one acre of land would be banned unless the project could be shown not to induce growth, harm air or water quality, or cause scenic damage. Gordon Hooper, chairman of the CTRPA who voted for the plan, remarked, "We have an undeniable obligation to not only property owners at the lake but also to the citizens of the state and the United States."[25] Hooper, a Tahoe City realtor, surprised many people by his strong environmental stand. The representatives from El Dorado County and the city of South Lake Tahoe voted against the proposal, arguing that the TRPA provided adequate control over development. South Tahoe interests immediately sought a court injunction to block the CTRPA action. Actually, no strict moratorium on building resulted; the CTRPA approved major projects as long as they met the standard of the interim plan.

By May 1975, the CTRPA had initiated discussions of its master plan, which provided that there would be no more than 150,000 people on the California side of the basin by 1985—many fewer than in a TRPA projection. The CTRPA incorporated Robert Bailey's land-capability system into its plan and noted that land capability and water quality standards could not be exceeded without an irreversible impact on the environment. Local people again protested vehemently, claiming that the plan would block economic progress, injure private property rights, and preempt the power of local government. Ed McCarthy, a Nevada realtor and chairman of the Council for Logic, stated, "It is no plan at all, but simply a no-growth philosophy."[26]

The CTRPA proposed a transportation plan in August that would include an extensive bus system and a sharp reduction in the use of automobiles. Large parking lots would be provided at entry points into the basin and a user fee assessed anyone who operated an automobile beyond these parking facilities. In addition, the plan emphasized the use of bicycle lanes and pedestrian paths.

By September, the agency had adopted both a regional plan and a transportation plan by narrow margins of 4–3. Perhaps most controversial was a provision against any further approval of subdivision lots until 85 percent of the existing lots within planning subdivisions had been built upon—a measure that some people believed could eliminate new subdivisions for the remainder of the century. Approximately twenty-one thousand unbuilt but subdivided lots existed on the California side of the basin. The CTRPA also "down-zoned" the density of all residential areas not yet developed. The three local representatives cast nay votes, preferring to support the less stringent TRPA plan.

Comparisons between the TRPA and the CTRPA were inevitable. Each prepared a regional plan concerned with land use, transportation, conservation, recreation, and public services and facilities. Of course, the TRPA plan applied to the entire basin, whereas CTRPA jurisdiction stopped at the California border. The CTRPA staff agreed that a single bi-state agency (TRPA) would be best for the basin "if it could be made to work." Until that happened, the staff believed the California agency should continue. Nevada's own agency (NTRPA), reconstituted in 1973, could review and approve only matters outside TRPA authority: namely, the development of gambling casinos.

By 1976, CTRPA criticisms of the TRPA included 1) the failure to provide even a plan to meet the relatively low federal air quality standards, despite several years and $4 million in planning funds, 2) the adoption of a transportation plan that called for construction of more highways and depended on privately owned automobiles to accommodate increased tourism, 3) the failure to adhere to the intent of the land-capability map because of the sixty-day rule and prior approval of casino sites, and 4) the lack of a program to control erosion and surface runoff into the lake.[27] Critics also noted the TRPA's apparent lack of concern about erosion and other processes leading to environmental degradation in the basin, or about the incremental environmental change brought on by separate developments, which often would not conform to the regional plan.

The CTRPA also had its critics. A report by a group called Economic Research Associates, commissioned by local governments, noted that restricting construction on the California side of the border put greater pressure for development outside the basin, on such places as Martis Valley, Squaw Valley, and especially Carson Valley. Further, the CTRPA plan most affected the owners of undeveloped property, the public service agencies, the construction industry, and the local basin governments and residents. Complaints about the CTRPA plan cited 1) the lack of compensation to property owners for economic losses, 2) the failure to relieve traffic congestion at Stateline, 3) the decentralization of commercial zones due to a rule that no more than 30 percent of the land on a site could be made impervious, 4) the inadequacy of facilities for older people and an overemphasis on campgrounds, 5) the inadequacy of recreational facilities, including ski resorts, and 6) the inadequacy of low- and moderate-priced housing. Nevertheless, a large majority of summer home residents expressed their approval of the tough approach of the CTRPA, and 80 percent of visitors reportedly favored restrictions on development at Tahoe.

South Lake Tahoe filed a suit against the CTRPA in federal court challenging the validity of its 85-percent build-out rule. The city also initiated legislation to abolish the agency. Five hundred irate citizens walked out of a city council meeting when no action was taken on a proposal to ignore CTRPA rules altogether. John Vostrez, the CTRPA executive officer, argued that critics of the agency did not consider the economic costs of environmental degradation in their calculations, including their calculations of the health of the local economy. Vostrez explained, "Visitors come here looking for a unique environment. If they find the area degraded, they will go elsewhere. The whole economy revolves around the Tahoe environment."[28] Although Vostrez believed that the government should purchase private property that was declared permanently unbuildable, he insisted this did not mean that anyone should make a profit or benefit from land speculation simply for purchasing property at Lake Tahoe.

Water Quality and the 208 Plan

The CTRPA took the brunt of criticism from local citizens and business interests, but it was not alone in acting to try to slow development. In April 1977, the Lahontan Regional Water Quality Control Board imposed a limit of five hundred new homes that could be constructed at south Tahoe that season because the sewage treatment plant did not meet discharge requirements. Increasing its load risked violating state water quality standards and contracts with the Forest Service and California state parks. In June, the State Department of Real Estate ordered an immediate halt to the sale of 290 unimproved lots owned by developers to protect unknowing buyers from purchasing property that could possibly never be developed because of lack of available sewer connections.

The construction of new treatment plants or the expansion of existing plants would take several years, and financing them would depend largely on state and federal funding. Roy Hampson, executive officer of the Lahontan board, predicted that the sewage capacity problem would "determine the destiny of Lake Tahoe for the next decade, perhaps longer."[29]

But the maintenance of water quality in the basin involved much more than improved sewage treatment plants. In 1972 Congress passed the Federal Water Pollution Control Act (public law 92–500), better known as the Clean Water Act, with the objective of restoring and preserving the integrity of the nation's water. Under the act, an agency could seek a grant for 75 percent of the construction costs of publicly owned sewage treatment facilities. Grants required compliance with provisions for the preparation of regional water pollution control plans under section 208 of the act.

Each plan had to identify existing and potential water quality problems and measures for correcting them. In California, the State Water Resources Control Board was given planning responsibilities, and in Nevada the Department of Conservation and Natural Resources had parallel duties. In 1974, California and Nevada jointly selected the TRPA as the agency responsible for preparing the "208 plan" for the Tahoe Basin, and the Environmental Protection Agency provided an initial $650,000 grant to the TRPA for the project. Three years later, the TRPA issued a draft 208 plan which identified several major water pollution problems—including erosion from old logging operations and roads, development in stream environment zones, construction on steep and unstable slopes, and runoff from parking lots and other areas stripped of vegetation.

The TRPA draft proposed a basin user fee to help fund the plan. It also recommended zoning changes to prevent development in stream environment zones and lands with a high erosion hazard. Further, it called for a moratorium on the development of existing subdivisions in stream environment zones until detailed plans to protect these environmentally sensitive areas could be developed. The TRPA Governing Body, however, in approving the final 208 plan, eliminated the user fee, the proposed zoning changes, and the moratorium. In other words, the Governing Body, bowing to local and state economic pressures, eliminated the means for effective implementation of the plan.

Nevada approved the revised plan in 1978 with very restrictive conditions (conditions that were never met), but the California state board rejected it. The board warned that the plan had no means of implementation, did not contain an effective erosion control program, and would accelerate the deterioration of water quality. Before the year ended, the board revoked its designation of the TRPA as the agency responsible for 208 planning at Tahoe and assumed that responsibility itself on the California side of the lake.

Although approval of a 208 plan for the basin remained unresolved, efforts continued to protect water quality through improved sewage systems. In addition to the South Tahoe Public Utility District plant, three other treatment plants served the basin in the 1970s: the Douglas County Sewer Improvement District, the Incline Village General Improvement District, and the Tahoe-Truckee Sanitation Agency (TTSA). The first two pumped effluent from the Nevada side of the basin to Carson Valley. The TTSA, serving the north and west shores in California, Alpine Meadows, Squaw Valley, and the Truckee area, utilized an export trunk line to a plant in Martis Valley near Truckee.

The new TTSA plant, completed in 1978, replaced an interim disposal system in which effluent treated at Tahoe City had been pumped a short distance for disposal at Cinder Cone, a volcanic formation on Forest Service land. The water percolated through cinders there before emerging in springs that flowed back into the Truckee River outside the basin. Sewage spills into Lake Tahoe as well as overflow at Cinder Cone had added urgency to completion of the new plant.

Debate mounted over the appropriate size of the TTSA sewage system and its impact on future growth within the basin. A CTRPA study concluded that the TTSA project was not intended to induce additional growth, although it allowed for a slight additional capacity over the existing system. The critical decision would be whether the enlarged sewer capacity would serve existing lots or allow for new subdivisions. In either case, a large interceptor sewage line that paralleled the Truckee River provided room for greatly expanded future flow from north Tahoe.

In 1980, the TTSA proposed a major expansion of its sewage system that would provide three thousand more sewer permits for north Lake Tahoe and eight thousand for the Truckee area. This would allow a population increase of some forty thousand by 1990 and would result in more traffic, noise, deterioration of air quality, and other impacts. Although a final environmental impact report in 1981 provided for an expanded system, it called for fewer sewer permits at north Lake Tahoe than originally envisaged. In the meantime, the Lahontan board, the League to Save Lake Tahoe, and others have monitored the sewage permit process to see that appropriate action is taken to mitigate the impact of additional growth. In spite of all efforts, however, sewage spills have continued to plague the sewage systems at Tahoe, and several spills have reached the lake.

Attempts to Revise the TRPA Compact

Although several agencies continued efforts to protect the water quality of Lake Tahoe, the agency most critical to the area's future remained the Tahoe Regional Planning Agency. Although the TRPA had been established in a spirit of optimism, hope that it might stem the tide of environmental degradation faded quickly. In spite of all the real and feared restrictions on growth, the trend of the early 1970s was toward continued development, especially because the TRPA allowed frequent variances to its regional plan and ordinances. In fact, the rate of growth of multiple and single-family dwellings did not diminish under the TRPA. The north shore became a focal point for condominiums; and the permanent population, as well as new housing units, increased at least 40 percent in four years in the basin as a whole.[30]

The League to Save Lake Tahoe responded to all this activity, including TRPA approval of the lake's largest shopping center at Tahoe Vista on the north shore, by withdrawing its endorsement of the agency in summer 1973. The league and the Sierra Club together sued the TRPA, claiming that it had violated the bi-state compact by approving a faulty regional plan and ordinances that allowed excessive development. The *Los Angeles Times* remarked acidly that the TRPA so far seemed incapable of planning anything but "gambling casinos and shopping centers," and the *San Francisco Chronicle* called the agency an "impotent pygmy."[31] The *Sacramento Bee* added that perhaps the time had finally arrived for the federal government to take over.[32] Not all California newspapers agreed with these assessments of TRPA performance, however. An editorial in the local *Tahoe Daily Tribune* commended the TRPA, stating that "the agency stands as a bulwark of increasing stature against the debilitating forces of special interest."[33]

Many Californians blamed Nevada for the failure of the TRPA.

A housing project at Tahoe Keys, known locally as The Rabbit Hutches, overlooks a dredged canal, formerly the site of extensive marshland. James Hildinger.

They called for independent action by California because it appeared that the TRPA could not or would not stand up to large developers. Assemblyman Z'Berg proposed a bill to tighten control of development on the California side of the basin. Three of the five Californians on the TRPA voted against a proposed "loop" road at Stateline needed to facilitate the expansion of Nevada's casinos. And, most important, California turned increasingly to CTRPA to restrict growth.

The TRPA responded to the criticism by establishing a six-member team to study the agency. Its report, released in July 1974, contained several recommendations that Californians welcomed, including 1) an end to the dual-majority voting system, 2) a shift of the balance of power to state representatives and a vote on the Governing Body for the federal representative, 3) stiffer penalties for violation of the TRPA ordinances, and 4) restriction of casinos to land they already occupied. Approval of these changes, of course, would depend on cooperation of the two states.

Richard Heikka, executive director of the TRPA, defended the agency. He noted many accomplishments, including sharp restrictions on the use of about thirty-four thousand acres in the basin, regulation of such activities as grading, shoreline development, and tree-cutting, and assistance in the completion of sewage facilities to pump all effluent outside the basin. Other sources also supported the TRPA. Both the California and Nevada supreme courts declared the agency constitutional, which meant that counties on both sides of the state line would be expected to abide by its decisions. In 1974 the TRPA was named the areawide planning organization for waste treatment, under section 208 of the Clean Water Act, and so it received a $650,000 grant from the EPA for a two-year study toward an areawide waste treatment management plan.

The following year, the U.S. District Court ruled in favor of the TRPA in the inverse condemnation suits brought against it. The court absolved county governments of any legal responsibility for TRPA actions, a decision that could encourage county authorities to take a more active role in upholding TRPA ordinances. The court also ruled that causing land to lose value did not alone make the TRPA land-use ordinance unconstitutional. Because the TRPA had no power of eminent domain, the court ruled that it was not subject to inverse condemnation suits. In brief, the TRPA held its ground against its critics and retained the legal authority it had originally been granted.

When the state of California lost in its effort to block construction of new casinos at south Tahoe, the court advised that the state's only remedy lay with the legislative branches of Nevada and California. Thus, creation of an effective bi-state agency to control growth at Tahoe depended on revision of the bi-state compact that had created the TRPA in the first place, and particularly on changes in the membership and voting provisions that had hindered its effectiveness.

The problem was how to devise a new compact acceptable to both state legislatures. When Nevada State Senator Thomas "Spike" Wilson introduced a bill that would have made future development projects dependent on approval by a majority of

TRPA members from each state, Nevada legislators rejected the measure. They objected to any provision that would give Californians a veto over the future of gambling at Tahoe. The following year, in 1976, when California legislators approved an act to reduce the power of local representation on the TRPA and require a dual majority for approval of any project, local officials and Nevadans opposed it. The next year, Nevada Governor Mike O'Callaghan initiated legislation to limit the expansion of gambling, require approval by both states of any development proposal, and eliminate the separate state regional agencies. Officials of California Governor Brown's office rejected the legislation. They wished to eliminate dominance by local representatives to the TRPA, and to continue the CTRPA until the TRPA proved its ability to protect environmental quality at Tahoe.

In retrospect, efforts to revise the bi-state compact failed in large part because of the unwillingness of each side to trust the good faith of the other. Nevada believed it had made important concessions in restricting the possible expansion of casinos, an action that opened the door to a U.S. Forest Service proposal for purchase of the remaining approved sites. Nevada had also agreed to give up the sixty-day rule that had prevented California from blocking projects on the Nevada side of the lake. Expecting California to give up the CTRPA and place the state's funds, time, and energy behind a single agency—TRPA—therefore seemed only reasonable. Any remaining problems could be settled by future amendments to the compact.

California, on the other hand, believed any further construction of casino-hotels would be environmentally disastrous and regarded the CTRPA as the only real line of defense, at least on the California side of the basin. Besides, the continuation of local control of the TRPA boded ill for the future. The Brown administration, filled as it was with activists uncomfortable with pragmatic politics, found Nevada's compromise unacceptable. Unwilling to wait any longer, California turned to the federal government in hope of a solution.

The National Recreation Area Proposal

California's Governor Brown, Assemblyman Eugene Gualco, Senator Alan Cranston, and Assembly Speaker Leo Mc-Carthy spearheaded the movement for increased federal involvement at Tahoe. When Secretary of the Interior Cecil Andrus came west on a visit in June 1977, he made clear his willingness to work to break the impasse. "I hesitate to stick the federal nose into a state problem," he remarked, "but if that is the only way it can be resolved, we're not all that bashful."[34] McCarthy wrote to federal and state officials formally requesting that the U.S. government take control of the lake. In his unusual letter, he recommended that California withdraw from the TRPA and support the CTRPA until a comprehensive federal plan for preserving the lake could be formulated.

Arguing that Tahoe was no less a national treasure than the Everglades of Florida or the Point Reyes National Seashore in California, Huey Johnson, California's Secretary of Resources, stated that "establishment of a national recreation area managed by the U.S. Forest Service is the only course which promises a solution."[35] A national recreation area (NRA), in his opinion, would preserve the lake and surrounding land, provide a means to purchase private lands that were prohibited from being developed, improve land management, and allow continued public use of the basin.

The national recreation area concept already had a successful track record in the Cuyahoga Valley of Ohio, the Sawtooth Valley of Idaho, the Golden Gate in California, and elsewhere. Under Johnson's proposal, private development including casinos would be limited, and a plan would be developed to "restore and preserve the magnificence of Lake Tahoe." The Johnson plan received favorable comment in most parts of California, met with skepticism and caution in Nevada, and aroused hostility from local government officials and business interests within the basin.

In July, key members of the California and Nevada congressional delegations met in Senator Cranston's office in Washington, D.C., and they agreed to seek federal funds to purchase the Kahle and Jennings hotel-casino sites at Stateline. But that was the extent of their agreement on federal intervention. Cranston failed in an effort to gain acceptance of a formal moratorium on casino construction elsewhere at the lake. Nor did the group support his request for a federal task force to ensure that federal funds spent in the basin would be used for purposes consistent with protecting the environment. Under these circumstances, Andrus, agreeing with Cranston's hands-off policy, left Tahoe to the regional, state, and local governments.

Environmentalists had two main alternatives: continue negotiations on revision of the bi-state compact, in spite of past disagreements and the fact that the Nevada legislature would not meet until 1979, or continue to pursue increased federal involvement, in spite of the steadfast opposition of Nevada's congressional delegation and the apparent hesitancy of federal officials to take any initiative. They pursued both avenues. The League to Save Lake Tahoe launched a campaign in support of Johnson's NRA proposal, and Charles Warren, chairman of President Jimmy Carter's council on Environmental Quality, carried on "shuttle diplomacy" between California and Nevada in efforts to revamp the TRPA.

After several months of negotiations, Warren optimistically announced agreement between the two states. Key provisions included a fourteen-member governing body in which state appointed members dominated, automatic denial of applications for projects that did not receive a majority vote from each state delegation, and a ban on new casinos. Most environmentalists hailed the Warren proposal as a major step forward, and the agreement had the support of both governors Brown and O'Callaghan. Warren needed approval only from the two state legislatures and from Congress.

The momentary optimism began to fade late in the year, when representatives of the major south shore casinos met to adopt a common policy. They called for "substantial changes" in the Warren proposal. John Gianotti, Harrah's vice-president for community relations, announced that it would be "very difficult" to obtain legislative support from Nevada unless California made major concessions, particularly regarding the continuation of local control and the elimination of the CTRPA. He warned Californians to be under no illusions: "We're never going to leave this lake. Gaming is here, it's going to be here and we're going to stay here."[36] The editors of the *Sacramento Bee* responded by calling the Nevadan pursuit of self-interest "reprehensible" and a path that could turn Tahoe into "just another tacky resort."

A concerned Warren warned: "If the two legislatures do not approve the agreement or pass different provisions, the entire effort to preserve Lake Tahoe will be disbanded and either the lake will be overwhelmed by gambling and development interests or the federal government will intrude, and establish the area as a national recreation area."[37] At the same time, a poll of more than six hundred Nevadans by the San Francisco firm of Corey, Canapary, and Galanis revealed that the majority strongly favored the kind of TRPA reform that had been agreed upon by the governors. Nevada State Senator Joe Neal, who favored the agreement, called the Tahoe issue one of "profit versus the environment" and stated that Nevada gambling interests dominated the state legislature. An ad hoc group of Nevada legislators headed by a Yerington casino owner and including State Senator Keith Ashworth, an executive of the Del Webb Corporation (which owned Sahara Tahoe), drafted its own alternative legislation.

The chances of agreement lessened early in 1979, when the newly elected governor of Nevada, Robert List rejected the position of outgoing Governor O'Callaghan. List criticized the Warren plan, attacking its "unwarranted interference" in Nevada's internal affairs.[38] Although negotiations continued throughout the spring of that year, the handwriting was on the wall. The Warren agreement, when placed before the Nevada legislature, received so many last-minute amendments that all efforts at compromise failed. California's chief negotiator, State Senator John Garamendi, blamed the "overwhelming power of the gambling industry," which, he said, "hovered around the table like vultures around a carcass."[39]

Thus by summer 1979 the situation at Tahoe had reached a

Gambling casinos rise high above forest and meadowland on Tahoe's south shore. James Hildinger.

stalemate. The Nevada legislature had adjourned, not scheduled to meet again until 1981. The federal government remained on the sidelines, unwilling to play a decisive role unless invited by both states, and Nevada steadfastly opposed federal intervention.

In the meantime, Tahoe experienced further growth and a resulting decline in environmental quality. The Park Tahoe casino, approved by the TRPA under the sixty-day rule in 1973, had opened its doors to business in summer 1978. The Stateline area reportedly had enjoyed more than a 60-percent increase in gambling tables and slot machines in a four-year period, aided by expansion within existing casinos. Proposals for massive parking structures by the big four (Harrah's, Harvey's, Sahara Tahoe, and Park Tahoe) threatened to more than double parking space to house 14,600 cars. Harrah's proposed seven-level garage alone would surpass the existing garage at the San Francisco International Airport and would be only slightly smaller in capacity than the four parking structures at the Los Angeles International Airport combined. The TRPA, once again, proved unable or unwilling to say no.

Nevada Senator Laxalt, speaking before a joint session of the Nevada legislature, had said there was "no way" a federal recreation area could be established as long as he and Senator Cannon remained in office. The Ninth Court of Appeals had ruled that construction of the high-rise hotel-casinos at Stateline could proceed. In November 1979, the U.S. Supreme Court allowed the decision to stand without comment, opening the door for major expansion. James Bruner, Jr., of the League to Save Lake Tahoe expressed bitter disappointment and looked to federal intervention as the only hope for preventing "ruination" of Tahoe "as we know it."

As the 1970s came to a close, the TRPA appeared to be dying a slow death. California refused to provide more funds, and the state's two appointed representatives resigned. The executive director followed, and the crippled agency could no longer carry out the duties mandated for it. California had lost hope of reforming the TRPA and so turned to the CTRPA to control growth on the California side of the lake. Nevada, on the other had, continued to fund the TRPA and called for acceptance of its amendments to the bistate compact.

Officials of the city of South Lake Tahoe and the five counties in the basin had by then formed the Tahoe Basin Association of Governments, an ad hoc group ready to fill the void left by the crippled TRPA. The association maintained support for home rule and favored a strengthened NTRPA. It also condemned the CTRPA, refused to send delegates to sit on its board, and announced that it would not recognize or enforce its ordinances. A lower court ruling, however, upheld the right of the CTRPA to pass and enforce ordinances, and directed local governments to abide by them.

Federal Involvement at the End of the 1970s

Faced with the ineffectiveness of the TRPA, the intransigence of local groups toward the CTRPA, and the unfavorable court verdicts on casino expansion, the League to Save Lake Tahoe and most environmentalists turned to federal intervention as the one remaining hope for Tahoe. Huey Johnson noted optimistically, "Sometimes it takes a half-dozen years, but I have never seen a national recreation proposal that's failed."[40] Nonetheless, the movement for an NRA encountered immediate resistance, and a long and difficult struggle loomed, once again, on the horizon.

Meanwhile, state and federal agencies had remained active in the Tahoe Basin. State agencies had issued occasional orders throughout the 1970s, for example, to slow or prevent additional sewer hookups until local utility districts complied with federal water quality standards. At the same time, the Environmental Protection Agency provided substantial grants to allow expansion of existing sewage disposal facilities—which helped prevent spills into the lake and the Truckee River but of course also opened the door to new construction and additional housing.

The EPA issued a major report, the *Lake Tahoe Study,* which had been requested under the 1972 Clean Water Act, sometime in the mid-1970s. Although the EPA found that federal management of Tahoe public lands was adequate for their protection, it noted that federal agencies could not control activities on private lands. It therefore recommended that Congress designate the basin an "area of national environmental significance" and declare a federal policy for the preservation of the ecological integrity of Lake Tahoe. Congress took no action, and federal agencies continued to defer to the TRPA in plans for the regulation of private land use in the Tahoe region. Thus federal agencies supported the efforts of state, regional, and local governments to resolve environmental problems, but they took no initiative to implement a national policy where there was none.

The EPA report did suggest further study of the impact that more urbanization would have on the basin and recommended the development and establishment of "environmental thresholds" to keep growth within the bounds of federal and state standards. The report argued that treating environmental problems in isolation when in fact they were interrelated no longer seemed reasonable. Instead of measuring air and water quality against some fixed standard, for example, the rate and direction of the changes could be studied. Then corrective action could be taken before a certain "threshold" of environmental quality had been exceeded.

In order to provide a clearly stated federal policy for the Tahoe Basin, the Western Federal Regional Council appointed a small task force to draft a statement that, in August 1978, was issued as the *Federal Policy for the Lake Tahoe Basin*. It declared the basin "a unique scenic and recreation resource of regional and national significance," and it called for an expanded federal role to encourage others to cooperate in maintaining environmental quality standards and to protect the uniqueness of Tahoe, stating that all federal activities and programs in the basin would be integrated and coordinated. With twenty-one federal agencies, from the Forest Service to the Coast Guard, having responsibilities in the basin, coordination would be a major undertaking. The report urged agreement on proposed revision of the bi-state compact and, meanwhile, continued federal support of the TRPA.

At about the same time, the Forest Service issued a *Land Management Plan* for national forests in the basin. It placed highest priority on protecting the water quality of Lake Tahoe, as well as on preserving the diversity and health of the biotic communities at the lake. It also allowed for the expansion of recreational facilities on public lands to better meet the needs of visitors. Among many specific recommendations, the report called for the expansion of public ownership in the basin to approximately 85 percent of the land, and for use of the land-capability system as a guide in the development and use of federal lands. The Forest Service had no control over the use of private lands, so it recommended continued cooperation with state, regional, and local governments to resolve environmental problems there.

A final Forest Service environmental impact statement in 1980 favored a plan providing that roadless areas in the basin be allocated for a variety of recreational opportunities. The plan proposed a small expansion of wilderness acreage, but it also provided for increased recreational development, primarily in heavily used areas near water attractions served by public transportation. In addition, a substantial increase in winter use was considered through the expansion of existing ski resorts at Heavenly Valley and Homewood and construction of a new resort in Ward Valley adjacent to the existing resort of Alpine Meadows. The policy of the Forest Service was to assure that opportunities for outdoor recreation reflected the public's "fair share" of capacity for use of national forest lands in the basin.

The Western Federal Regional Council generally kept a low profile, but it closed the decade on a dramatic note by issuing the *Lake Tahoe Environmental Assessment*. More than any previous study or report, this document clarified the trends at Tahoe. Based on the years 1970–1978, the study reported that such "people-related inputs" as capital and energy had increased by 125 percent. As would be expected, the influx of goods, money, and people had stimulated rapid growth in housing, transportation, public utilities, and recreational facilities. Employment had more than doubled, and the growing demand for goods and services was maintaining the pressure for more development. Government at all levels was doing its best to meet the needs of both visitors and residents in the basin, thus allowing if not encouraging the process of growth.

The permanent population of the basin by 1980 neared 60,000. Estimates of peak summer population, including tourists, varied from 124,000 by the south Tahoe visitors' bureau to 223,000 by the Forest Service. With more than seven million people within a four-hour drive of Tahoe, a reduction in the traffic seemed unlikely. It had in fact increased 80 percent during the study period.

Already the basin was violating national ambient air quality standards for carbon monoxide and ozone, and it barely met federal standards for particulates. Water quality also continued to decline rapidly in violation of federal and state nondegradation policies. Algal concentrations had increased 150 percent between 1969 and 1975, and in ten years the clarity of the water had decreased 6–13 percent.

Trends in land use were also alarming. The area of urban development had increased by 78 percent since 1970. In fact, since settlement first began in the basin, approximately 75 percent of all marshes, 50 percent of meadowlands, and 15 percent of forests had been converted to urban use or had been significantly damaged by human activity. The removal of vegetation disturbed the forest ecosystem and allowed increased erosion. Not surprisingly, the nitrogen runoff, a key element in the threat to the lake's water purity, was highest from the most developed land.

Clearly, the gambling industry contributed significantly to the environmental problems, including the sharp decline in air and water quality. An estimated 61 percent of visitors to the basin gambled, and the gambling industry continued to dominate the economy of the area. As the Western Federal Regional Council's report noted: "Gaming accounts for about 78 percent of the jobs, 41 percent of the houses, 31 percent of the tax revenues, and 43 percent of the sewage flows."[41]

What most disturbed the council were the *trends* at Lake Tahoe. The accumulation of seemingly minor decisions and activities had caused environmental problems of major magnitude. Yet there seemed no end in sight to the process by which separate decisions, often by well-meaning people, led inevitably to the degradation of the land and the lake. And, as the council noted, the federal government ironically had added to the problems. Between 1970 and 1977, for example, it had spent $34.5 million for sewage systems in

Development of high-density housing on steep hillsides, shown here near the top of Kingsbury Grade, continues despite the dangers of soil erosion and pollution of Lake Tahoe. James Hildinger.

the basin, $7.8 million for transportation, and $7.4 million for outdoor recreation facilities—and through each action had encouraged growth.

By the same token, however, the federal government had an opportunity to influence significantly future trends at Tahoe. Although the government had no direct control over urban activities, it had a substantial indirect influence. As the council's report noted: "Federal decisions to fund wastewater treatment plants, build highways, provide low and moderate income housing, provide expanded medical facilities, and provide for airport expansion all influence the nature and extent of urban development that can take place on private lands."[42]

In particular, the EPA had the power to approve state management and implementation of plans to meet federal air and water quality standards. To a significant degree, Tahoe's future rested on the ultimate decision of the EPA on proposed expansion of the basin's waste disposal system. Expansion of the system would lead inevitably to more urbanization and its consequences, including further deterioration of water quality; so many environmentalists had difficulty imagining how the EPA could approve the use of federal funds for such a purpose.

The council's report offered a clear statement of the causes and results of urbanization at Tahoe. Certainly ample material existed to document conclusively the processes that had led to development, as well as to the current environmental condition of Tahoe. Effective action was long overdue.

Regional Forester Zane G. Smith concluded that environmental deterioration was "worse than any of us thought it was." He expressed displeasure and disappointment that California and Nevada "can't get their act together." Smith revealed his interest in creating a national recreation area, adding, "I don't think we want to stand around and wait forever."[43]

1980 and Beyond

The report of the Western Federal Regional Council helped produce a flurry of attempts to resolve the myriad problems that were apparent as the 1980s began:

a proposal for a Lake Tahoe national scenic area;
a bill to sell federal land near Las Vegas to provide funds for the purchase of environmentally sensitive land at Tahoe;
a California state bond issue for $85 million for the same purpose;
an update of the CTRPA regional plan and proposals to curb growth;
a 208 plan by the California State Water Resources Control Board for controlling erosion in the basin;
creation of a Tahoe federal coordinating council;
revision of the bi-state compact that had created the TRPA.

California Congressman Vic Fazio introduced legislation early in 1980 to create a national scenic area at Lake Tahoe. Under his proposal, the Forest Service would formulate a scenic plan within two years. In the meantime, the service would administer a moratorium on all major construction. Following approval of the plan, local government could either comply with its provisions or face loss of federal aid. The Forest Service would have the power to stop harmful development and to purchase undeveloped private property for the national scenic area.

The League to Save Lake Tahoe, led by executive director James Bruner, Jr., launched a national campaign to support the Fazio bill. After a decade of failure by the TRPA and local and state governments to halt environmental decline in the basin, Bruner regarded increased federal control as the best hope to save the lake from further degradation. Several major newspapers agreed, and a *Washington Post* editorialist argued, "Tahoe's scenic qualities are on a par with those of Yosemite, Yellowstone and the Grand Canyon. They should have the same protection."[44] But the measure was defeated because of vehement opposition from Nevada's representatives and many local people.

While controversy surrounded the national scenic area proposal, environmentalists and local residents joined forces in 1980 to successfully support the Burton-Santini bill permitting the sale of approximately nine thousand acres of Bureau of Land Management property near Las Vegas. Most of the expected revenue, estimated at approximately $150 million, would be used to purchase environmentally sensitive, privately owned property in the basin. Although a California bond issue for the same purpose was narrowly defeated that year, it gained approval two years later.

In the meantime, the CTRPA had continued its efforts to contain growth on the California side of the basin. An emergency ordinance early in 1980 temporarily barred construction in stream zones and environmentally sensitive areas. Late in the year, after nearly two years of preparation, the CTRPA adopted a revised version of its 1975 regional plan. It established strict controls over construction on environmentally fragile lands, banned construction on fifty-two hundred California lots, and recommended significant changes in Tahoe's transportation system. To help finance the improvements, CTRPA staff suggested a basin user fee. The CTRPA staff hoped that major components of the agency's plan would be incorporated in a new bi-state plan to be developed by the TRPA.

During 1980 the California State Water Resources Control Board unveiled its 208 plan calling for prohibition of construction on 75 percent of the existing undeveloped lots on the California side of the basin. Carla Bard, chairwoman of the board, explained the necessity for strong action, as sedimentation from construction sites was polluting the lake at an alarming rate. Runoff from developed land and roads had increased one hundred to a thousand times natural levels. "It's as if," Bard commented, "each day of the year 22 dump trucks back up to the lake and unload."[45]

Under the plan, new subdivisions would be prohibited, lots in high erosion areas or near streams or marshes would be declared unbuildable, and erosion control projects costing an estimated $95 million would be carried out over several years. But funding for the plan and cooperation among agencies in maintaining high-quality standards throughout the basin remained in doubt.

To foster solutions to water quality and other pressing problems —solutions dependent on the cooperation of numerous government agencies—President Carter signed an executive order in October 1980 creating the Lake Tahoe Federal Coordination Council. The council had the duty of determining the carrying capacities of the basin and seeing that federal actions did not contribute to further environmental degradation. The council also could have improved the coordination between federal agencies and state and local agencies in the basin. The Reagan landslide in the November election, however, foreshadowed a sharp shift in federal environmental policy. Favoring state and local control, Reagan quickly rescinded the order creating the council.

Although efforts to increase federal responsibility in the basin failed, local Forest Service officials worked quietly behind the scenes to resurrect negotiations on the bi-state compact that had created the TRPA. Through numerous phone calls to influential persons and quiet visits with most of the principals, they assisted in arranging private meetings in Forest Service offices between California State Senator John Garamendi and Assemblyman Victor Calvo and Nevada State Senator "Spike" Wilson and Assemblyman Joe Dini. Following a candid discussion in January 1980, these legislators arranged for staff to clarify the differences that separated the two states, and the gap between them narrowed quickly.

In May, President Carter, in the midst of campaigning for the California primary election, announced his intention to strengthen the federal role in the basin, particularly if the bi-state compact were not strengthened. The following month Governor Brown, encouraged by federal interest, agreed to resume talks with Nevada officials, and Nevada's Governor List, fearful that the national scenic area proposal might gain momentum, rallied to support a revamped TRPA. Following approval of the revised compact by the California legislature, List called the Nevada legislature into a special one-day session during which it approved the proposal overwhelmingly. Finally, Congress passed the measure, which became law in December 1980.[46]

The new compact represented a compromise. The TRPA Governing Body was expanded from ten to fourteen voting members in order to reduce the power of representatives of local government. California acquired state over local representation by a four to three margin; the Nevada delegation was split three to three with a seventh member, either a state or local representative, to be selected by the other six. Voting procedures were also altered, depending on the issue under consideration. Approval of a proposed new regional plan and ordinances, for example, required an affirmative vote by at least four of the seven members of each state's delegation on the Governing Body. Approval of new projects, on the other hand, required five of the seven members from the state in which the project would be located, plus nine of the total fourteen members. The new procedures eliminated the sixty-day rule that had allowed for approval by default of projects on which the Governing Body could reach no decision. Either state could block unwanted changes in the proposed regional plan; but projects could be approved that might have the support of the majority of only one state. For example, if all members from one state approved a project on their side of the basin, it would take only an affirmative vote by two of the seven members of the other state to gain approval.[47]

The compact required a threshold and carrying capacity study to determine what kinds of development would produce undesirable and unacceptable environmental damage in the basin. After months of debate, in August 1982 the Governing Body approved stringent threshold standards for water and air quality, soil conservation, vegetation, noise, wildlife, fisheries, recreation, and scenic resources. The next step, implementation of these standards, awaited adoption of a new regional plan that would set the parameters for growth at Tahoe in the years ahead.

The compact gave the TRPA new life; at the same time, a provision stipulated that California's strong CTRPA would be phased out upon the adoption of ordinances to implement the new regional plan. Increasingly, as the TRPA has acquired added responsibilities, the future of the basin has appeared to rest in its hands. Protecting Lake Tahoe will require a major commitment of public funds and strict regulatory control in order to reduce nutrients and sediments reaching the lake. The ability of the TRPA to respond to this challenge remains to be seen.

Trends of recent years provide an unmistakable warning: as land is disturbed, degradation of the water of Lake Tahoe increases. Charles Goldman reports that the water lost 25 percent of its clarity in only fourteen years. He warns that this serious and "totally predictable" change in Lake Tahoe could destroy most of the lake's clarity in only forty years. Tahoe, once world renowned, could become "very ordinary."[48] The future quality of the environment of Lake Tahoe remains seriously in doubt.

Conclusion

The Lake Tahoe basin has been altered markedly since John Frémont first sighted the lake from a mountain peak in 1844. Although Lake Tahoe itself looks much the same today when seen from such a distance, closer inspection of the lands along its shores reveals the magnitude of human impact.

Change has come slowly. After thousands of years of summer residence at Tahoe, the Washo Indians left essentially no mark on the land, except for an occasional bedrock mortar or arrowhead. Their hunting, fishing, and gathering economy did not deplete the abundance of fish and other foods in the basin, nor did the Indians significantly alter the ecosystems of the meadows, forests, and marshes. During the early settlement of the west, whites largely bypassed Tahoe. Then construction of the Comstock Road to Nevada's mines fostered the rapid rise of a freight and tourist business in Tahoe Valley. With completion of the Central Pacific Railroad, Tahoe settled back into relative tranquillity—until lumbermen invaded the basin and cut nearly all the accessible timber. Early photographs reveal the extent to which the shoreline and surrounding hills were denuded; the resulting erosion and sedimentation undoubtedly were substantial. Nevertheless, the logging era passed relatively quickly. By the early years of the twentieth century, a second growth of timber covered the mountain slopes and the lake had recuperated from most of the damage to the quality and clarity of its water.

During the next half-century, the Tahoe Basin underwent slow growth as a summer resort area. Scattered cottages and a few lodges along the shoreline were served at first by trains to Tahoe City and steamships on the lake, and later by growing numbers of automobiles and a few buses. Most people assumed that Tahoe would remain a rustic, quiet summer retreat indefinitely. But then a series of events, including the population explosion in California, the completion of improved highways to the basin, the rapid expansion of winter recreation activities, and especially the construction of year-round casino-hotels, combined to produce a rate of urbanization that no one had expected or prepared for. By the early 1960s, a small city was emerging on the shores of south Tahoe. The Crystal Bay Development Company had begun the construction of Incline Village, and small communities elsewhere around the lake mushroomed in size.

As a result of this urban boom, all aspects of environmental quality within the Tahoe Basin declined. Emissions from vehicles on the congested roads created smog, reduced visibility, and often exceeded the national ambient air quality standards for carbon monoxide and ozone. Marshes and meadowlands, the habitat of many wildlife species, increasingly succumbed to the bulldozer. Even more alarming, the crystal-clear waters of Lake Tahoe revealed signs of increased pollution in spite of the introduction of a modern sewage disposal system that pumped effluent out of the basin. The growth of algae in the lake appeared to be increasing at an exponential rate, and the clarity of its water lessened.

The total impact of urbanization, like the fact of Tahoe's growth, had not been foreseen. Here was development with no apparent end in sight. The water of Lake Tahoe was given no hiatus to recover from the onslaught of nutrients from sewage, construction sites, landfills, dredging, storm run-off from parking lots, and the like. Even when the damage was not visible to the casual observer, anyone accustomed to swimming at Tahoe could not help noticing the steady accumulation of slippery green vegetation on the once clean rocks along the shoreline. Nor could one ignore the traffic congestion, or the parade of neon lights and billboards on the approach to the south shore casinos. Those who had known

Tahoe in an earlier day felt deeply the loss of serenity and beauty that once had been its hallmark.

No one had proposed or consciously planned that the Tahoe Basin become urbanized; but a multitude of individual and governmental decisions—and the attraction of Tahoe's scenic wonders—inevitably flooded the basin with people. Of course alternatives have existed, then as now. But with the passage of time, setting aside all or a major portion of the basin as a public park or forest has become increasingly difficult and expensive.

Tahoe has long been regarded as a scenic asset of national significance, and it could have been one of the nation's first and finest national parks. Its beauty and promise as an outdoor recreation center rivaled Yosemite. Only the misfortune of circumstances, especially the concern that large landowners of timberland in the basin might benefit unduly from a lieu land exchange, blocked a national park proposal. And in later years, the National Park Service itself defeated suggestions for a national park by arguing that the basin no longer had the pristine condition required for such designation.

Although Congress failed to set aside the Tahoe Basin as a national park, the federal government did protect large tracts of timberland within national forests. Over the years the Forest Service has added to the publicly owned lands at Tahoe. Since 1973 and the creation of a single management unit for all national forests in the basin, these lands have been managed in an orderly fashion—primarily for the purpose of outdoor recreation. In addition, the states of California and Nevada have established several notable state parks, and their beaches and campgrounds have received very heavy use.

Despite efforts to protect portions of the basin from commercial development, most of the prized shoreline remains in private hands. On these lands the urbanization has taken place and the major difficulties have arisen. Local governments have been unable to resolve the environmental and social problems resulting from the essentially unchecked growth; it was expecting too much to hope that they could solve regional problems for which they lack the political capabilities and financial means. Also, it has become evident that political control at the local level more often than not has fallen to those whose short-term economic interests benefit from continued growth. Local government has a legitimate role at Tahoe, but only within the framework of an effective and enforceable regional plan based on the interests of a much broader spectrum of citizens and on long-term considerations.

Similarly, efforts at cooperation between Nevada and California have largely failed. Neither state has an unblemished record; the hotel-casinos of Nevada rest side by side with the subdivisions and strip development of California. State control has shortcomings in any case because the basin is a fragile ecosystem that would be best managed as a whole.

One choice remains untried: some kind of direct federal control. Many local and some state officials have long been suspicious of, if not hostile to, any kind of federal management of the Tahoe Basin, and the federal government has avoided such intervention. Yet if the TRPA under the revised bi-state compact fails once again, increased federal control appears to be the only viable authority that could enforce a regional plan dedicated to the environmental protection of Tahoe. Creation of a national scenic or recreation area would by itself be no panacea for Tahoe's problems, however. The effectiveness of such an area—like the effectiveness of the TRPA—would depend on adequate funding, political acceptability, cooperation in pursuit of goals, and administrative skill.

Despite the severity of Tahoe's environmental problems, much has been accomplished to protect the lake and its surroundings. The concerted efforts of many dedicated people have led to: stabilization of the lake level within a six-foot range; establishment of several state parks and extensive national forests; curtailment of highway construction throughout the basin, and protection of the mouth of Emerald Bay and its neighboring state parks from a freeway; restrictions on the expansion of new casinos; export of sewage effluent from the basin; extensive research yielding an improved understanding of the detrimental impact of people on the ecosystem of the basin; heightened public awareness of the environ-

Emerald Bay (foreground) would not have retained its remarkable scenic beauty without the efforts of concerned citizens. James Hildinger.

mental problems of Tahoe, resulting in increased political efforts to find solutions.

Some years ago, planners defined the carrying capacity of the land in the Tahoe Basin in relation to its ability to tolerate use without sustaining permanent damage. Although the concepts of environmental threshold and carrying capacity have often been disregarded by decision makers, they remain valuable. The principle of a carrying capacity could provide a workable base for the regulation of privately and publicly owned land—if it were properly understood and enforced.

Ideally, decisions affecting the environment of Tahoe should be made in accord with an environmental ethic that puts the health of the land before economic expediency. As American naturalist Aldo Leopold suggested many years ago: "Examine each question in terms of what is ethically and esthetically right, as well as what is economically expedient. A thing is right when it tends to preserve the integrity, stability, and beauty of the biotic community. It is wrong when it tends otherwise."[1]

Tahoe cannot be returned to its earlier days of quiet beauty and serenity. The demand for recreational opportunity alone precludes such a possibility. But it could evolve and be maintained in the future as an outdoor scenic and recreational area of high quality. The high-rise casino-hotels, which never should have been built in the midst of a scenic national treasure, might someday decline in importance, particularly if California decides to legalize gambling in selected locations elsewhere in the state. If that should happen, the urban problems that the casinos helped generate might be substantially reduced.

The heart of Tahoe's environmental problems is urbanization. The solution lies in the political arena. The citizen and taxpayer is the one who, ultimately, must decide what Tahoe should be. And in wrestling with the knotty problems of Tahoe they will be wrestling with but a part—albeit a dramatic part—of the larger problems of urbanization and environmental degradation that face Americans in all corners of the land. In their struggles to find solutions, as in the solutions they work out, those concerned with the Tahoe Basin are both providing warnings and pointing directions.

Notes

Preface

1. U.S. Congress, Senate Subcommittee on Air and Water Pollution of the Committee on Public Works, Hearings, *Environmental Problems of the Lake Tahoe Basin,* 92nd Cong., 2d sess., August 21, 1972, 57.

2. Charles R. Goldman, "Bad News from Lake Tahoe," *Cry California* 3 (Winter 1967–68): 12.

3. Joseph LeConte, *A Journal of Ramblings through the High Sierra of California* (San Francisco: Sierra Club, 1960), pp. 133, 138.

1 The Tahoe Basin: Natural History and Early Days

1. Warren L. d'Azevedo, ed., *The Washo Indians of California and Nevada* (Salt Lake City: University of Utah Press, 1963), p. v.

2. Brevet Col. J. C. Frémont, *The Exploring Expedition to the Rocky Mountains, Oregon and California* (Buffalo: Geo. H. Derby, 1852), p. 334.

3. G. H. G., "Lake Bigler," *Hutchings California Magazine* 2 (September 1857): 107.

4. "Description of Lake Bigler," *Daily Alta California* (San Francisco), July 7, 1859.

5. "Lake Tahoe," *Sacramento Daily Union,* August 13, 1863.

6. E. A. Sterling, "Report on the Forest Condition in the Lake Tahoe Region, California," June 1904, p. 4, copy in Forestry Library, University of California, Berkeley.

7. Quoted in "Mountain Vandalism," *Pacific Coast Wood and Iron* 12 (September 1889): 70.

8. Charles H. Shinn, "Report on the Proposed Addition to the Lake Tahoe Forest Reserve, California," October 31, 1902, p. 12, in Drawer 134, Research Compilation File, Records of the U.S. Forest Service, Record Group 95, National Archives, Washington, D.C. (hereinafter cited as RG 95).

2   *Urbanization of the*
     Tahoe Basin: 1900–1960

1. Lake Tahoe Railway and Transportation Company, *Tahoe Tavern, Lake Tahoe, California* [1905?], a promotional brochure, copy in Bancroft Library, University of California, Berkeley.

2. A. J. Wells, *Lake Tahoe and the High Sierra* (San Francisco: Southern Pacific, 1906), p. 9.

3. *Tallac* (n.d.), a promotional brochure, copy in Bancroft Library.

4. Wells, *Lake Tahoe,* p. 2.

5. "Great Project Designed to Draw Millions to State," *San Francisco Call,* May 18, 1912; and "California Will Share Its Scenic Gifts" (editorial), *San Francisco Call,* May 19, 1912.

6. According to one account, the summer tourist trade flourished as the wealthy from the San Francisco Bay Area, who could no longer afford to go to Europe, replaced the middle class, who could not afford to come to Tahoe. Conversation with Frank Globin as reported to the author by Kenneth C. Smith.

7. *Tahoe Vacation Guide* ([Tahoe City] published by *Tahoe Tattler* [1940]), copy in Bancroft Library.

8. "Toward a Unified Tahoe Area," *Tahoe Tattler,* September 2, 1938.

9. "Tahoe Nightlife," *Tahoe Tattler,* August 8, 1941.

10. *San Francisco Chronicle,* August 2, 1948.

11. State Engineers of Nevada and California, *Joint Report on the Use of Water in the Lake Tahoe Watershed* (June 1949), pp. 7–8.

12. John Ward, "South Lake Tahoe Resort Areas Mushroom," *Sacramento Bee,* February 25, 1957.

13. "South Tahoe Resort Construction Starts," *Sacramento Bee,* June 4, 1959.

14. "Industrial Development," in Industrial Committee, El Dorado County Chamber of Commerce, *The Economic Resources of Western El Dorado County* [1963?].

15. Raymond Smith, "A Preliminary Survey and Analysis of Planning and Development Problems: Lake Tahoe Portion of Washoe County, Nevada," Lake Tahoe Area Council, *Topic Report no. 5* (April 1960), p. 20.

3   *Parks and Forests*

1. John Muir, "Lake Tahoe in Winter," *Sierra Club Bulletin* 3 (May 1900): 122–23, repr. from the *San Francisco Bulletin*.

2. David A. D'Ancona, *A California-Nevada Travel Diary of 1876*, ed. William M. Kramer (Santa Monica: Norton B. Stearn, 1975), pp. 35–36.

3. Captain George M. Wheeler, *Report upon United States Geographical Surveys West of the One Hundredth Meridian* (Washington, D.C.: GPO, 1889), pp. 103–4.

4. "Lake Tahoe," *Truckee Tribune*, September 7, 1878.

5. The name Bigler, after California's third governor, was used only in official state government circles; others used the popular designation Lake Tahoe.

6. "Report of the Lake Bigler Forestry Commission," in *Appendix to the Journals of the Senate and Assembly in the Twenty-Sixth Session of the Legislature of the State of California,* pt. 5 (Sacramento, 1885), p. 12.

7. Telegram from White and Perkins to Secretary of the Interior, October 20, 1896, Box 151 (Division R, National Forests, Tahoe), Records of the Bureau of Land Management, Record Group 49, National Archives, Washington, D.C. (hereinafter cited as RG 49, Box 151).

8. Warren Olney to S. W. Lamoreaux, October 26, 1896, RG 49, Box 151.

9. Jordan to Cornelius N. Bliss, April 2, 1897, RG 49, Box 151.

10. Allen to Commissioner, September 24, 1897, RG 49, Box 151.

11. Mills to Binger Hermann, December 17, 1897, RG 49, Box 151.

12. "Remonstrance," n.d., RG 49, Box 151.

13. *United States Statutes at Large,* 31: 1953–54.

14. Muir, "The Wild Parks and Forest Reservations of the West," *Atlantic Monthly* 81 (January 1898): 17.

15. George B. Sudworth, "Stanislaus and Lake Tahoe Forest Reserves: California and Adjacent Territory," *Twenty-First Annual Report of the United States Geological Survey to the Secretary of the Interior, 1899–1900,* pt. 5: "Forest Reserves" (Washington, D.C.: GPO, 1900), p. 560. See also W. C. Bartlett, "A Year in Forest Reservations," *Overland Monthly* 35 (March 1900): 247–49.

16. Marsden Manson, "Observations on the Denudation of Vegetation: A Suggested Remedy for California," *Sierra Club Bulletin* 2 (June 1899): 298.

17. Gifford Pinchot, "Report on Examinations of the Forest Reserves," Senate Doc. 189, *Senate Documents Miscellaneous,* 55th Cong., 2d sess. (1897–98).

18. Stewart to Mills, September 4 and December 19, 1899, William M. Stewart Papers, Nevada Historical Society, Reno, Nevada. See also an editorial written by Mills entitled "Are We Unwittingly Destroying a State," *San Francisco Post,* June 21, 1899.

19. *San Francisco Examiner,* February 27, 1900.

20. Petition enclosed with letter from DeVries to Hermann, March 13, 1900, RG 49, Box 151.

21. "Senator Stewart's Reply," *San Francisco Examiner,* March 24, 1900.

22. Newhall's report, December 18, 1900, RG 49, Box 151.

23. Muir to Newhall, December 1, 1900, RG 49, Box 151. The directors of the Sierra Club, however, unanimously supported the expansion of forest reserves around Lake Tahoe in their resolution dated November 24, 1900, copy in ibid.

24. Charles H. Shinn, "Report on the Proposed Addition to the Lake Tahoe Forest Reserve, California," p. 12, RG 95.

25. California Water and Forest Association, *Should the Forests Be Preserved?* (1903), p. 6.

26. Hermann to Register and Receiver, Sacramento, December 24, 1902, RG 49, Box 151; "Proposed Extension of the Lake Tahoe Forest Reserve," n.d., handwritten draft, ibid.

27. California Water and Forest Association, *Should the Forests Be Preserved?* p. 12.

28. *Sacramento Evening Bee,* May 9, 1903.

29. Diary of Albert F. Potter, Conservation Library, Denver Public Library, Denver, Colorado.

30. Stewart to the President, October 8, 1903, RG 49, Box 151.

31. Acting Commissioner to Secretary of the Interior, January 18, 1904, and E. A. Hitchcock to Commissioner, February 17, 1904, RG 49, Box 151.

32. *Report of the Commissioner of the General Land Office, 1905* (Washington, D.C.: GPO, 1905), pp. 213–14; *Report . . . , 1906,* pp. 196–97; *United States Statutes at Large,* 34 (October 3, 1905): 3163.

33. Harold French, "The Fremont National Park," *Sierra Club Bulletin* 8 (June 1911): 141. See also "Tahoe National Park Aim of Knowland Bill," *San Francisco Call,* April 4, 1912.

34. Knowland to Walter L. Fisher, March 4, 1912, Box 630, File 12–0 Lake Tahoe, Central Classified File, Proposed National Parks (0–32), Records of the National Park Service, Record Group 79 (hereinafter cited as RG 79), National Archives, Washington, D.C.

35. Albright to Bliss, November 29, 1918, ibid.

36. Townsend to Albright, April 14, 1931, and Albright to Townsend, April 24, 1931, ibid.

37. Quotations above are from Toll to Director, April 30, 1932, attached to W. P. Mott, "Proposed Lake Tahoe National Park," December 13, 1935, Box 2951, File 0–51 Tahoe, Central Classified File 1933–49, Proposed National Parks (0–32), RG 79.

38. Most of the following discussion of land acquisition is based on [Andrew R. Schmidt], "The Role of the United States Forest Service and Other Federal Agencies in the Evolving Political, Social and Economic Microcosm of the Lake Tahoe Basin: An Historical Brief" (USDA Forest Service, June 1979), typescript copy in author's files, pp. 172–86.

39. Joseph H. Engbeck, Jr., *State Parks of California* (Portland: Graphic Arts Center, 1980), pp. 47–55.

40. Frederick Law Olmsted, *Report of the State Park Survey of California* (Sacramento: State Printing Office, 1929).

41. Jack P. Stowe, "Know Your Parks: Tahoe State Park," *News and Views* 14 (January 1957): 10; and author's interview of Joseph H. Engbeck, Jr., 1979.

42. Thomas W. Miller, "The Genesis and Programs of the Nevada State Park System," *Planning and Civic Comment* 24 (June 1958): 47–49.

43. U.S. Congress, Senate, *Congressional Record,* 74th Cong., 1st sess., 1935, 79: 4899; and 75th Cong., 1st sess., 1937, 81: 3574; and 77th Cong., 1st sess., 1941, 87: 3037.

44. *Park, Parkway and Recreational Area Study* (Carson City: State Printing Office, 1938), p. 80.

45. Houghteling to Gould, June 23, 1961, Margaret Wheat Papers, Nevada Historical Society, Reno. For a useful summary of events 1961–63, see the report of the California Commission on Interstate Cooperation, *Lake Tahoe Interstate Park* (Sacramento: Senate of the State of California, 1963).

46. Minutes of the first interstate park commission meeting, November 18, 1961, Nevada State Park Advisory Commission 1955–65 file. Office of Nevada Division of State Parks, Carson City, Nevada.

47. Elmo J. De Ricco, "Historical Report, Acquisition Program, Lake Tahoe State Park," January 23, 1968, Office of Nevada Division of State Parks; Samuel G. Houghton, "At Last! A Park for Lake Tahoe," *Nevada Highways and Parks* 25 (Spring 1965): 4–15, 58; and Theodore J. Wirth and Associates, *A Land Use Plan for Lake Tahoe State Park, Nevada* (n.p. [1969]).

4   *Water Use and Quality*

·1. "Tahoe Sanitary Problems Studied," *Reno Evening Gazette,* July 22, 1947.
2. "Renoan Proposes Two State Control For Lake Tahoe," *Sacramento Bee,* December 13, 1948.

5   *Planning and Conflict*

1. Raymond M. Smith, "An Exchange of Correspondence Relative to Philosophies of Future Planning for the Lake Tahoe Area," in Lake Tahoe Area Council, *Topic Report no.* 9 (May 1960), pp. 4–5; and Alvin S. Trivelpiece, "Aide Gives Brighter View of Tahoe on Nevada Side," *Sacramento Bee,* March 20, 1957.
2. Raymond F. Smith, "Objectives of a Planning Program at Lake Tahoe," in Lake Tahoe Area Council, *Topic Report no.* 7 (June 1960), p. 3.
3. *Lake Tahoe News,* May 16 and June 20, 1957.
4. California Assembly Committee on Natural Resources, Planning and Public Works, *Regional Planning in the Lake Tahoe Basin,* 1966, app., p. 284.
5. *Lake Tahoe* [December 1965?], copy in unprocessed file, Nevada Historical Society, Reno.
6. Typescript of CBS program entitled, "Can Lake Tahoe Be Saved?" Channel 2, Los Angeles, February 1, 1966.
7. Jeff Brown, "Tahoe Notebook," *Holiday* 38 (December 1965): 78.
8. "Monumental Challenge At Tahoe," *San Francisco Chronicle,* November 28, 1965.
9. "Orderly Development of Tahoe Is of Prime Interest," *Reno Evening Gazette,* January 12, 1957.
10. Quoted in W. Turrentine Jackson, *Early Planning Efforts at Lake Tahoe: The Role of Joseph F. McDonald, 1956–1963* (Davis: University of California Institute of Governmental Affairs, 1974), p. 14.
11. "Nevada Man Is Named Tahoe Council Planner," *Sacramento Bee,* August 26, 1959.
12. Robert A. Burco, *Policy and Planning in the Lake Tahoe Basin: The Case of Transportation* (Davis: University of California Institute of Governmental Affairs, 1973), on p. 43.
13. Ken R. White Company, *1985 Development Plan: Lake Tahoe, Douglas County, Nevada* (1964), pp. 32, 35.

14. "Lake Tahoe: The Future of a National Asset: Land Use, Water and Pollution," *California Law Review* 52 (August 1964): 619.

15. Edmond Constantini and Kenneth Hanf, *The Environmental Impulse and Its Competitors: Attitudes, Interests and Institutions at Lake Tahoe* (Davis: University of California Institute of Governmental Affairs, 1973), p. 28.

16. Quoted in Jackson, *Early Planning Efforts*, p. 57.

17. Engineering Science, Inc., *Comprehensive Study on Protection of Water Resources of Lake Tahoe Basin through Controlled Waste Disposal* (June 1963), p. 128.

18. A. W. West and K. M. Mackenthun, *Report on Pollution in the Lake Tahoe Basin, California-Nevada* (Cincinnati: U.S. Department of the Interior, Federal Water Pollution Control Administration, 1966), p. 38.

19. J. T. Leggett and F. R. McLaren, "The Lake Tahoe Water Quality Problem: History and Prospectus," *California Water Pollution Control Association Bulletin* 6 (October 1969): 6–8.

20. Charles R. Goldman, *Eutrophication of Lake Tahoe Emphasizing Water Quality* (Corvallis, Ore.: U.S. Environmental Protection Agency, 1974), p. 11.

21. Russell L. Culp and Harlan E. Moyer, "Wastewater Reclamation and Export at South Tahoe," *Civil Engineering* 39 (June 1969): 38.

22. James E. Pepper and Robert E. Jorgensen, *Influences on Wastewater Management on Land Use: Tahoe Basin, 1950–1972* (Washington, D.C.: U.S. Environmental Protection Agency, 1974), p. 2. See also Western Federal Regional Council Interagency Task Force, *Lake Tahoe Environmental Assessment* (1979), pp. 205, 211.

23. Alfred E. Heller, "Lake Tahoe: Time for Tough Federal Action," *Cry California* 1 (Winter 1965–66): 29.

24. California Assembly Interim Committee on Natural Resources, Planning and Public Works, *Regional Planning in the Lake Tahoe Basin*, January 1967, p. 22 (Assembly interim reports, 1965–67, vol. 25, no. 6). See also Gary J. Spradling, "Regional Government for Lake Tahoe," *Hastings Law Journal* 22 (February 1971): 708.

25. *Report of the Lake Tahoe Joint Study Committee* (March 1967), p. 7.

26. Ibid., p. 5.

27. "Tahoe Chamber Raps Regional Agency Plan," *Sacramento Bee*, July 10, 1967.

28. Editorials, *San Francisco Examiner*, May 18 and July 2, 1969.

29. "Z'Berg Opposes Compromise on Tahoe Compact," *Sacramento Bee*, January 25, 1968.

30. "Solon's Unit Kills Tahoe Bill," *Sacramento Bee*, March 21, 1968; "Reagan Blast Over Tahoe Bill," *San Francisco Chronicle*, March 22, 1968.

31. "Nevada Tahoe Plan Is Turned Down By Assembly Unit," *Sacramento Bee*, March 21, 1968.

32. Raymond G. Davis, *Regional Government for Lake Tahoe: A Case Study* (Davis: University of California Institute of Governmental Affairs, 1970), pp. 22–23.

33. Spradling, "Regional Government for Lake Tahoe," p. 731.

34. "Fight Over Tahoe's Trip to Moon," *San Francisco Chronicle*, July 8, 1969.

35. Raymond M. Smith, *Nevada Tahoe General Plan* (January 1970), pp. 15–16.

6   *The Tahoe Regional Planning Agency: The Emperor's New Clothes*

1. "Laxalt and Reagan Make It Official," *Tahoe Daily Tribune*, March 17, 1970.

2. Mike Hayden, *Guidebook to the Lake Tahoe Country*, 2 vols. (Los Angeles: Ward Ritchie, 1971), 2: 65.

3. William Bronson, "It's About Too Late for Tahoe," *Audubon* 73 (May 1971): 52.

4. For an analysis of efforts to coordinate the planning activities of the TRPA and its academic consultants, and a discussion of problems of communication with public interest groups, see James E. Pepper, "An Approach to Environmental Impact Evaluation of Land-Use Plans and Policies: The Tahoe Basin Planning Information System," Master's thesis, City Planning, University of California, Berkeley, 1972.

5. Robert G. Bailey, *Land Capability Classification of the Lake Tahoe Basin, California-Nevada* (South Lake Tahoe: USDA Forest Service in cooperation with the TRPA, 1974), p. 5.

6. Quoted in Kathleen Agena, "Tahoe," *Planning* 38 (January 1972): 8.

7. The figure of 134,000 was misleading: Smith considered neither the existing density of population nor subdivisions previously approved. If he had, his estimate would have been much higher.

8. William E. Felts and Geoffrey Wandesforde-Smith, *The Politics of Development Review in the Lake Tahoe Basin* (Davis: University of California Institute of Governmental Affairs, 1973), p. 11.

9. John D. Ayer, "A Trip through the Fiscal Wilderness," *California Journal* 3 (January 1972): 13–15.

10. Western Federal Regional Council Interagency Task Force, *Lake Tahoe Environmental Assessment* (1979), p. 208. See also U.S. Congress, Senate Subcommittee on Air and Water Pollution of the Committee on Public Works, Hearings, *Environmental Problems of the Lake Tahoe Basin,* 92d Cong., 2d sess., August 21, 1972, pp. 11, 17–21, 42.

11. Letter to Senator Edmund Muskie in ibid., p. 57.

12. "Preservation of Tahoe's Natural Areas Gains Widespread Attention," *Lake Tahoe* 4 (October 31, 1961): 1, 4.

13. "S. 2208: Introduction of a Bill," in U.S. Congress, Senate, *Congressional Record,* 91st Cong., 1st sess., 1969, 115: 13069.

14. *United States Statutes at Large,* 84 (September 26, 1970): 882.

15. Department of the Interior, Bureau of Outdoor Recreation, *Strategies to Save a Lake* (September 1971), p. 74.

16. Economic Research Associates, *Economic Analysis of Projected Growth for the Lake Tahoe Basin* (October 1971), pp. II-2 and II-3.

17. Quoted in Bronson, "It's About Too Late," p. 77.

18. Ibid., p. 61.

19. "Status of Casino Lawsuit," *Tahoe Reflections* (November 1974): 5.

20. Quoted in Chris Bowman, "Impact of Added Casinos Is Cited," *Sacramento Bee,* January 26, 1977.

21. Oliver Kahle, "An Economic Assessment," *Tahoe Reflections* (November 1974): 6.

22. "Tahoe Ruling Pleases List, Not Younger," *Sacramento Bee,* October 7, 1975.

23. Quoted in Ira Heyman, "The Great 'Property Rights' Fallacy," *Cry California* 3 (Summer 1968): 33.

24. Gale Cook, "Storm of Emotions Buffet Lake Tahoe," *San Francisco Chronicle,* June 23, 1974.

25. "Tough Tahoe Building Rules OKd," *San Francisco Chronicle,* July 13, 1974.

26. "Tahoe Plan Views Differ," *Tahoe Daily Tribune,* June 26, 1975.

27. "Regional Report–CTRPA News," *Tahoe Reflections* (March 1976): 6.

28. Quoted in Cilla Brown, "Tahoe Planning Goals Are Widely Different," *Sacramento Bee,* February 9, 1976.

29. David Johnston, "Building Boom to End at Lake Tahoe," *Los Angeles Times,* March 28, 1977.

30. Raymond M. Smith, "Building Patterns: Lake Tahoe" (April 9, 1974), typed copy in the Tahoe Collection, El Dorado County Free Library, South Lake Tahoe Branch.

31. Editorials, *Los Angeles Times,* November 4, 1973, and *San Francisco Chronicle,* September 30, 1973.

32. *Sacramento Bee,* July 15, 1973.

33. "TRPA Deserves Tyler Award," *Tahoe Daily Tribune,* November 30, 1973.

34. "Andrus Weighs Tahoe Snafu," *Sacramento Bee,* June 16, 1977.

35. "Lake Tahoe Tomorrow," California Resources Agency news release, December 12, 1977, copy in author's files.

36. "Casino Fight," *Sacramento Bee,* November 18, 1978.

37. "Nevada's Tahoe Stand Draws Ire," *Sacramento Bee,* January 19, 1979.

38. "State of the State Address," *Nevada State Journal,* January 18, 1979.

39. "Nevada Relents—OKs BiState Pact," in "This World" in the *San Francisco Chronicle,* June 3, 1979.

40. "U.S. Role Urged at Tahoe," *San Francisco Chronicle,* May 23, 1979.

41. Western Federal Regional Council, *Lake Tahoe Environmental Assessment,* p. 192.

42. Ibid., p. 205.

43. "Lake Tahoe Nearing Crisis Stage, Forest Officials Say," *Sacramento Bee,* August 16, 1979.

44. "Save Lake Tahoe," *Washington Post,* January 24, 1980.

45. Quoted in "Building Ban Sought," *Lake Tahoe News,* January 23, 1980.

46. *United States Statutes at Large,* 94 (December 19, 1980): 3232.

47. The compact forbade any new casinos not previously approved, but casinos already built could expand the area devoted to gambling up to 15 percent within existing buildings. Earlier in the year, the Forest Service purchased Ted Jenning's twenty-acre site for the Tahoe-Palace hotel-casino for $11.5 million. In 1982, Douglas County, led by County Commission Chairman Ken Kjer, and the state of Nevada purchased the Kahle site for $2.8 million.

48. Tom Martens, "'Alarming Deterioration' in Lake Tahoe Clarity," *Tahoe World,* May 28, 1982.

Conclusion

1. Aldo Leopold, *A Sand County Almanac* (New York: Oxford University Press, 1949), pp. 224–25.

Bibliographical Essay

This book is based primarily on published and unpublished records located in the following libraries and archives: the general and specialized libraries of the University of California at Berkeley, including the Agriculture, Anthropology, Bancroft, Biology, Earth Sciences, Environmental Design, Forestry, Graduate Social Science, and Law libraries; the Water Resources Center Archives located on the University of California campus in Berkeley; the University of Nevada Library in Reno; the Nevada Historical Society in Reno; the Nevada State Library in Carson City; the California State Library in Sacramento; the Institute of Governmental Affairs Library at the University of California in Davis; the U.S. Forest Service headquarters library at South Lake Tahoe; the Tahoe Regional Planning Agency library at South Lake Tahoe; and the National Archives in Washington, D.C. The most valuable single collection consulted, the Lake Tahoe Area Council library, is currently located in the El Dorado County Free Library, South Lake Tahoe Branch.

Bibliographies

Two useful bibliographical guides to the study of Lake Tahoe are available. Maureen Trimm, comp., *Lake Tahoe—A Bibliography: Its History, Natural History and Travel Guides* (Sacramento: Mountain Valley Library System, 1977) is the result of a cooperative effort by twenty-five academic, public, and special libraries constituting the Sierra Libraries Information Consortium. This bibliography, arranged alphabetically by author, includes the location of each citation in the cooperating libraries in northern California and western Nevada. James R. Jones, comp., *Inventory of Research Activities in the Lake Tahoe Area:*

A Bibliography, 1845–1976 (South Lake Tahoe: Lake Tahoe Area Research Coordination Board, 1976), issued by the board and the Nevada State Library, is a computerized list of 1,098 citations directly related to environmental research on the Lake Tahoe area. Jones divides the 219-page volume into seven main topics (air, land, water, vegetation, animal life, socio-economic, and other factors) and then into subtopics within each category. An extensive subject and author index and a location guide to each document add greatly to the usefulness of this bibliography.

General Historical Studies

Despite the extensive published material on Tahoe, broad general studies of the Tahoe Basin and its history are limited in number. Edward B. Scott, *The Saga of Lake Tahoe* (Crystal Bay, Calif.: Sierra-Tahoe Publishing, 1957), emphasizes the nineteenth century and devotes a short chapter to every historically important community in the Tahoe Basin. Bliss Hinkle and George Hinkle, *Sierra-Nevada Lakes* (Indianapolis: Bobbs-Merrill, 1949), is also most useful on early events at Tahoe. John and Ricky Warriner, *Lake Tahoe: An Illustrated Guide and History* (San Francisco: Fearon, 1958), depends heavily on the Scott and Hinkle studies.

There are several more recent and scholarly studies. Donald J. Pisani, "Storm Over the Sierra: A Study in Western Water Use," Ph.D. diss., Department of History, University of California, Davis, 1975, deals authoritatively with the struggle to control Tahoe's water from the 1860s to the 1970s. Paul F. Mackey provides a valuable interpretive essay, "Evolution of Land Use Patterns in the Lake Tahoe Basin with Emphasis on the Spatial Patterns Resulting from Early Transportation and Mining Developments," in J. R. Evans and R. A. Mathews, eds., *Geologic Studies in the Lake Tahoe Area, California,* annual field trip guidebook of the Geological Society of Sacramento (1968), pp. 67–81. Paul Francis Mungan, "A History of the Recreational Development at Lake Tahoe and Its Effects upon the Environment," Master's thesis, Recreation Administration, Sacramento State College, 1971, is descriptive, sketchy, and based on limited sources. The Tahoe Regional Planning Agency and U.S. Forest Service, *Cultural and Historical Significance of the Lake Tahoe Region: A Guide for Planning* (South Lake Tahoe, 1971), emphasizes the early construction of roads and contains good maps of logging activities and historical and archaeological sites.

Newspapers

Many newspaper articles are cited in the notes, as well as later in this bibliography. The most useful newspapers consulted were published in cities and towns in northern California and western Nevada, particularly San Francisco, Sacramento, South Lake Tahoe, Reno, and Carson City. Indexes exist for the *San Francisco Chronicle* and the *Los Angeles Times,* but only for the past few years. The California State Library in Sacramento has a card index (of uneven quality) for major San Francisco newspapers in the early twentieth century. The Nevada Historical Society has begun a project to index selected Nevada newspapers.

1   The Tahoe Basin:
     Natural History and Early Days

Brief descriptions of Tahoe's geology and natural history have appeared in recent years. See, e.g., *Report of the Lake Tahoe Joint Study Committee* (March 1967), pp. 42–46; J. R. Crippen and B. R. Pavelka, *The Lake Tahoe Basin: California-Nevada,* U.S. Geological Survey Water-Supply Paper no. 1972 (Washington, D.C.: GPO, 1970), pp. 2–23; and U.S. Environmental Protection Agency, *The Lake Tahoe Study* [1975?] pp. 13–21, 49–54. John H. Burnett discusses the "Geology of the Lake Tahoe Basin" in *California Geology* 24 (July 1971): 119–30. Also useful is N. J. Hyne et al., "Quarternary History of Lake Tahoe, California-Nevada," *Geological Society of America Bulletin* 83 (May 1972): 1435–48. The Tahoe Regional Planning Agency and the U.S. Forest Service jointly published a series of pamphlets in 1971 on various aspects of Tahoe's physical environment as a guide for planning. This series includes titles on climate, land resources, fisheries, geology, hydrology, limnology, wildlife, soils, and vegetation.

An excellent description of Indian life and cultural change after contact with whites is presented in James F. Downs, *The Two Worlds of the Washo* (New York: Holt, Rinehart and Winston, 1966). Also useful is [Jo Ann Nevers] *Wa She Shu: A Washo Tribal History* (Reno: Inter-Tribal Council of Nevada, 1976), which is based in part on recent interviews with Washo. An introduction to the extensive archaeological and anthropological literature is provided in Warren L. d'Azevedo, ed., *The Washo Indians of California and Nevada* (Salt Lake City: University of Utah Press, 1963). In particular, note d'Azevedo's preface and a review of research to 1963 by John A. Price. Material specifically on Washo activity in the Tahoe Basin can be found in Stanley A. Freed, "Washo Habitation Sites in the Lake Tahoe Area," *University of California Archaeological Survey Reports,* no. 66 (February 1966): 78–83; the previously cited Tahoe Regional Planning Agency and U.S. Forest Service, *Cultural and Historical Significance of the Lake Tahoe Region: A Guide for Planning* (South Lake Tahoe, 1971), pp. 18–28; and recent unpublished studies by the Nevada Archaeological Survey of the University of Nevada in Reno (Jonathan O. Davis, Robert Elston, and Gail Townsend, "A Preliminary Archeological Reconnaissance of Fallen Leaf Lake" [1974], and Robert Elston et al., "The Archeology of the Tahoe Reach of the Truckee River" [1977]).

Several studies provide valuable information on early explorations, surveyors, and road builders in the Tahoe Basin. Francis P. Farquhar, *History of the Sierra Nevada* (Berkeley: University of California Press, 1965), is excellent on nineteenth-century events. Several general studies mentioned earlier have specific material on Tahoe. See Edward B. Scott, *The Saga of Lake Tahoe* (Crystal Bay, Calif.: Sierra-Tahoe Publishing, 1957), Paul F. Mackey, "Evolution of Land Use Patterns in the Lake Tahoe Basin . . . ," in J. R. Evans and R. A. Mathews, eds., *Geologic Studies in the Lake Tahoe Area, California,* annual field trip guidebook of the Geological Society of Sacramento (1968), pp. 67–74; and TRPA and U.S. Forest Service, *Cultural and Historical Significance,* pp. 4–12. See also John Debo Galloway, "Early Engineering Works Contributory to the Comstock," *University of Nevada Bulletin,* 41 (June 1947): 23–102. Stewart Mitchell's "Crossing the Sierra," *California Highways and Public Works* 28–29 (September 9, 1950): 49–68, emphasizes routes across the northern Sierra.

Reports of explorers and government surveyors provide some of the earliest eyewitness accounts of the Tahoe Basin. For example, see Brevet Col. J. C. Frémont, *The Exploring Expedition to the Rocky Mountains, Oregon and California* (Buffalo: Geo. H. Derby, 1852), p. 334; William M. Eddy, *Annual Report of the Surveyor General* (of California) (December 15, 1852), copy in Bancroft Library; George H. Goddard, "Report of a Survey of a Portion of the Eastern Boundary of California," *Annual Report of the Surveyor-General of the State of California* (1856), copy in Bancroft Library; William Brewer's journal in Francis P. Farquhar, ed., *Up and Down California in 1864* (New Haven: Yale University Press, 1930); and the report of Lt. M. M. Macomb on a survey trip of 1876 in George M. Wheeler, *Report upon United States Geographical Surveys West of the Hundredth Meridian* (Washington, D.C.: GPO, 1889).

The general studies mentioned earlier, particularly Scott's *The Saga of*

Lake Tahoe, also provide detailed information on Tahoe's early settlements. Firsthand accounts of visits to Tahoe are too numerous to list. Newspapers, especially those published in San Francisco, Sacramento, Truckee, Reno, and Carson City, provide a wealth of information. See, e.g., "Tahoe As It Is," June 25, 1872; "Navigation on Lake Tahoe," June 14, 1873; "The Hotels around Lake Tahoe," July 17, 1873; "Resources of Tahoe," June 2, 1875; "Trip to Lake Tahoe," June 30, 1877; and "Lake Tahoe and Its Surroundings," June 26, 1880—all in the *Truckee Republican.* Also note "Lake Tahoe As A Resort," *Sacramento Daily Record-Union,* July 6, 1889. For a valuable case study of land ownership and development in the vicinity of Camp Richardson, see [John Townley] *Historical and Architectural Research: South Lake Tahoe Estates* (San Francisco: U.S. Forest Service [1974?]). William Brewer's description of the Washoe trade is contained in Farquhar, ed., *Up and Down California,* pp. 438–39.

Mining never became an important activity in the basin. Agriculture is discussed in newspaper accounts. For additional information on the impact of grazing, see Tahoe Regional Planning Agency and U.S. Forest Service, *Land Resources of the Lake Tahoe Region: A Guide for Planning* (South Lake Tahoe, 1971), pp. 17–18, 21. For fishing, see Tahoe Regional Planning Agency and U.S. Forest Service, *Fisheries of Lake Tahoe and Its Tributary Waters: A Guide for Planning* (South Lake Tahoe, 1971); Hubert Howe Bancroft, *History of Nevada, Colorado, and Wyoming, 1540–1888* (San Francisco: History Company, 1890), p. 241; Chancey Juday, "Notes on Lake Tahoe, Its Trout and Trout Fishing," *Bulletin of the Bureau of the Fisheries* 26 (1906): 133–46; and Almo J. Cardone and Ted C. Frantz, "The Lake Tahoe Sport Fishery," *California Fish and Game* 52 (October 1966): 240–62.

The materials available on lumbering and railroads at Tahoe are extensive. In addition to the general works already cited, Donald J. Pisani, "Lost Parkland: Lumbering and Park Proposals in the Tahoe-Truckee Basin," *Journal of Forest History* 21 (January 1977): 4–17, provides a valuable appraisal of logging and preservation efforts in the basin in the nineteenth century. The technical aspects of the logging industry are well treated in David F. Myrick, *Railroads of Nevada and Eastern California* (Berkeley: Howell-North, 1962), 1: 416–37; Gilbert H. Kneiss, *Bonanza Railroads* (Stanford: Stanford University Press, 1941), pp. 52–68; John Debo Galloway, "Early Engineering Contributory to the Comstock," *University of Nevada Bulletin* 41 (June 1947): 23–102; and Swift Berry, *Lumbering in the Sugar and Yellow Pine Region at California,* U.S. Department of Agriculture Bulletin no. 440 (Washington: GPO, 1917). Constance Darrow Knowles's unpublished manuscript "A History of Lumbering in the

Truckee Basin from 1856–1936" is instructive on logging practices in the vicinity of the Tahoe Basin and contains valuable detailed information; available in the Forestry Library at the University of California, Berkeley. Newspapers, particularly the *Truckee Republican* and the *Carson Daily Appeal,* reported regularly on logging activity at Tahoe.

Several reports by government agencies and forestry agents provide graphic descriptions of the impact of unwise logging practices: *Fifth Biennial Report of the State Forester of the State of California* (Sacramento: State Printing Office, 1914), pp. 48–49; Charles H. Shinn, "Report on the Proposed Addition to the Lake Tahoe Forest Reserve, California," October 31, 1902, in Drawer 134, Research Compilation File, Records of the U.S. Forest Service, Record Group 95, National Archives, Washington, D.C.; and E. A. Sterling, "Report on the Forest Fire Condition in the Lake Tahoe Region, California," June 1904, copy in Forestry Library, University of California, Berkeley. For a useful guide to newspaper and periodical articles on this topic, see U.S. Forest Service, California Forest and Range Experiment Station, *Bibliography of Early California Forestry* (n.p., n.d.); vols. 9 and 10 deal with El Dorado County and vols. 39 and 40 with Placer County.

Other materials on the lumbering era appear in scattered sources. For example, Duane L. Bliss is discussed in an anonymous article, probably from the files of Hubert H. Bancroft, in the Duane L. Bliss Papers, Bancroft Library; Samuel Clemens' account of his visit to Tahoe is included in *Roughing It* (Hartford, Conn.: American Publishing, 1884), pp. 168–77; James Horace Gardner provides a brief account of logging at south Tahoe in "Pioneer Days in Tahoe Region," *Timberman* 30 (August 1929): 178–79; and Alan Briggs briefly discusses the same topic in "Logging, Fishing Once Thrived at South Lake Tahoe," *Tahoe Daily Tribune,* February 28, 1975.

2   *Urbanization of the*
     Tahoe Basin, 1900–1960

There is no general study of the Tahoe Basin in the twentieth century. Edward B. Scott's *Saga of Lake Tahoe* (Crystal Bay, Calif.: Sierra-Tahoe Publishing, 1957), which concentrates on the nineteenth century, contains only fragmentary information after 1900. George Wharton James, *The Lake of the Sky: Lake Tahoe* (Pasadena: George Wharton James, 1915), provides a description of life at Tahoe in the early twentieth century. A series of articles in the *Sacramento Union* (May 17, 24, and 31, 1953) traces changes in tourism at Tahoe from the 1920s to the early

1950s. For the years immediately after World War II, see W. Turrentine Jackson and Donald J. Pisani, *From Resort Area to Urban Recreation Center: Themes in the Development of Lake Tahoe, 1946–1956,* Environmental Quality Series no. 15 (Davis: University of California Institute of Governmental Affairs, 1973), a study based largely on newspaper records. The Lake Tahoe Area Council's collection, at the El Dorado County Free Library, South Lake Tahoe Branch, contains newspaper clippings on Lake Tahoe from the late 1950s and early 1960s.

Changes in attitude toward nature and travel in the American West in the early twentieth century are discussed in such books as Earl Pomeroy, *In Search of the Golden West* (New York: Alfred A. Knopf, 1957), and Peter J. Schmitt, *Back to Nature: The Arcadian Myth in Urban America* (New York: Oxford University Press, 1969). Tourism at Lake Tahoe at the turn of the century is described in several promotional brochures located in the Bancroft Library. See, e.g., Lake Tahoe Railway and Transportation Company, *Lake Tahoe* (1899), and *Tahoe Tavern, Lake Tahoe, California* [1905?]; *Sierra Highlands* (San Francisco: H. S. Crocker, n.d.); A. J. Wells, *Lake Tahoe and the High Sierra* (San Francisco: Southern Pacific, 1906); and Southern Pacific Company, *The Tahoe Country* (1915). Newspapers are a good source of information on tourism, although data is scattered and difficult to find. The variety of resorts at Tahoe in the 1930s, e.g., is revealed in a full page of advertisements in the *San Francisco Chronicle,* June 20, 1934. For a list of resorts at Tahoe, see Lake Tahoe Sierra Association, *Lake Tahoe* [1940], copy in Bancroft Library.

Information on transportation can be pieced together from such sources as the following: Marco Varozza, *Report of the Lake Tahoe Wagon Road Commissioner, 1898* (Sacramento, 1899); Stewart Mitchell, "Crossing the Sierra," *California Highways and Public Works,* 28–29 (September 9, 1950): 64–69; "Lake Tahoe via Pierce Arrow Stage and Oakland, Antioch and Eastern Railway," an advertisement [1919], copy in Bancroft Library; "Fine Highway Will Soon Link Tahoe Resorts," *San Francisco Call,* December 1, 1912; "Last Link to be Built for All Year Road," *Tahoe Tattler,* July 7, 1939; *Tahoe Vacation Guide* ([Tahoe City] published by *Tahoe Tattler* [1940]), copy in Bancroft Library; "The Lake of the Sky," July 12, 1925, and "Two Roads to Lake Tahoe," August 7, 1927, in the *San Francisco Examiner;* and Bliss Hinkle and George Hinkle, *Sierra-Nevada Lakes* (Indianapolis: Bobbs-Merrill, 1949), pp. 354–55. Proposals for an electric railway from Reno to Tahoe are noted in David F. Myrick, *Railroads of Nevada and Eastern California* (Berkeley: Howell-North, 1962), 2: 867–73, and in articles in the *Daily Nevada State Journal* (Reno) on August 6 and September 24, 1905, and July 17, October 17, and December 16, 1906. Also see "Electric Railroad to Tap Important Resorts," *San Francisco Chronicle,* August 22, 1907.

Mention of proposed subdivisions is made in "Beautiful Lake Tahoe and Emerald Bay," *Daily Nevada State Journal,* August 12, 1906; and "Great Project Designed to Draw Millions to State," *San Francisco Call,* May 18, 1912; James, *The Lake of the Sky,* pp. 230–31. For a personal account of promotional activities at the north shore between 1927 and 1933, see Norman H. Blitz, "Memoirs of the 'Duke of Nevada,'" an interview by Mary Ellen Glass, November–December 1967, typescript copy, Special Collections, University of Nevada Library, Reno.

The north Tahoe zoning conflict is discussed in "North Tahoe Splits on Re-Zoning," August 19, 1938, and "Club to Present Program to Re-Zone to County Board: Opponents to Fight," August 26, 1938, in the *Tahoe Tattler.* Later issues of zoning and building codes are discussed in Jackson and Pisani, *From Resort Area to Urban Recreational Center.* Newspapers are once again an indispensable source. See, e.g., a series of articles by William B. Carr, Jr., that explains the controversy over a proposed north Tahoe shopping center, in the *Sacramento Bee,* April 19 and 21–24, 1959.

For historical information on skiing, see J. H. Hildebrand, "A History of Ski-ing in California," *British Ski Year Book,* ed. Arnold Lunn, vol. 10 (1939), pp. 64–78; Hal Cole, "Skiing at Tahoe: a 120-year Saga," *Tahoe Daily Tribune,* February 28, 1975; and J. E. "Jerry" Carpenter, *California Winter Sports and the VIIIth Winter Olympic Games, 1960, at Squaw Valley* (San Francisco: Fearon, 1958). Also see "McGlashan Known as Journalist" and Arthur Broughton, "Donner Summit's Ski Areas Opened in '30s," March 28, 1975, and Bill Jensen, "Hilltop, Granlibakken Were 1st Areas," April 16, 1976, in *Sierra Sun Bonanza* (Truckee).

There is no history of the gambling industry at Lake Tahoe. Russell R. Elliott, *History of Nevada* (Lincoln: University of Nebraska Press, 1973), pp. 248, 278–83, 334–37, briefly discusses the history of gambling in Nevada. A brief sketch of Harvey Gross appears in W. K. Bixler, *A Dozen Sierra Success Stories* (Tahoe Valley: Sierra Magazine, 1964), pp. 75–84. For a critical evaluation of the strategies used to attract customers to Tahoe casinos, see Keith Munroe, "The New Gambling King and the Social Scientists," *Harper's Magazine* 224 (January 1962): 35–41. Newspapers provide useful information; for example, see John Morris, "Gaming: Logging Camps to Big Industry," and "Cal-Neva Known for Rustic Look," in *Tahoe Daily Tribune,* February 28, 1975. Also note "Hard Work, Drive Toward Perfection Key to Success" and John Morris, "Harvey Gross Key Figure in Tahoe Growth," in *Tahoe Daily Tribune,* July 2, 1976; and Bill Friel, "Gambling: A Key to the Reno–Lake Tahoe Success Story," *Oakland Tribune,* March 17, 1974.

Statistical data for 1945–60 is contained in such documents as the following: State Engineers of Nevada and California, *Joint Report on the Use of Water in the Lake Tahoe Watershed* (June 1949); "Statistical Data," compiled by the South Lake Tahoe Chamber of Commerce [c. 1970]; [South Shore, Lake Tahoe, Chamber of Commerce] *Lake Tahoe* [1965?], copy in unprocessed files, Nevada Historical Society, Reno; and "Industrial Development" in Industrial Committee, El Dorado Chamber of Commerce, *The Economic Resources of Western El Dorado County* [1963?].

3 Parks and Forests

This chapter is based on my article "Preservation Efforts at Lake Tahoe, 1880 to 1980," *Journal of Forest History* 25 (April 1981): 78–97.

For an account of preservation efforts at Tahoe before 1900, see Donald J. Pisani, "Lost Parkland: Lumbering and Park Proposals in the Tahoe-Truckee Basin," *Journal of Forest History* 21 (January 1977): 4–17. Early action by California in regard to forestry at Tahoe is explained in C. Raymond Clar, *California Government and Forestry,* vol. 1 (Sacramento: Division of Forestry, Department of Natural Resources, State of California, 1959) pp. 83–96; and Gerald D. Nash, "The California State Board of Forestry," *Southern California Quarterly* 47 (September 1965): 292–95. Also see *Report of the Lake Bigler Forestry Commission to Governor George Stoneman* (Sacramento: James J. Ayres, Supt. State Printing, 1884). This report also appears in *Appendix to the Journals of the Senate and Assembly of the Twenty-Sixth Session of the Legislature of the State of California,* pt. 5 (Sacramento, 1885), pp. 5–15.

Substantial records exist for the critical years (1896–1905) during which the most serious efforts were made to establish a national park or forest reserve within the Tahoe Basin. The best and most extensive collection is contained in pts. 1–2, Box 151 (Division R, National Forests, Tahoe), Records of the Bureau of Land Management, Record Group 49, National Archives, Washington, D.C. This file contains correspondence, filed reports, petitions, and other important material. Included is correspondence of senators George C. Perkins, Stephen M. White, and William M. Stewart; field reports of B. F. Allen and C. S. Newhall; statements by the secretaries of the Department of the Interior, commissioners of the General Land Office, and lesser officials who held office during this period; petitions for and against preservation efforts by prominent California and Nevada citizens and organizations; and miscellaneous correspondence from interested parties, including Warren Olney and John Muir of the Sierra Club and William Thomas of the California Water and

Forest Association. The William M. Stewart Papers, including materials of Charles J. Kappler, at the Nevada Historical Society, Reno, also contain extensive records, particularly relating to Stewart's national park proposal.

The events of 1896–1902 are well documented in the collections just noted, but there is a notable gap in the critical record of 1902–1905, when major acreage was set aside in the expanded Lake Tahoe Forest Reserve. Department of the Interior records for Tahoe are sparse for 1904 and 1905, and U.S. Forest Service records do not begin in detail until 1907. Among existing documents for this period, the following are especially useful: Charles H. Shinn, "Report on the Proposed Addition to the Lake Tahoe Forest Reserve, California," October 31, 1902, in Drawer 134, Research Compilation File, Records of the U.S. Forest Service, Record Group 95, National Archives, Washington, D.C.; and the diary of Albert F. Potter (1903) in the Conservation Library of the Denver Public Library, Denver, Colorado. An extensive earlier report, based on an 1899 reconnaissance, has limited value because the Lake Tahoe Forest Reserve is not discussed separately: George B. Sudworth, "Stanislaus and Lake Tahoe Forest Reserves: California, and Adjacent Territory," *Twenty-First Annual Report of the United States Geological Survey to the Secretary of the Interior 1899–1900,* pt. 5: Forest Reserves (Washington, D.C.: GPO, 1900), pp. 499–561.

Although no administrative history of the national forests in the Tahoe Basin exists, extensive administrative records are deposited both in the National Archives and in the Federal Archives and Records Center, San Bruno, California. In addition, the Forest Service office for the Tahoe National Forest in Nevada City, California, has retained some historical records. [Andrew R. Schmidt] "The Role of the United States Forest Service and Other Federal Agencies in the Evolving Political, Social and Economic Microcosm of the Lake Tahoe Region, A Historical Brief" (USDA Forest Service, 1979), typescript copy in author's files, emphasizes recent events but contains some references to the early days in the national forests.

Information on national park proposals at Tahoe, except for Stewart's proposal in 1900, is sparse. The best data on later proposals is contained in File 12–0 Lake Tahoe, Box 630, Proposed National Parks (0–32), Central Classified File, Records of the National Park Service, Record Group 79, National Archives; and in File 0–51 Tahoe, Box 2951, Proposed National Parks (0–32) Central Classified File 1933–49, ibid.

Joseph H. Engbeck, Jr., *State Parks of California* (Portland, Ore.: Graphic Arts Center, 1980) provides a valuable history of the California state park system. *News and Views,* published monthly by the California state park system, has some material on parks at Tahoe, e.g., Jack P. Stowe, "Know Your Parks: Tahoe State Park," 14 (January 1957): 10–13; Keith Carpenter, "Know Your Parks: Emerald Bay State Park," 14 (May 1957): 5–7; and "New Tahoe Park Named," (August 1978): 2. Newspapers contain considerable data on negotiations leading to the acquisition of property for the California parks in the Tahoe Basin: e.g., "Gift to State," *San Francisco Chronicle,* June 29, 1928; "Tahoe Lands OK'd for Park Project," *San Francisco Examiner,* December 16, 1928; "CCC Boys Put Rubicon Point Park in Shape," *Tahoe Tattler,* June 28, 1935; "State Will Expand Emerald Bay State Park," *Sacramento Bee,* August 21, 1953. Although no history of an individual California state park at Tahoe has been written, some information on the parks is available in "Unit History Emerald Bay" and "Memorandum to All Area Managers from Department of Parks and Recreation District 3, July 1, 1974," both at headquarters library, Sugar Pine Point State Park; see also W. James Barry, "Burton Creek Project," in the same collection. The status of state park proposals at Tahoe in the 1960s is reviewed in Resources Agency, Department of Parks and Recreation, Division of Beaches and Parks, *Lake Tahoe Region Study* (May 1965).

The early history of the movement to establish state parks in Nevada is discussed in Thomas W. Miller, "The Genesis and Programs of the Nevada State Park System," *Planning and Civic Comment* 24 (June 1958): 47–49, and in Nevada State Planning Board and the Nevada State Park Commission, *Park, Parkway and Recreational Area Study* (Carson City: State Printing Office, 1938). Extensive material on Nevada parks is contained in the Thomas W. Miller Papers, Special Collections, University of Nevada Library, Reno. The history of the establishment of the Sand Harbor State Beach can be traced through the "Minutes," Nevada State Park Commission, Office of the Nevada Division of State Parks, Carson City. Several articles of interest were published in the Reno and Carson City newspapers.

The efforts to establish a bi-state park are outlined in "Summary and Chronology: Lake Tahoe Interstate Park Discussions," in Report of the California Commission on Interstate Cooperation, *Lake Tahoe Interstate Park* (Senate of the State of California [Sacramento], 1963). The origin of the bi-state concept is discussed in a letter from Joseph Houghteling to Leslie Gould, June 23, 1961, in the Margaret Wheat Papers, Nevada Historical Society, Reno. The minutes of the first interstate park comission meeting, November 18, 1961, are contained in the Nevada State Park Advisory Commission 1955–1965 file, Office of Nevada Division of State Parks, Carson City, Nevada.

Information on the establishment of the Lake Tahoe Nevada State Park is contained in the minutes of the Nevada State Park Commission, noted earlier. Also useful is Samuel G. Houghton, "At Last! A Park for Lake Tahoe," *Nevada Highways and Parks* 25 (Spring 1965): 4–15, 58, and Donald B. Alexander, "Close Call At Lake Tahoe," *Parks and Recreation* 1 (February 1966): 146–48. Arguments in support of the park are contained in Nevada Wildlife Federation, "Proposed Lake Tahoe Park Fact Sheet" (n.p., n.d.). For a list of private lands on the Nevada side of the basin, see Myron Wall and Associates, *Recreation Land Classification,* prepared for the Nevada Department of Conservation and Natural Resources (August 1963). See also *Information Report: Proposed Lake Tahoe Park,* prepared at the request of Governor Grant Sawyer by the State Department of Conservation and Natural Resources (Carson City: December 17, 1963). Background on the condemnation suit against Whittell is presented in Elmo J. De Ricco, "Historical Report, Acquisition Program, Lake Tahoe State Park" (Office of Nevada Division of State Parks, Carson City, 1968). For planning efforts, see Theodore J. Wirth and Associates, *A Land Use Plan For Lake Tahoe State Park, Nevada* [1969].

4   Water Use and Quality

Probably more has been written about environmental problems related to the water of the Tahoe Basin than about any other issue except the Tahoe Regional Planning Agency. The topic of water can be divided into two subtopics: 1) the question of water rights, or who should be allowed to utilize the water and for what purpose, and 2) the question of water quality, a problem related primarily to the influx of people to the basin after World War II. The most extensive single work on the history of water use in the Tahoe region is Donald J. Pisani, "Storm Over the Sierra: A Study in Western Water Use," Ph.D diss., Department of History, University of California, Davis, 1975. The best general article on the allocation and use of Tahoe water, as well as the early response to water pollution problems, is Carl R. Pagter and Cameron W. Wolfe, Jr., "Lake Tahoe: The Future of a National Asset—Land Use, Water, and Pollution," *California Law Review* 52 (August 1964): 563–622. This article is based in part on a collection of forty documents located in G37935, J4-3, supp., in the Water Resources Center Archives, University of California, Berkeley.

For material on von Schmidt's proposal to divert water to California, see Pisani, "Why Shouldn't California Have the Grandest Aqueduct in the World? Alexis von Schmidt's Lake Tahoe Scheme," *California Historical*

Quarterly 53 (Winter 1974): 347–60. The original proposal is contained in A. W. von Schmidt, *Report to the Lake Tahoe and San Francisco Water Works Company* (San Francisco: Alta California, 1871). Also see James A. Waymire, *Diverting Water from Lake Tahoe for Use in California* [San Francisco: Argus, 1907?].

The topic of water use, particularly for irrigation, is treated extensively in several articles by Pisani: "Federal Reclamation and Water Rights in Nevada," *Agricultural History* 51 (July 1977): 540–58; "Conflict over Conservation: The Reclamation Service and the Tahoe Contract," *Western Historical Quarterly* 10 (April 1979): 168–89; "Western Nevada's Water Crisis, 1915–1935," *Nevada Historical Society Quarterly* 22 (Spring 1979): 3–20; and "The Strange Death of the California-Nevada Compact: A Study in Interstate Water Negotiations," *Pacific Historical Review* 47 (November 1978): 637–58.

W. Turrentine Jackson and Pisani have written two studies that deal more specifically with Tahoe: *A Case Study in Interstate Resource Management: The California-Nevada Water Controversy, 1865–1955* (Davis: California Water Resources Center, 1973); and *Lake Tahoe Water: A Chronicle of Conflict Affecting the Environment, 1863–1939* (Davis: University of California, Institute of Governmental Affairs, 1972). Other articles on water rights prior to World War II include Mary Ellen Glass, "Hot Summer in the Sierra: An Early Contest for Resource Rights at Lake Tahoe," *California Historical Quarterly* 51 (Winter 1972): 306–14; and Richard G. Lillard, "Trouble over Tahoe Water," *Progress-Bulletin* (Los Angeles City College) 1 (April 1942): 19–28. Also note Bliss Hinkle and George Hinkle, *Sierra-Nevada Lakes* (Indianapolis: Bobbs-Merrill, 1949), pp. 336–45.

Brief historical sketches of water resources and use at Tahoe are contained in J. R. Crippen and B. R. Pavelka, *The Lake Tahoe Basin: California-Nevada*, U.S. Geological Survey Water-Supply Paper no. 1972 (Washington, D.C.: GPO, 1970); and Tahoe Regional Planning Agency and U.S. Forest Service, *Water Resources in the Lake Tahoe Region* (South Lake Tahoe, 1971). Legal issues are discussed in Keith Creighton King and Earl Warren, Jr., "The Tahoe Controversy: Compact or Litigation?" (1959), mimeographed, copy in author's files. See also Norris Hundley, Jr., "The Dark and Bloody Ground of Indian Water Rights: Confusion Elevated to Principle," *Western Historical Quarterly* 9 (October 1978): 455–82.

Useful data on early efforts for reclamation in western Nevada are contained in "Truckee-Carson Project: Outline History, 1906–1912," in the Truckee-Carson Project files, Records of the Bureau of Reclamation,

Record Group 115, Denver Federal Archives and Record Center. See also U.S. Congress, House, *Truckee–Carson–Lake Tahoe Project,* 62nd Cong., 2d sess., 1912, H. Doc. 451, pp. 130–41.

Contemporary articles on the water controversy in the early twentieth century include G. S. Arnold, "The Lake Tahoe Controversy," *California Outlook* 10 (April 1, 1911): 9–10; "Public Use of the Waters of Lake Tahoe," in George Wharton James, *The Lake of the Sky: Lake Tahoe* (Pasadena: George Wharton James, 1915), pp. 353–58; and Stewart Edward White, "Easy Dollar! Shoot It Quick!" *Saturday Evening Post,* August 14, 1920, pp. 32–34, 90. Newspaper articles are, once again, a valuable source of information.

Two excellent articles explore the issue of Tahoe's water use and quality in the years after World War II: John Ayer, "Water Quality Control at Lake Tahoe: Dissertation on Grasshopper Soup," *Ecology Law Quarterly* 1 (Winter 1971): 3–61; and Pagter and Wolfe, "Lake Tahoe." Also see Joan Gibson Reid, "Pollution of Lake Tahoe: A Brief Summary," a staff report to the California Assembly Interim Committee on Water (November 1, 1965); Carl F. Grove and Robert A. Sowers, "An Analysis of the Carrying Capacity of the California/Tahoe Region: Water Quality Element," in [CTRPA] *An Analysis of the Carrying Capacity of the California/Tahoe Region* (1977), 3–23; J. T. Leggett and F. R. McLaren, "The Lake Tahoe Water Quality Problem: History and Prospectus," *California Water Pollution Control Association Bulletin* 6 (October 1969): 6–11; and Deane Seeger, "Sewage Disposal and Water Pollution Control in the Lake Tahoe Basin, 1960–1964," Lake Tahoe Area Council, *Topic Report* (64–1), in the Tahoe Collection, El Dorado County Free Library, South Lake Tahoe Branch. Further references on water quality in the 1960s and 1970s appear in the bibliography to chaps. 5 and 6. A list of many of the government publications related to Tahoe water is presented in James R. Jones, comp., *Inventory of Research Activities in the Lake Tahoe Area: A Bibliography, 1845–1976* (South Lake Tahoe: Lake Tahoe Area Research Coordination Board, 1976).

5   *Planning and Conflict*

Most of the important events of the 1950s and 1960s, especially the efforts to establish some form of regional government within the Lake Tahoe Basin, are discussed in W. Turrentine Jackson, *Early Planning Efforts at Lake Tahoe: The Role of Joseph F. McDonald, 1956–1963,* Environmental Quality Series no. 18 (Davis: University of California Institute of Governmental Affairs, 1974), and W. Turrentine Jackson and

Terry L. Dailey, *Environmental Planning Efforts at Lake Tahoe: The Evolution of Regional Government, 1963–1968,* Environmental Quality Series no. 19 (Davis: University of California Institute of Governmental Affairs, 1974). McDonald's papers are located in Special Collections, University of Nevada Library, Reno. As noted earlier, the best and most extensive collection of documents relating to environmental questions about Lake Tahoe in the postwar era is the Lake Tahoe Area Council's collection, El Dorado County Free Library, South Lake Tahoe Branch. In that collection see Walter J. Hopp and Gail F. Linn, "Tahoe's Environmental Problems and Regional Controls with a History and Analysis of the Tahoe Regional Planning Compact" (September 1970), mimeographed. Newspapers provide an especially rich resource for information on these years; see, e.g., a series of five articles on environmental concerns at Tahoe by Donald M. Richardson in the *Sacramento Bee,* June 3–7, 1963.

For discussion of local response to urban problems, see W. Turrentine Jackson and Donald J. Pisani, *From Resort Area to Urban Recreation Center: Themes in the Development of Lake Tahoe, 1946–1956,* Environmental Quality Series no. 15 (Davis: University of California Institute of Governmental Affairs, 1973). Two useful local publications are Fred M. Schultz, "Early History of the Lake Tahoe Area Council," Lake Tahoe Area Council, *Topic Report* no. 2 (December 1959); and Raymond M. Smith, "Survey of the Planning Agencies within the Lake Tahoe Basin," Lake Tahoe Area Council, *Topic Report no.* 6 (May 1960).

The literature on waste disposal is extensive. See the bibliography to chap. 4, especially the articles by Ayer, Pagter and Wolfe, Seeger, and Reid. A useful analysis is James E. Pepper and Robert E. Jorgensen, *Influences of Wastewater Management on Land Use: Tahoe Basin, 1950–1972* (Washington, D.C.: U.S. Environmental Protection Agency, 1974). For a description of the sewage disposal system, see Russell L. Culp and Harlan E. Moyer, "Wastewater Reclamation and Export at South Tahoe," *Civil Engineering* 39 (June 1969): 38–42.

The Emerald Bay Bridge controversy is discussed in newspaper accounts including those of the *Lake Tahoe News, Tahoe Daily Sierra Tribune, Mountain Democrat* (Placerville), *Placerville Times, Reno Evening Gazette, Nevada State Journal* (Reno), *Sacramento Bee, San Francisco Examiner,* and *San Francisco Chronicle.* The position of Newton Drury is also stated in *News and Views* 14 (November 1957): 2–3.

Economic and population trends in the 1960s can be traced in such publications as Economic Research Associates, *Economic Analysis of Projected Growth for the Lake Tahoe Basin* (October 1971); [South Shore, Lake Tahoe, Chamber of Commerce] *Lake Tahoe* [1965?], copy in unprocessed file, Nevada Historical Society, Reno; Raymond M. Smith,

"Reconnaissance Report: Lake Tahoe Basin Area," mimeographed, prepared for the Nevada Tahoe Regional Planning Commission (1968), copy in the Tahoe Collection, El Dorado County Free Library, South Lake Tahoe Branch; and "California: After 19 Million, What?" *Population Bulletin* 22 (June 1966): 29–57.

The complex story of the creation of the Tahoe Regional Planning Agency is discussed succinctly in Gary J. Spradling, "Regional Government for Lake Tahoe," *Hastings Law Journal* 22 (February 1971): 708–15. An expanded account that closely follows Spradling's article is included in chap. 3 of Jackson and Dailey, *Environmental Planning Efforts at Lake Tahoe.* For other accounts of the formation of the TRPA and a discussion of its initial problems, see Raymond G. Davis, *Regional Government for Lake Tahoe: A Case Study* (Davis: University of California Institute of Governmental Affairs, 1970), and Don E. Lane, "Portrait of Conflict: The Tahoe Regional Planning Agency" (n.d.), mimeographed, copy in author's files. For further references on the TRPA, see the bibliography for chapter six.

6   *The Tahoe Regional Planning Agency: The Emperor's New Clothes*

The sources for the 1970s, particularly newspapers, periodicals, and government publications, are voluminous. The TRPA attracted national interest, much of it critical. See, e.g., Dewey Anderson, "Lake Tahoe: Then and Now," *National Parks Magazine* 44 (April 1970): 4–11; William Bronson, "It's About Too Late for Tahoe," *Audubon* 73 (May 1971): 46–80; Steven Brandt, "What's Going Wrong at Tahoe," *Sierra Club Bulletin* 56 (December 1971): 8–10; Gary J. Spradling, "Regional Government for Lake Tahoe," *Hastings Law Journal* 22 (February 1971): 705–31; Steven Brandt, "It's the Public's Turn at Tahoe," *Sierra Club Bulletin* 58 (April 1973): 22–24; Tahoe Research Group, "Tahoe's Troubled Waters," *Natural History* 84 (January 1975): 60–67; Thomas Graham, "Tahoe Regional Planning," *Sierra Club Bulletin* 60 (March 1975): 25–31; Charles R. Goldman and Thomas H. Cahill, "Danger Signs for Tahoe's Future," *Cry California* 10 (Spring 1975): 30–35; Sherwood Stockwell, "Balancing Private and Public Interests: Conservation and Development at Lake Tahoe," *Urban Land* 35 (March 1976): 3–12; Walt Anderson, "The Tahoe Troubles," *Cry California* 13 (Summer 1978): 27–31; James W. Bruner, Jr., "What Will We Tell Our Kids about Lake Tahoe," *National Parks and Conservation Magazine* 54 (May 1980): 9–12; Hal Rubin, "The Umpteenth Attempt at Preserving Lake Tahoe,"

California Journal 12 (January 1981): 21–23; and Rubin, "Lake Tahoe: A Tale of Two States," *Sierra* 66 (November-December 1981): 43–47. A useful review of the TRPA from 1965 to 1977 and of issues and trends in 1977 is included in William R. Eadington and James S. Hattori, "Public Policy and Lake Tahoe: Economic Issues and Legislative History," *Nevada Review of Business and Economics* 1 (Spring 1977), 2–10.

Cathleen Agena provides an insightful look at the earliest years of TRPA's efforts at planning in "Tahoe," *Planning* 38 (January 1972): 3–16. Laurel W. Ames covers much the same topic in "The Real Life Adventures of a Planning Agency," *California Journal* 3 (January 1972): 12, 16–17. In the same issue, John D. Ayer discusses economic causes of Tahoe sub-urbanization in "A Trip through the Fiscal Wilderness," 13–15. For a review of the TRPA compact and legal issues up to 1975, see "Tahoe Regional Planning Agency: An Overview," (September 1975), mimeo-graphed, copy in the TRPA office, South Lake Tahoe. Paul Meyer, *What Is TRPA? A Bureaucratic Hassle, An Eco-Sell-Out, or a Pragmatic Problem Solver?* [Davis: University of California Institute of Governmental Affairs, 1975], covers the same time period. Dr. Robert Twiss provides an insider's view of the TRPA in "Regional Planning: 1970, 1975, and Where Do We Go From Here," *Proceedings: Lake Tahoe Research Seminar VI* (September 29, 1975), 26–37. For a useful discussion of problems of early planning efforts by the TRPA and consultants, see James E. Pepper, "An Approach to Environmental Impact Evaluation of Land-Use Plans and Policies: The Tahoe Basin Planning Information System," Master's thesis, City Planning, University of California, Berkeley, 1972. Two other docu-ments of particular value for study of the early 1970s are Economic Re-search Associates, *Economic Analysis of Projected Growth for the Lake Tahoe Basin* (October 1971); and Raymond M. Smith, *Nevada Tahoe General Plan* (January 1970).

The actual day-to-day activities of the TRPA are revealed in TRPA records and in newspaper accounts. In addition, the United States Office of Management and Budget published monthly reports on the TRPA in "5520 Wildland Studies," copies in U.S. Forest Service headquarters, South Lake Tahoe. Sari Sommarstrom provides an excellent case study of the TRPA and the planning process involving the shore zone and water quality in "The Land-Water Interface in Inland Lake and Its Implications for Ecological Planning," Ph.D. diss., Resource Planning and Conser-vation, University of Michigan, 1976. A valuable collection of material is contained in U.S. Congress, Senate Subcommittee on Air and Water Pollution of the Committee on Public Works, Hearings, *Environmental Problems of the Lake Tahoe Basin,* 92nd Cong., 2d sess., August 21, 1972; this document includes *The Lake Tahoe Plan and Effectuating Ordi-*

nances, TRPA and Forest Service reports on nearly all aspects of social and environmental concerns in the Tahoe Basin in 1971, and testimony from the hearings. The "Smith plan" is presented in Tahoe Regional Planning Agency, *Proposed Regional Plan: Lake Tahoe Region, California-Nevada* (South Lake Tahoe, 1971). Most of the scientific and government reports of the first half of the decade are listed in James R. Jones, comp., *Inventory of Research Activities in the Lake Tahoe Area: A Bibliography, 1845–1976* (South Lake Tahoe: Lake Tahoe Area Research Coordination Board, 1976).

Federal policy in the Tahoe Basin is stated in part in U.S. Environmental Protection Agency, *The Lake Tahoe Study* [1975?], based on conditions in the basin in 1973 and 1974; and [Western Federal Regional Council] *Federal Policy for the Lake Tahoe Basin* [August 1978], a memorandum of the consensus of eleven federal agencies and departments. "The Role of the United States Forest Service and Other Federal Agencies in the Evolving Political, Social and Economic Microcosm of the Lake Tahoe Region: An Historical Brief" (USDA Forest Service, 1979), typescript copy in author's files, is informative, particularly about recent planning efforts in the basin; the author, Andrew R. Schmidt, led the Forest Service Planning Team in the early 1970s. Also see U.S. Department of Agriculture, Forest Service Region 4 and 5, *Multiple Use Management Plan for National Forest Lands: Lake Tahoe Basin* (1962); USDA Forest Service, California Region, Lake Tahoe Basin Management Unit, *Land Management Plan: Part 1* (1978); USDA Forest Service, Pacific Southwest Region, Lake Tahoe Basin Management Unit, *Draft Environmental Impact Statement: Land Management Plan: Part 2* (1978), and *Final Environmental Impact Statement: Land Management Plan: Part 2* (1980). Other government publications of particular interest include the Bureau of Outdoor Recreation's suppressed draft report, *Strategies to Save a Lake* (September 1971); U.S. Department of the Interior, *Lake Tahoe: A Special Place* (January 1973); and Robert G. Bailey, *Land Capability Classification of the Lake Tahoe Basin, California-Nevada* (South Lake Tahoe, USDA Forest Service in cooperation with the TRPA, 1974). Robert S. Wood, *Desolation Wilderness* (Berkeley: Wilderness Press, 1970) pp. 7–18, provides historical data on that geographic area.

The Institute of Governmental Affairs at the University of California, Davis, published an Environmental Quality Series, several volumes of which were cited earlier. Another volume, Charles Finkelstein's *Planning and Politics: A Staff Perception of the Tahoe Regional Planning Agency,* no. 21 (November 1974), provides a personal view of the TRPA's first eighteen months, during which the author served as its planning co-ordinator; the appendix contains two TRPA staff papers of particular interest, "Tahoe: A Second Look, August 6, 1970," and "Tahoe: An Eleventh Hour Look," (n.d.). Other volumes include Edmond Constantini and Kenneth Hanf, *The Environmental Impulse and Its Competitors: Attitudes, Interests, and Institutions at Lake Tahoe*, no. 29 (October 1973), which explains the diversity of views and political fragmentation that made coordinated and effective planning most difficult; also William E. Felts and Geoffrey Wandesforde-Smith, *The Politics of Development Review in the Lake Tahoe Basin*, no. 16 (May 1973), a study of the first eighteen months of the TRPA's existence and of the factors that influenced its performance. Also of note is Robert A. Burco, *Policy and Planning in the Lake Tahoe Basin: The Case of Transportation*, no. 17 (August 1973); and Kenneth Hanf and Geoffrey Wandesforde-Smith, *Institutional Design and Environmental Management: The Tahoe Regional Planning Agency*, no. 24 (August 1972).

The Lake Tahoe Environmental Education Consortium, the TRPA, the Tahoe Research Group, and the Research Coordination Board published *Tahoe Reflections* from 1974 to 1976 under a three-year federal grant. This periodical, established as a community-development project, was presumably a nonpartisan effort in environmental education, but it gradually assumed a perspective sympathetic to environmentalists. The periodical contains considerable material on a variety of environmental issues.

The significance of gambling to Nevada's economy is explained in W. R. Eadington, "Gambling and Nevada's Economy: Current Trends and Future Prospects," *Nevada Review of Business and Economics*, 2 (Summer 1978): 6–15. The TRPA staff has provided a well-documented article, based on its study of conditions in 1974, entitled "Impacts of Potential Hotel/Casino Expansion at Lake Tahoe," *Nevada Review of Business and Economics* 1 (Summer 1977), 11–19. Also most informative is Daryl Lembke's article "Nevada Favors Ban on More Tahoe Casinos," *Los Angeles Times*, July 11, 1974.

Legal issues involving the TRPA are reviewed in Jeff Rabin, "Tahoe Caught in Legal Crossfire," *Western Law Journal* 1 (September/October 1979): 22–23. The issue of private property rights is explained in Ira Michael Heyman, "The Great 'Property Rights' Fallacy," *Cry California* 3 (Summer 1968): 29–33; and Thomas H. Crawford, "'Property Rights' Revisited: A New Look at an Old Illusion," *Cry California* 13 (Summer 1978): 32–36.

The TRPA versus CTRPA controversy is best revealed in newspaper accounts. See, e.g., Al Donner, "Tahoe Boils with Agency Strife," *Sacramento Union*, April 18, 1977. The CTRPA has a small library at South Lake Tahoe that contains information on its operation and publications. Two documents are especially important: CTRPA, *Regional Plan for Lake Tahoe, California* (August 29, 1975); and CTRPA, *Land Use Ordinance* (September 19, 1975). Useful secondary accounts include Ginny McPartland, "Changing of the Tide in the Lake Tahoe Basin," *California Journal* 7 (January 1976): 9–11, 27; and Harriet Nathan and Phyllis Barusch, "Tahoe: The Bistate Stalemates," *Cry California* 11 (Summer 1976): 24–28. For a critical view of the CTRPA, see Economic Research Associates, *Socioeconomic Impact of the California Tahoe Regional Planning Agency Plan and Land Use Ordinance* (January 27, 1976). For the CTRPA's controversial transportation proposal, see CTRPA, *Regional Transportation Plan Summary* (May 1977). For a comparison of the CTRPA and TRPA transportation plans, see "Trans-Plans Explained," *Tahoe Reflections* (November 1975), p. 4. A critique of the TRPA by the CTRPA staff appears in "Regional Report," *Tahoe Reflections* (March 1976), p. 4. Local criticism of the CTRPA is summarized in Bruce P. Grego's letter to the editor of the *Tahoe Daily Tribune,* August 1, 1977. Contrasting approaches to the housing problem at Tahoe are revealed in CTRPA, *Housing Policy Evaluation: Draft* (October 1976), and Dillingham Development Company, *South Lake Tahoe Basin Market Study for Low Income Housing* (March 1976).

Many documents and studies deal with water quality and the 208 plan in the 1970s. The following are particularly useful: U.S. Environmental Protection Agency, *Wastewater Treatment and Conveyance System, North Lake Tahoe–Truckee River Basin (Tahoe-Truckee Sanitation Agency): Final Environmental Impact Statement* (September 17, 1974); Sari Sommarstrom, "An Analysis of the Carrying Capacity of the California Tahoe Region: Sewage Capacity Element," in [CTRPA] *An Analysis of the Carrying Capacity of the California/Tahoe Region* (November 1977): Kaiser Engineers, *Water Quality Control Plan Report: North Lahontan Basin (6A),* prepared for the State Water Resources Control Board and Lahontan Regional Water Quality Control Board (April 1975); State of California, State Water Resources Control Board, *Lake Tahoe Basin Water Quality Plan,* 3 vols. (September 1980); and Tahoe Regional Planning Agency, *Lake Tahoe Basin Water Quality Management Plan: Draft Environmental Impact Statement* (February 1981).

Efforts to revise the TRPA compact between 1975 and 1980 are covered at length in newspaper accounts. No legislative history of the period has been written, but several sources are especially helpful on the subject, including the *Sacramento Bee* and *Keep Tahoe Blue,* the publication of the League to Save Lake Tahoe.

The proposal for a Lake Tahoe national lakeshore can be studied in newspaper accounts. For the bill to study such a lakeshore, see U.S. Congress, Senate, *Congressional Record,* 91st Cong., 1st sess., 1969, vol.

115, pt. 10: 13069–70; 91st Cong., 2d sess., 1970, vol. 116, pt. 11: 15358–60; 92d Cong., 2d sess., 1972, vol. 118, pt. 18: 23162–64. The enabling act for the study is in *United States Statutes at Large,* 84 (September 26, 1970): 882. Legislation authorizing a complete study of the need for extending federal control in the basin is contained in *United States Statutes at Large,* 86 (October 18, 1972): 833. The two reports that resulted, *Strategies to Save a Lake* and *The Lake Tahoe Study,* are noted above.

Huey Johnson's proposal for a national recreation area is explained in "Lake Tahoe Tomorrow," a news release from the California Resources Agency, December 12, 1977, copy in author's files, and in "Partners to Save Lake Tahoe: Public Involvement and a New Federal Role," his speech presented to the annual meeting of the League to Save Lake Tahoe, Tahoe City, August 27, 1977, copy in the Tahoe Collection, El Dorado County Free Library, South Lake Tahoe Branch. Also see Ron Roach, "U.S. Control over Tahoe Basin Proposed," *Los Angeles Times,* January 3, 1978; *Keep Tahoe Blue* (July 1977): 3–5; and TRPA, *Tahoe Basin National Recreation Feasibility Study* (1976). The TRPA's short-lived proposal for an NRA or national park is discussed in "Emerald Bay National Recreation Area: A Proposal" (n.d.), in 5520 National Recreation Area file, U.S. Forest Service headquarters, South Lake Tahoe; and Cilla Brown, "Tahoe Agency Drops Plan for Park Area," *San Francisco Chronicle,* October 28, 1976.

For an assessment of the environmental quality of the Tahoe Basin at the end of the 1970s, see [CTRPA] *An Analysis of the Carrying Capacity of the California/Tahoe Region* (November 1977), and Western Federal Regional Council Interagency Task Force, *Lake Tahoe Environmental Assessment* (December 1979). For a selected list of recent scientific and governmental studies of the basin, see the bibliography in Tahoe Regional Planning Agency, *Environmental Impact Statement for the Establishment of Environmental Threshold Carrying Capacities* (1982). Events of 1980 and beyond are most easily traced through newspaper accounts and interviews with participants.

Index